REVOLUTION FROM ABOVE

REVOLUTION FROM ABOVE

Military Bureaucrats and Development in Japan, Turkey, Egypt, and Peru

Ellen Kay Trimberger

Transaction Books
New Brunswick, New Jersey

Copyright © 1978 by Transaction, Inc.,
New Brunswick, New Jersey 08903

Library of Congress Catalog Number: 76-1771
ISBN: 0-87855-136-0 (cloth).
Printed in the United States of America.

Library of Congress Cataloging in Publication Data

Trimberger, Ellen Kay, 1940-
    Revolution from above.

    Originally presented as the author's thesis, University of Chicago.
    Bibliography: p.
    Includes index.
    1. Revolutions—Case studies. 2. Sociology, Military—Case
studies. 3. Armed Forces—Political activity—Case studies. I. Title.
JC491.T68 1977   301.5'93   76-1771
ISBN 0-87855-136-0

Contents

Preface

This book grew out of a dissatisfaction with the existing sociological theory of revolution—dissatisfaction with the attempts to develop a general theory of revolution based on ahistorical functionalism,[1] and with the more historically based comparative studies focused only on the great Western revolutions.[2] Instead of abstractly reviewing the existing literature, I wanted to provide an alternative methodological and substantive approach through the study of "unusual" attempts at revolution in the non-Western world. An article on "Japan's Aristocratic Revolution"[3] caught my interest, as did a book stressing the special comparability of Japanese and Turkish society.[4] Further research proved that revolutions in these two countries—the Meiji Restoration of 1868 in Japan and the Ataturk takeover of 1923 in Turkey—did indeed appear to be both unusual and comparable. From the beginning, I was concerned with Japan and Turkey primarily as cases from which to develop theoretical generalizations about social change. Using a structuralist and materialist framework, I have not examined similarities or differences in their cultures.[5] Influenced first by Weberian and later by Marxist theory, generalizations drawn from the historical study of Japan and Turkey reflect both traditions, but fit neither framework.[6]

The following chapters develop a model of revolution from above by military bureaucrats as distinct from either coup d'etat or mass—bourgeois or socialist—revolution from below. The original model of revolution from above was subsequently modified by application to more current attempts at development through military initiative in Nasser's Egypt and Velasco's Peru. Initially, I considered revolutions from above as exceptional events, possible in only very few societies. I now believe that the preconditions for this type of social change are becoming increasingly prevalent in many

Third World countries. Attempts at industrialization and modernization through state, and increasingly military, direction is on the contemporary agenda. It now seems that mass revolutions from below are the truly exceptional or rare historical phenomena. My research suggests that a revolution from below is only possible when the state apparatus loses both its capacity to support the status quo and to generate a revolution from above. While the present study concentrates primarily on creating a model of one type of revolution, its analysis of the relationship between bureaucratic state structures and class forces has broader implications for the theoretical study of revolution and of the state.

I wish to thank my dissertation committee at the University of Chicago—Morris Janowitz, Edward Shils, and Urie Zolberg—for their support. Valuable comments on, and criticisms of, the dissertation manuscript were made by William Kornhauser, Dankwart Rustow, Robert Bellah, and Roberta Ash among others. More recently, the following colleagues and friends have provided supportive encouragement and helpful critiques: Theda Skocpol, James O'Connor, Irving Louis Horowitz, Susan Eckstein, Erik Wright, Raymond Franklin, Douglas Dowd, David Eakins, Clarence Lo, John Mollenkopf, Patricia Fagan, and Richard Flacks.

Notes

1. This approach is best typified by Neil J. Smelser, *Theory of Collective Behavior* (New York: Free Press, 1963); and Chalmers Johnson, *Revolutionary Change* (Boston: Little Brown, 1966).

2. See Crane Brinton, *The Anatomy of Revolution* (New York: Vintage Books, 1938); and Lyford Edwards, *The Natural History of Revolution* (Chicago: University of Chicago Press, 1967).

3. By Thomas C. Smith in *Yale Review* 50 (1961).

4. See Robert Ward and Dankwart Rustow (eds.), *Political Modernization in Japan and Turkey* (Princeton: Princeton University Press, 1964).

5. For example, both Japan and Turkey historically and today have a strong military ethos in their culture. While this may have had a common impact on their revolutions, I have not analyzed such factors.

6. The recent publication of Jon Halliday's *A Political History of Japanese Capitalism* (New York: Pantheon, 1975) marks the first important English-language study of Japanese development from a Marxist perspective. Like me, Halliday stresses state structure and its relationship to class forces as an important variable determining the course of Japan's modernization. But we differ considerably in our specific interpretation of these forces in Tokugawa and early Meiji Japan. Halliday also attributes far less importance to the Restoration as a key event in Japanese development. My analysis attempts to integrate the Japanese experience with that of other non-Western nations, emphasizing both the unique and more general characteristics of the Japanese road to industrial capitalism.

Chapter 1
Bureaucrats
and Revolution

In 1868 in Japan and 1923 in Turkey some of the highest military and civil bureaucrats in the old regime organized movements to overthrow the government in violent, but brief, civil war. After taking power, they abolished the traditional aristocracy, consolidated centralized nation states, and initiated industrialization. Through analysis of these two transformations, this book develops a model of revolution from above and explores the causes and consequences of such change. In chapter 5 this model is modified by application to the Nasser regime of 1952-70 in Egypt and the military government established in 1968 in Peru.

Unlike many paradigms and ideal types in sociology, this model of revolution from above is not independent of historical determinants. The model tries to specify certain social structural relationships necessary to a definition and causation of this type of social change. It also shows how certain elements, preconditions, and especially consequences, of revolution from above may be altered by historical developments. This emphasis on both structural and historical determinants of revolution from above indicates that there can be no general theory of revolution (or of social change) applicable to all societies at all times. Any general theorizing about the causes and consequences of different types of revolution is invalidated by the distinct historical and international contexts in which particular revolutions occur. Every revolution is unique in some respects, and each revolution changes the paramaters facilitating and hindering the next one. Just as industrialization has different prerequisites and results depending on the timing and sequence in which it occurs,[1] so does revolution. Just as industrialization after the English case could only succeed by deviating from the English pattern, so do successful revolutionaries use techniques distinctly different from those of their predecessors. As a result, all general theories of revolution have been useless as

1

analytic or predictive tools.[2] We cannot predict the outbreak or outcome of revolution. All we can do is develop the conceptual tools which will permit some analysis of the internal and international structural constraints within which revolutionaries (and counterrevolutionaries) must operate.

Another theoretical preconception of the present study is that both the causes and consequences of revolution from above—or any revolution—are determined by structural relationships internal to a national society and by the international context of that society. Thus the explanatory model presented here seeks to link macroanalysis at the national level with external (transnational) variables.[3]

Revolution from Above as a Type of Revolutionary Change   There is much dissension among scholars and interpreters as to whether the Ataturk regime, Meiji Restoration, Nasserism, and the Velasco takeover in Peru were really revolutionary. Those who deny the revolutionary quality of these events most often focus on the lack of a mass movement and mass upheaval.[4] In using this criterion, they adopt the "great" revolutions as the model for such social change. For example, scholars in Japan have engaged in a long battle over whether the Meiji Restoration was a bourgeois revolution or not, without considering any alternative model.[5]

Rather than quibbling over alternative ways to define revolution, I hope the analysis in subsequent chapters will justify the utility of a simple process definition. A definition of revolution based on the process that occurs is independent of the causes and long-range consequences of such events. It permits one to distinguish revolution from reform and coup d'etat, but also allows one to define distinct types of revolution based on different participants and processes. Such a definition allows for the development of independent theories about the causes and consequences of different types of revolution.

Using these criteria, a revolution can be defined as an extralegal takeover of the central state apparatus which destroys the economic and political power of the dominant social group of the old regime. Such a takeover of government depends at least on the threatened use of force and is usually violent. What distinguishes revolution from reform or coup d'etat is the destruction of the dominant social group. This destruction is a fundamental precondition for the innovative and positive change associated with revolution. The nature and degree of change resulting from revolutions depends both on process variables and on societal and international structural relationships independent of the revolutionary process.

A revolution from above is defined by a specific type of revolutionary process. Five characteristics define a revolution from above:

1. The extralegal takeover of political power and the initiation of economic, social, and political change is organized and led by some of the highest military and often civil bureaucrats in the old regime.
2. There is little or no mass participation in the revolutionary takeover or in the initiation of change. Mass movements and uprisings may precede and accompany revolution from above, but military bureaucrats who take revolutionary action do so independently from, and often in opposition to, such movements.
3. The extralegal takeover of power and the initiation of change is accompanied by very little violence, execution, emigration, or counterrevolution.
4. The initiation of change is undertaken in a pragmatic, step-at-a-time manner with little appeal to radical ideology. Both the third and fourth characteristics are the result of control and use of a bureaucratic apparatus for radical aims.
5. Military bureaucrats who lead a revolution from above—as opposed to a coup d'etat—destroy the economic and political base of the aristocracy or upper class. This destructive process is basic to both revolution from above and from below. The following chapters demonstrate that the Meiji Restoration, Nasserism, and military government in Peru after 1968 all meet this criterion of a revolution. The Ataturk regime was only marginally revolutionary. Ataturk destroyed the political, but only part of the economic, base of the notables of the Ottoman Empire. The inclusion in our study of this marginal—or abortive—revolution from above illustrates the importance of class destruction as a defining element of revolutionary change.

A primary contribution of this book is to stress the revolutionary potential of the state apparatus under certain specific internal and international conditions. The increasing power of the state in the twentieth century, the prevalence of military governments in the Third World, and the need for state initiative in the industrialization of late-developing nations have become almost clichés. But no analytic consensus has developed on whether state action can be "progressive" and if so, under what conditions. What distinguishes "progressive" military rule from reactionary military dictatorship? Why do some states succeed in fostering sustained economic development while many others fail? If the increasing civil and military power of the state makes revolutions from below increasingly problematic, are revolutions from above still possible and with what results? This book will provide some preliminary answers to these questions. It will also develop concepts and a style of analysis that may aid in future examination of such problems.

Bureaucratic Autonomy from Class Domination as a Precondition for Revolution from Above   The most important concepts developed in this study are: (1) a relatively autonomous bureaucratic state apparatus; and (2) a dynamically autonomous state bureaucracy. These concepts were derived inductively from the observation that revolution from above was made possible in Tokugawa Japan and Ottoman Turkey because state and military bureaucrats were not merely an instrument of a dominant economic class. Historically, the status groups which staffed the state apparatus in these two societies became urbanized and separated from control over the means of production in the countryside. In a crisis situation, their separation from vested economic interests and their personal dependence on the power of the state led bureaucratic leaders to sacrifice traditional status groups to a strategy to save the state through revolutionary means.

A bureaucratic state apparatus, or a segment of it, can be said to be relatively autonomous when those who hold high civil and/or military posts satisfy two conditions: (1) they are not recruited from the dominant landed, commercial, or industrial classes; and (2) they do not form close personal and economic ties with these classes after their elevation to high office. Relatively autonomous bureaucrats are thus independent of those classes which control the means of production. In the twentieth century, multinational corporations and international capitalists invest in Third World countries and often ally themselves with a segment of the national bourgeoisie. Relatively autonomous bureaucrats must be free of connections and control by both internal and international class interests.

Relatively autonomous bureaucrats have a distinctive class position in that they have a particular relationship to the means of production. But they have no possibility of becoming a dominant class within the existing social order because they have no control over the means of production. Relatively autonomous bureaucrats can, however, use their control over state resources—coercive, monetary, and ideological—to destroy the existing economic and class order. Even in polities where the state bureaucracy is subordinate to a party and parliamentary system controlled by such class interests (as in Peru and Egypt prior to revolutions from above), relatively autonomous military officers have the potential for breaking this institutional subordination by force. This is why the military, as opposed to the civil bureaucracy, is indispensable for a revolution from above. This definition of bureaucratic autonomy implies that the method of recruiting military officials, their class interests once in power, and the structural relations between the state bureaucracy and other political institutions, are all important determinants of what bureaucrats can and will do, especially in crisis situations.

It is only in a crisis situation—when the existing social, political, and economic order is threatened by external forces and by upheaval from below—that relatively autonomous bureaucrats are likely to take such radical initiative. In so doing they become dynamically autonomous, acting to destroy an existing economic and class order. Dynamically autonomous bureaucrats enter the class struggle as an independent force, rather than as an instrument of other class forces. The outcome of such radical bureaucratic initiative depends on the international competition between states and also on the domestic class constellation.

Why and under what conditions do state bureaucrats become relatively autonomous in precapitalist or early capitalist societies? This study does not presume a definitive answer valid for all historical periods, but it does lead to the conclusion that such autonomy is likely to occur when there is no consolidated landed class, as in nineteenth-century Japan and Turkey, or when a landed oligarchy is in economic and political decline. In the latter case, the rising bourgeoisie must also be weak and/or dependent on foreign interests, as in twentieth-century Egypt and Peru.

To clarify the concept of a relatively autonomous bureaucratic apparatus as a precondition for the dynamic autonomy leading to revolution from above, it shall be briefly distinguished from the classic discussion of bureaucracy by Marx and Weber, and also from some contemporary analyses of relative state autonomy in capitalist society.

Marx and Weber on Bureaucrats and Social Change Both Marx and Weber in their analyses of nineteenth-century European modernization saw the bureaucratic state apparatus as primarily a passive instrument to be used by individuals or classes for conservative political ends. Bureaucratic organization played a radical role in the creation of a capitalist economy, but its political functions were very different.

Marx characterized the nineteenth-century French state as follows: "The executive power, with its enormous bureaucratic and military organization, with its ingenious state machinery, embracing wide strata, with a host of officials numbering a half million, enmeshes the body of French society like a net and chokes all its pores."[6] According to Marx's analysis, this state apparatus reached the height of its power in France under the military dictatorship of Louis Bonaparte in the 1850s. Here executive power triumphed over parliament, and the state apparatus became independent of class control. Under the Bonapartist state "the bourgeoisie had already lost, and the working class had not yet acquired the faculty of ruling the nation."[7] But the autonomous reign of bureaucrats under Bonaparte did not lead to revolution from above. His reign was both temporary and conservative. Bonapartism occurred in a predominantly capitalist country; revolution from above in an agricultural or dependent capitalist society.[8] Louis Bonaparte supported the economic interests of the capitalist bourgeoisie. Unlike bureaucratic revolutionaries, he did not uproot any class interest or try to change the economy in fundamental ways.

Marx was probably correct in his analysis of the French state. His more general insight that state structures are usually dominated by the capitalist class was also true in nineteenth-century Europe. But Marx was not justified in generalizing these observations into a theory of state power in all industrial and industrializing nations. An autonomous bureaucratic state is not always an unstable and conservative regime. The growth of bureaucracy may have very different political and social consequences in late-developing nations in the twentieth century than it did one hundred years ago in European states.[9]

Weber, like Marx, saw the growth of state bureaucracy as stifling both human innovation and radical social change. Weber portrayed the model bureaucrat as a narrow professional geared to routine and interested primarily in secure, step-by-step promotion in a career. He was not the type of man who could become a revolutionary hero or even an innovative leader. For Weber, "qualities of political leadership have never been born and brought to fruition anywhere in the world under a system of unchecked rule by bureaucracy."[10] Weber felt that political leadership could come only from a man who had a private means of income that would free him from work. Such a man could live "for politics," as compared to the servile officials who had to live "from politics."[11]

Weber saw the charismatic individual—the very antithesis of the bureaucrat—as the initiator of revolutionary breakthroughs. This charismatic hero could arise in any era, under very different social conditions. Weber had no causal or historical explanation for revolutionary change. For him it was the great individual independent of complex structures who made great breakthroughs. The bureaucrat from lowly origins, economically dependent on the state apparatus, was the most conservative.[12] In our study it is such bureaucrats who became revolutionaries. Ataturk, Nasser, and Velasco, as military leaders had some charismatic qualities, but they combined them with the rational attributes of organizers and administrators. The Meiji revolutionaries were not at all charismatic.

Weber concluded that the growth of the state bureaucracy meant "the place of revolution is taken by coup d'etat."[13] A coup replaces the top state leadership without altering either the structure of political authority or the exercise of economic power. In contrast, civil and military officials in Japan and Turkey used their bureaucratic positions to organize a revolutionary movement which differed fundamentally from a coup d'etat.

Weber's analysis of bureaucracy was probably a correct interpretation of the late nineteenth- and early twentieth-century German state. Here state bureaucrats were conservative, but this was more likely due to their close ties to the landed Junker class than to conditions inherent in rational administration. Both Weber and Marx made generalizations about the role of the bureaucratic state that were too narrowly tied to the experience of the European polity.

The Concept of Relative State Autonomy in Recent Literature The definition of a relatively autonomous state apparatus developed here is distinct from that proposed recently by both a Marxist structuralist (Nicos Poulantzas) and a structural-functionalist (Samuel Huntington). Let me briefly consider their analyses, in order to clarify my concept derived from a study of bureaucratic revolutions in the transition to capitalism.

Nicos Poulantzas in *Political Power and Social Class* defines two ways in which the state is autonomous from class forces. First, and most important, is his concept of a relatively autonomous state. Poulantzas says that under the capitalist mode of production it is functionally necessary for the state to be structurally independent of class forces in order to maintain and protect the interests of the capitalist class.[14] The capitalist state is relatively autonmous to the extent that it is capable of transcending the parochial, individualized interests of specific capitalists and capitalist class factions. But for Poulantzas a relatively autonomous state apparatus is not free to abrogate the structural requirements of the capitalist economy, even in a crisis situation. Poulantzas declares that this relative autonomy is a structural characteristic of the capitalist state. He maintains that the class origins or ties of state bureaucrats are of no consequence for understanding state actions.

For Poulantzas, a second and more unstable state autonomy occurs only where there is a balance between competing classes or factions within the dominant class so that none of them are dominant.[15] It is only under these rare circumstances that the state would cease to function as a political organizer of the capitalist class. Poulantzas does not consider the impact of extranational forces. Thus the state apparatus rarely has power independent of social class power.[16] As Ralph Miliband says: "Poulantzas' failure to make the necessary distinction between class power and state power . . . deprives the state of any kind of autonomy at all and turns it precisely into the merest instrument of a determined class."[17]

In contrast, the definition presented here assumes that control of the governing apparatus is a source of power independent of that held by a class because of control over the means of production. Hence it can make a big difference in state policy whether those who control state power are independent of, or closely tied to, those who exercise control over the means of production. It is important whether those who control state power are personally committed (by vested interests) to the present organization of the economy.

Samuel Huntington defines autonomy as one of the four characteristics of a modern political system. An autonomous political system, he says, is "insulated from the impact of non-political groups and procedures."[18] A political organization that is the instrument of a particular social group—family, clan, or class—lacks autonomy. Yet Huntington sees political parties as the most important instruments to create a modern and autonomous polity: it is political parties which most successfully seek to aggregate and overcome narrow interests.[19] Huntington thus assumes that all political parties are autonomous; he never considers that many modern parties articulate the interests of the capitalist class in a way that makes them *seem* a general interest.[20] While Poulantzas sees the state apparatus as completely controlled by economic forces, Huntington sees the political system as completely independent of the national or international economy. Ultimately, Huntington's analysis is a sophisticated polemic in support of a strong, stable state which seems autonomous—appears to be articulating general interests—but is actually upholding rule by the capitalist class.

Other non-Marxist and nonfunctionalist political sociologists—especially those like Reinhard Bendix[21] and Edward Shils[22] working in the Weberian tradition—have stressed the importance of the political system in sponsoring modernization and economic development. But they have not specified what type of state organization is most likely to sponsor successful development. They have talked of a strong, effective, bureaucratized, or centralized state, but have not considered how such a state apparatus relates to other sources of power in society, especially class-based power.

Neither the Marxist nor non-Marxist political sociology of Third-World societies has looked at the relationship between the state apparatus and dominant classes as an independent variable determining the type and rate of change in the transition from agrarian to industrial societies. Nor have they integrated this internal analysis with a consideration of the international context.

Effect of Internal and International Variables in Determining the Results of Revolution   Enumerating and evaluating the results of any revolution has always been controversial. This is especially true when one has to decide how to weigh the technical needs of modernization (economic development and efficient government) versus the more humane values of equality, democracy, and social welfare. Because of their bureaucratic base, revolutions from above are especially suited to technical achievements and particularly vulnerable to the neglect of human needs. These tendencies were enhanced because military bureaucrats in all four countries sought to control and depoliticize, rather than mobilize, the masses in the process of social change. Even in technical terms, the results of most of these revolutions are disappointing. In assessing long-term results of revolutions from above we see the limitations of their bureaucratic and elitist form. The conclusion of chapters 4 and 5 is that the reluctance of military leaders to mobilize mass participation in economic development was primarily responsible for the failure of most of these revolutions to achieve their nationalist aims.

Military bureaucrats in all four countries used the state apparatus in an attempt to foster capitalist industrialization independent of foreign control. Japan has been more successful at capitalist industrialization than any other non-Western country. This success can be attributed both to Japan's early start at industrialization before the consolidation of imperialist control and to the strong and autonomous state apparatus that stimulated economic development by accumulating capital from the peasants. But even Japan's economy became subordinate to Western capitalism in a manner which constricted Japan's industrialization to a narrow sector, geared it to military expansion, and promoted great social and economic inequality. Chapter 4 will demonstrate how Japan became the first sub-imperialist country. "Japan remained in an essentially 'third world' relationship with the West commercially, while holding the position of an 'advanced' capitalist country vis-à-vis the rest of Asia."[23] It was this contradictory position that led directly to Japan's destructive entry into World War II.

Even though military bureaucrats in Turkey, Egypt, and Peru employed many of the same techniques to stimulate economic growth as their earlier Japanese counterparts, none of these countries has even approached self-sufficient industrialization. All three countries have some industry, but all remain primarily dependent suppliers of raw materials upon the international market. All rely upon foreign private and public investment with their proverbial economic and political strings. The economic problems faced by these countries in the twentieth century were much greater than those of Japan in 1868. Turkey, Egypt, and Peru were more intimately tied to the world capitalist economy as subordinates. The advanced capitalist countries had much greater control over the world economy in 1930, 1950, and 1970 respectively than they did in 1870.

Every revolution from above, like each revolution from below, has to invent new strategies for industrialization, adapted not only to idiosyncrasies in national social structure, but more importantly to changes in the international balance of power. Late industrialization and delayed revolutions face increasingly greater obstacles to successful modernization. After 1850 the only way any country could hope to industrialize autonomously without foreign domination of their economy was through a temporary withdrawal from the world market and a sustained effort at internal mass mobilization for a vast productive effort. Even this strategy is likely to succeed only in populous countries with vast natural resources. But in none of these revolutions from above did military bureaucrats even attempt such mass mobilization.

The failure to mobilize a mass base hindered long-range attempts at independent industrialization in another way. An autonomous political system, even if it instills mass apathy, is inherently unstable. To consolidate their political power, bureaucratic revolutionaries need a secure social base. Rather than mobilize working-class or peasant support, autonomous state bureaucrats in all four countries eventually compromised with a class that was opposed to autonomous capitalist industrialization. Bureaucrats in Japan and Turkey agreed to share power with a precapitalist landed class. In Egypt and Peru bureaucrats coalesced with a rising capitalist class, but one whose economic interests were allied with capitalists in the advanced countries in a manner detrimental to the integrated economic growth of their own nation. Once bureaucrats formed a political alliance with such a class, they also lost their reforming zeal for autonomous national development. It was not that autonomous bureaucrats chose to share power with these classes or to compromise their original economic aims. Rather, the organized power of such classes forced the bureaucrats either to mobilize the masses for further revolutionary action or to consolidate a status quo in which their own power and status was no longer in danger. Chapter 5 considers whether bureaucrats in future attempts at revolution from above might act any differently.

Notes

1. For a good exposition of this point see Reinhard Bendix, "Tradition and Modernity Reconsidered," *Comparative Studies in Society and History* 9 (1967).

2. For an excellent critique of past theorizing on the great revolutions and presentation of an alternative approach see Theda Skocpol, "Explaining Revolutions: In Quest of a Social-Structural Approach," in *The Uses of Controversy in Sociology*, eds. Lewis Coser and Otto Larsen (New York: Free Press, 1976); and "France, Russia, China: A Structural Analysis of Social Revolutions," *Comparative Studies in Society and History* (April 1975).

3. Most often macroanalysis of social change is limited to either internal or external analysis. For example, Barrington Moore's important comparative study of revolutions looks almost exclusively at internal class variables. *The Social Basis of Dictatorship and Democracy* (Boston: Beacon Press, 1966). Conversely, dependency theories of continuing Latin American underdevelopment provide explanations which focus primarily on the external relationships of Latin American countries to more advanced capitalist nations. See André Gunder Frank, *Capitalism and Underdevelopment in Latin America* (New York: Monthly Review Press, 1967).

Immanuel Wallerstein in *The Modern World-System: Capitalist Agriculture and the Origins of the European World-Economy in the Sixteenth Century* (New York: Academic Press, 1974) stresses the importance of structural relations between nations, but he also includes a consideration of variables internal to societies.

4. Samuel Huntington characterizes Ataturk as an effective reformer, but not a revolutionary. *Political Order in Changing Societies* (New Haven: Yale University Press, 1968), p. 269. Barrington Moore (1966) is ambivalent about whether the Meiji Restoration is revolutionary, while W.P. Wertheim contends it was not. *Evolution and Revolution* (Baltimore: Penguin Books, 1974), p. 168.

5. See Jon Halliday, *A Political History of Japanese Capitalism* (New York: Pantheon, 1975), p. 313.

6. Karl Marx, "Eighteenth Brumaire of Louis Bonaparte," in *Marx and Engels: Basic Writing on Politics and Philosophy*, ed. Lewis Feuer (New York: Doubleday, 1959), p. 336.

7. Ibid., p. 365.

8. A revolution from above may be similar to the idea of a "passive revolution" developed by Gramsci to describe Italy's unification and modernization in the nineteenth century. I do not know enough Italian history to make the comparison. See Antonio Gramsci, *Selections from the Prison Notebooks* (New York: International Publishers, 1971) pp. 45-47, 104-14.

9. Supporting this idea is the following observation: "The later Leninist notion of the Communist party-state as a force for social change, an instrumentality of a long-range revolutionary transformation of society from above, is in this respect a serious modification of Marxist theory." Robert C. Tucker, "Marx as a Political Theorist," in *Marx's Socialism*, ed. Shlomo Avineri (New York: Lieber-Atherton, 1973), p. 134.

10. Max Weber, *Economy and Society*, ed. Guenther Roth and Claus Wittich (New York, Bedminster Press, 1968), p. 1413.

11. Max Weber, "Politics as a Vocation," in *From Max Weber*, eds. Hans Gerth and C. Wright Mills (New York: Oxford University Press, 1958), pp. 84-85.

12. Arthur Mitzman, *The Iron Cage: An Historical Interpretation of Max Weber* (New York: Grosset and Dunlap, 1969), p. 177.

13. Weber, *Economy and Society*, p. 989.

14. Poulantzas gives the clearest definition in an article, "The Problem of the Capitalist State," in *Ideology in Social Science*, ed. Robin Blackburn (New York: Vintage Books, 1973).

15. Nicos Poulantzas, *Political Power and Social Class* (London: New Left Books, 1973), p. 262.

16. Poulantzas, "The Problem of the Capitalist State," p. 115.

17. Ralph Miliband, "Poulantzas and the Capitalist State," *New Left Review* 82 (1973): 87.

18. Huntington, p. 20.

19. Ibid.

20. Ralph Miliband says: "The conservative parties, for all their acceptance of piecemeal reform and their rhetoric of classlessness, remain primarily the defense organizations in the political field of business and property. What they really "aggregate" are the different interests of the dominant classes . . . . [But] these interests require ideological clothing suitable for political competition in the age of mass politics; one of the special functions of the conservative political parties is to

provide the necessary clothing." *The State in Capitalist Society* (New York: Basic Books, 1969), p. 187.

21. Reinhard Bendix, *Nation-building and Citizenship* (Garden City: Double-day, 1969).

22. Edward Shils, "Political Development in the New States," *Comparative Studies in Society and History* 2 (1960).

23. Halliday, p. 61.

Chapter 2
The Process
of Revolution
from Above

U pon first consideration it might appear that there is no basis for comparing a revolution in 1868 in Japan with one in 1919 in Turkey. Turkey in
the 1860s and afterwards comprised the ruling center of a large empire;
Japan was a small semicentralized state. Turkey could look back on
centuries of political and economic intervention by European powers;
Japan had been isolated for two centuries (until 1853) from all but minimal
contact with the West. The Ottoman Empire contained a myriad of diverse
national, ethnic, and religious groups; the Japanese were a racially, reli-
giously, and culturally homogeneous people. These structural differences
did have an impact on the long-range results of revolution. Despite them,
there are striking similarities in the processes of the Meiji Restoration and
Ataturk Revolution which define them as revolutions from above.

The immediate motivation and ideological basis for revolution in Japan
and Turkey was nationalism inspired by the direct threat of Western
domination and takeover. In both Japan in 1867 and Turkey in 1919
military and civil bureaucrats, dissatisfied with the ineffective and vacillat-
ing policy of dynastic leaders (Shogun and Sultan) in dealing with the West,
launched unauthorized nationalist movements. Although these movements soon developed the objective of seizing power from the government, they did not at first envision major social, economic, or even
political change. Many traditionalists who supported the anti-Western
movement did not expect (or desire) the radical measures which resulted.

In both countries, radical nationalist leaders were drawn from high
military and civil officials without direct decision-making power in the
central government. Bureaucrats from the large, semiautonomous domains in western Japan initiated extraordinary action; officials in the
central Tokugawa bureaucracy for the most part supported the status quo.
Turkish military officers commanding provincial armies, in coalition with

party bureaucrats of the local branches of the major political party, took the radical initiative. Members of parliament and many governors and provincial administrators joined them, but the civil and religious bureaucrats in the capital generally remained conservative. The relatively decentralized political system of Togukawa Japan and Ottoman Turkey necessitated a provincial base of power for revolution from above. In more centralized states military bureaucrats in the capital city can lead a revolution without provincial organization.

Organization and Tactics **PREEMPTING THE ORGANS AND**
to Defeat the Old Regime **SYMBOLS OF THE OLD REGIME** The
and Consolidate Political Power strategy created by bureaucratic revolutionaries to overthrow the old re-
gime differs significantly from that used in mass urban or rural guerrilla revolutionary movements. In a revolution from above there is no mass uprising which triggers the collapse of the old regime. Nor is there the anarchy and social upheaval resulting from competition among antagonistic revolutionary groups (as in the French, Russian, and Mexican revolutions). Rather, rebel bureaucrats preempt organs and personnel of the established regime to fight those remaining loyal to the existing government. Depending on historical circumstances, such opposition may involve only military units organizing secret cells within the bureaucracy, or it may entail, in addition, the appropriation of civil bureaucratic and legislative organs, party structures, and monetary resources. Because those who lead a revolution from above have high positions in the old regime, they can also manipulate traditional symbols for their antiestablishment ends.

Revolution in Turkey began with the organization by Mustafa Kemal (later called Ataturk, father of the Turks) of a resistance movement in rural Antolia after Turkey's surrender to the Allies in 1919. Kemal's status as a general and his fame as a victorious commander in the war permitted him to obtain appointment from the sultan to be sent officially to the interior of the country. He was instructed to maintain order and supervise the orderly demobilization of the Ottoman armies, but he had no such intention. Even before leaving Istanbul he had collaborated with five leading army and navy officers to lay a plan for the resistance movement.

As a bureaucrat, Kemal "all his adult life drew a regular (if modest) government salary. His instinct, moreover, was to solve any and all problems by organization. One organization, the War Ministry of Istanbul, had sent him to Anatolia, and Kemal had taken a personal hand in the staff work that prepared his mission. On arrival, he established contact with another set of organizations—groupings of local notables and members of the defunct Union and Progress Party."[1] Moreover, "Kemal's leadership in these early years was based on receiving and imparting information, on consulting with associates who formed a network over the country, on harmonizing and concerting the actions of the most diverse regions, social groups and individuals. It was a virtuoso performance of leadership by conciliation, by connection, by communication."[2]

This organizational expertise could be put to use because Turkish troops stationed in Anatolia preserved their discipline and a clear chain of command, but were not under close supervision from Istanbul.[3] More importantly, the former Young Turk Union and Progress party had built up an extensive party organization that spread to even the small towns.[4] These local party organs, led by school teachers, administrative officials, intellectuals, and landowners,[5] spontaneously formed local defense units and became the civilian backbone of Ataturk's movement, at a time when most of the central bureaucrats and their provincial representatives in Anatolia were "cool or at best cautiously correct toward the nationalist cause."[6] It is significant that Ataturk's first move—even before making military plans to counter the Greek invasion—was to organize a national congress to unite all these local civilian defense organizations into a central organization led by a representative committee. Soon he established a true countergovernment.

Kemal and the Representative Committee of the Defense Organization called for elections to a new National Assembly to meet in Anatolia. The election order—addressed to the commanding general of the army corps, provincial administrators, and governors—called for the election of five representatives from each province to attend the extraordinary assembly along with those deputies from the Istanbul Parliament who had escaped to Anatolia. Soon 106 deputies from Istanbul joined 232 newly elected provincial delegates to form the first Grand National Assembly.[7] That this situation of dual power (which lasted two and a half years) was still an elite affair dominated by military and civil bureaucrats is seen from the composition of this first Turkish Grand National Assembly: 43 percent of the 437 deputies were government officials (23 percent civil bureaucrats, 15 percent military officers, and 5 percent educators) and 17 percent were religious officials. Eighteen percent of the delegates were independent professionals (law, medicine, and journalism), with only 13 percent of the deputies in trade and banking, and 6 percent in agriculture (most with large estates).[8] There were no peasants or workers. Government officials held 50 percent of the leadership positions in the First Assembly, with more military than civil bureaucrats in these top posts.[9] Another indicator of the connection of these deputies with the state is that 70 percent of the representatives in the assembly (and 88 percent of the top leaders) had a university education.[10] Thus the nationalist movement and countergovernment were controlled by high-level bureaucrats who dominated lower officials and local interest groups.

Ataturk also manipulated traditional values and symbols for his own ends. He obtained a decree from religious officials that the sultan had betrayed the Islamic faith by submitting to infidel (Western) demands. But later, "the Allied occupation of Istanbul provided a convenient pretext for carrying out the nationalist struggle in the name of the Sultan and for discounting the Sultan's anti-nationalist acts and proclamations as having been obtained under duress. The official statements from the rebels in Anakara were all couched in terms of monarchist loyalty, and frequently blended a religious-Muslim with a nationalist-Turkish appeal."[11]

In Japan, revolutionary civil war was a direct result of Western military intervention in 1863 on the side of the central government to subdue two dissident provinces which objected to Western trading concessions. Humiliated by the fact that Western military might had to be used to chastise internal dissidents, the central shogunal government subsequently organized a military campaign against the province of Choshu. This move propelled the most radical bureaucrats in several provinces (especially Choshu and Satsuma) to reject the authority of the shogunate and organize an alternative government based on provincial military and administrative organs and claiming legitimacy for the traditional (and for two hundred and fifty years, purely ceremonial) emperor.

The establishment of an alternative center of authority in Japan and Turkey, controlled by some of the highest officials of the old regime, mobilized around traditional organs of the government, and claiming legitimacy on the basis of a nationalism partly derived from traditional values, precipitated civil war. But the duration and social upheaval of these revolutionary wars were limited for a number of reasons.

NEUTRALIZATION OF THE ARISTOCRACY The high status and official authority of rebel bureaucrats—along with their use of nationalistic appeals which incorporated traditional political symbols and values—enabled them to mobilize a small core of elite supporters and neutralize the rest of the traditional aristocracy. Most of the daimyo and samurai in Japan—as the Ottoman state and religious elite—were against any radical change, but they refused to take up arms either in support of the rebels or the dynasty. Their neutrality arose out of a fear of national disunity at a time of intense foreign threat. The use of traditional political organs and symbols by the rebels also produced confusion as to whether they were really illegitimate or revolutionary. The indecisiveness of the Ottoman elite paralleled that of the daimyo and samurai: "One may speculate that most of the han [provincial governments] remained in the grip of the same inertia that had immobilized them since 1853. That the Bakufu [Ottoman Empire] was about to fall seemed obvious; to support it would be folly, yet to openly oppose it might still be dangerous. An air of incipient change hung over the country; better to wait until events were more clearly defined than to act rashly."[12] The existence of large numbers of neutral elites, however, gave de facto support to the legitimacy of the rebels and their usurpation of part of the government and army.

NEUTRALIZATION OF THE MASSES Because they could organize a revolutionary movement based on officials and organs of the old regime, bureaucratic revolutionaries did not need to mobilize mass support. Some commoners participated in both the revolutionary and conservative armies in Japan and Turkey, but only under elite control. In Japan the unorganized masses remained neutral.[13] In Turkey, spontaneous mass violence was inspired by the sultan's appeal to traditional religious fanaticism, but this communal killing was unorganized and apolitical, and violence quickly petered out. Insofar as the revolutionaries had to recruit soldiers or obtain food from the immediate population, they had the resources to pay and/or the authority to obtain them voluntarily. What the revolutionaries did need, at a minimum, was some assurance that most of the peasants would not voluntarily aid the sultan and shogun or willingly (without coercion) take up arms against the revolutionary forces. Such neutralization of the rural masses was easy to obtain because the political forces of the old regime were concentrated in the capital city with only minimal control over the countryside.[14] Moreover, tacit support of the masses was assured by the limited foreign intervention in the conflict between the rebels and government. The collaboration of government officials with a foreign power increased the nationalistic appeal of the rebels, as did a military stand by the revolutionaries against foreign troops. Under such conditions, bureaucratic revolutionaries had no need or incentive to use force to obtain mass neutrality. If the revolutionary threat, however, had triggered massive foreign intervention, the revolutionaries would have been forced to mobilize mass support for a conventional civil war or a guerrilla movement in order to survive. In this case, revolution from above would either fail or change into some form of mass revolution with an increased level of violence.

All the tactics used by bureaucratic revolutionaries—preempting the organization and symbols of the old regime, neutralizing the aristocracy and the masses—mitigated violence and upheaval in the revolutionary process. The demoralization of the dynastic head of the old regime and those officials who remained loyal to him prevented them from mounting an effective resistance to the countergovernment. The sultan's army in Turkey was defeated in one battle with the nationalist forces in 1920. This battle was not decisive, but further confrontation was suspended because of the invasion by the Greek army. After the nationalist armies defeated the Greeks, both the strength and prestige of the nationalists was so high that the sultan fled the country without taking another armed stand. Likewise, the two Japanese civil wars—in 1864 and 1868—involved only two or three large battles, and in 1868 the shogun voluntarily surrendered his power (although some of his followers held out). Violent confrontation was limited not only because the conservative supporters of the old regime in Japan and Turkey failed to stand and fight, but also because the rebels did not pursue their military advantage to impose a decisive military victory. Rather, the old regimes were terminated by political maneuver of the rebel countergovernments. It was both the character of radical bureaucrats and the unique strength and quasi legitimacy of the alternative regimes that permitted the radicals to abolish the old regimes through political and nonviolent means.

Because military and civil bureaucrats did not stage a coup, but rather established a countergovernment in the process of overthrowing the old regime, they were able to initiate rapid change after taking power. Not only had they already mobilized elite support and appealed to the masses for legitimacy through nationalist symbols, but the bureaucrats had themselves been radicalized in the process. Those who took to the hills to organize a countergovernment did not take with them a comprehensive ideology or even a clear conception of revolutionary change. But the immediate problems created by setting up a rebel regime destroyed their commitment to, and identity with, sanctioned political values and familiar procedures of rule. The intense interaction among a small cadre of rebels stimulated a search for new organizational forms and appropriate political values.

Yet this process of organization in Japan and Turkey—and divergent procedures in Egypt and Peru—cannot explain why these bureaucrats became not just nationalists, but revolutionaries. The purpose of this chapter is to document their continuing radicalization. The next chapter will try to explain it.

Ataturk and the Choshu-Satsuma coalition used their experience as bureaucrats to structure their selection of methods to initiate change. The way they used their authority and organizational resources is first seen in the manner in which they eliminated the old regime and consolidated their own power through political manipulation of their more moderate supporters. The Japanese moderates included the Tosa and Hizen bureaucrats and some court nobles; the Turkish moderates were led by some of Kemal's close military and civil bureaucratic associates with higher social status.

POLITICAL MANIPULATION OF MODERATE SUPPORTERS Moderates in a preindustrial revolution can be defined as those who favor only reform (and not abolition) of the old regime by forming some sort of constitutional monarchy. Moderates also stress the importance of civil liberties, preservation of aristocratic prerogatives, and only gradual social and economic change. Radicals, in contrast, are committed to complete elimination of the old regime and rapid social and economic change.

Because revolutionary bureaucrats have politico-organizational experience and control administrative and military resources, they retain a stronger position vis-à-vis their moderate supporters than is true of revolutionaries who arise outside the structure of state power. In contrast to the French and Russian revolutions, moderates in the Meiji and Ataturk revolutions were always subordinate to the radicals, and there was never a complete polarization between moderates and radicals.

According to Crane Brinton, the downfall of the moderates in the French and Russian revolutions arose from their position as leaders after the abdication of the old regime—positions for which they were ill prepared by their background and style of action. The moderates, committed to consultation and deliberation in solving problems, were faced with a chaotic society, opposed by both strong radical and conservative forces, and threatened by foreign troops. They were also hindered by political structures inherited from the old regime. Unable to take decisive action to resolve the social disorder and please both Right and Left opposition, they sanctioned the destruction of the conservatives. It was after the exodus of the conservative aristocracy that the radicals—with organized mass support—overthrew the moderates and initiated a reign of terror and virtue.[15]

In the Japanese and Turkish revolutions the moderates were never called upon to exercise leadership in a revolutionary situation. The radicals, as bureaucrats in positions of power, themselves initiated action against the old regime. From the beginning moderate supporters (who were also primarily bureaucrats) were placed in a position subordinate to the radicals—a position in which they could preserve their own indispensability to the radicals vis-à-vis the conservatives. But also a position in which they could be manipulated by the radicals to support more drastic change.

The action of radicals in the Japanese and Turkish revolutions from above also differed from that of their counterparts in the French and Russian revolutions. Starting from a position of power and with considerable experience in exercising it, radical bureaucrats in Japan and Turkey achieved their goals through manipulation of elites rather than mass mobilization. Revolutionary leaders in Japan and Turkey were not intellectuals or idealists; they were efficient and practical realists. "Kemal's own ideals were tempered by expediency and above all by his ruthless sense of realities . . . . He was a realist, who thought in terms not of gestures but of actions thoughtfully conceived, scientifically planned, and systematically executed."[16] Likewise, Okubo Toshimichi, the architect of the Meiji Restoration, has been called the "Bismarch of Japan"—a tough-minded realist, practical and unemotional."[17] Like Ataturk, Okubo "almost singlehandedly during the critical period of the spring of 1868 to 1871, held the government together, coaxing and flattering jealous colleagues and suspicious han into devoting themselves to the national ideal."[18] The leaders of the Meiji Restoration were "men of affairs . . . characterized by ruthlessness, a readiness to use violence, but also a political realism that made them calculate the consequences of what they did."[19]

Radical bureaucrats were motivated to eliminate the decentralized state in Japan and the multiethnic empire in Turkey for both nationalistic and personal reasons. In order to counter Western encroachment they knew that they needed strong, efficient political institutions that could engender widespread support and eliminate internal political divisions. As one of the Meiji leaders put it: "If we cannot rule at home we will be unable to set matters to right abroad."[20] At the same time, the personal power of the radical bureaucrats in Japan would have been limited by the preservation of the traditional polity. Their power no longer rested on the domains from which they came, but on control of the nucleus of a central bureaucratic and military machine under the emperor figurehead. Their status inferiority to the feudal daimyo and the necessity of manipulating personal and factional favors in a number of domains could only limit their personal power.[21] Similarly, the personal power of Ataturk's bureaucratic and military followers would be limited in a constitutional monarchy where the sultan-caliph and his dynastic family and personal servants could still influence political decision making.

Given this motivation, radical bureaucrats in Japan and Turkey eliminated the structures of the old regime through political means rather than the use of extensive military or mass violence. To do this they first used tactical timing to introduce changes through incremental steps. In dismantling the old regime the revolutionary bureaucrats never revealed their total plan for a new polity and society, but introduced each change as a limited reform. Simultaneously, the revolutionary leaders used bureaucratic controls to eliminate the power of the conservatives and then to manipulate moderate support for more radical change.

Ataturk first concentrated on winning the war for independence by using a nationalist appeal that did not discuss postwar polity. He gained the support of a wide social spectrum including some of the most conservative elite. During the war in 1921, he influenced the Ankara National Assembly to pass a constitutional act which stated that sovereignty belonged to the nation and that the Grand National Assembly administered the Turkish state.[22] But this act did not specify the form of the state; many of the deputies interpreted the aim as some form of constitutional monarchy which would preserve the sultan caliph. After the war was won militarily, a crisis was created by the Allied invitation to both the Ankara Assembly and the sultanate to send delegations to a peace conference in Lausanne. The sultan accepted. "At this the deputies [in the Grand National Assembly] exploded in wrath. Sixteen orators in succession denounced it as a maneuver of the Sultan to divide the country in the eyes of the foreigners. They rehearsed at length the crimes of his government."[23] Ataturk took advantage of the crisis to propose that the sultanate be separated from the caliphate so that the monarch's political authority (as sultan) could be abolished, while his religious authority (as caliph) would be maintained. The assembly accepted this. Only later—after Ataturk had consolidated control over the assembly through the formation of a political party—was the republic proclaimed, and subsequently the caliphate also eliminated.

Abolition of the traditional polity in Japan proceeded in a similar incremental manner. At first the anti-Tokugawa movement proposed "some kind of Emperor-centered feudalism, operating through a baronial council.... This very vagueness made it possible to incorporate into the movement a great variety of social groups, ranging from Court nobles to feudal lords to lesser samurai and even well-to-do commoners."[24] After militarily defeating the Tokugawa forces, their lands (one-fourth of Japan) were put directly under the control of bureaucrats appointed by the central government. This was not seen as a threat to the other lords or to the samurai, for many interpreted this as making "the Emperor his own Shogun, the most powerful of the country's feudal lords."[25] A second step in the centralization of power occurred when the four daimyo of the han that dominated the new government (Satsuma, Choshu, Tosa, and Hizen) were convinced by the Meiji leaders to voluntarily and publicly return their lands to the emperor. Yet this act too could be interpreted in a traditional manner, for their letter to the emperor said: "The lands in which we live are the Emperor's lands. The people we govern are the Emperor's people. How then can we lightly treat them as our own? We now surrender our land registers to the throne, asking that the Court dispose of them at will, bestowing that which should be bestowed, taking away that which should be taken away."[26] The tone of this document was traditional. "There was nothing in it to suggest that the lands, once surrendered, would not be returned to those who already held them in fief, where this was merited."[27] Moreover, the action by the four lords alleviated the fears of other lords that they would establish a new shogunate. Hence, most of the other daimyo were convinced to surrender their lands after assurances that they would be continued as imperial governors of their domains, with power to appoint all provincial officials. They would also retain their traditional income and status, and samurai stipends would be paid by the central government.[28] Only several years later were the former daimyo removed as provincial governors and ordered to reside in Tokyo. Later still, the 302 former domains were reduced to 72 with new names and new geographical boundaries which did not coincide with the feudal units.[29]

Proceeding in this incremental manner—which at first concentrated on changing only the political organization of the regime without attacking the socioeconomic basis of the traditional polity—minimized opposition to each specific change. Opponents of one were unable to combine with opponents of another.[30] Tactical timing by the bureaucratic revolutionaries—which led to swift introduction of each change when the time was ripe—further prevented the crystallization of effective opposition.

Because of their own control of bureaucratic and military resources, the radical bureaucrats in Japan and Turkey felt free to establish parliamentary institutions in which members of the traditional elite with both moderate and conservative views would be represented. The wide spectrum of social interests represented in the first Turkish Grand National Assembly meant that Ataturk had to use persuasion and influence through long discussions and debates with the delegates to gain his objectives. But he also knew that these delegates had no independent base of power. As the war for independence neared its end, however, he organized a hierarchical and bureaucratic political party to exercise control over the delegates.

In Japan the samurai bureaucrats from Satsuma, Choshu, Tosa, and Hizen who took over the emperor's palace by force, established a new central administration in which court nobles and daimyo were appointed to the top posts.[31] While the radical samurai leaders accepted lower positions in the new government, they controlled the new centralized provincial administration and the new military forces. These samurai bureaucrats had learned to manipulate the daimyo in their han in putting together the anti-Bakufu coalition. They now used the same techniques with the emperor and court nobles, who, along with the daimyo had long been figureheads without real governing experience. At the same time the samurai bureaucrats had the emperor issue a Charter Oath which established a national assembly for all daimyo and high-ranking samurai. The Charter Oath proclaimed the principle of government by consultation, but did not give the assembly legislative power. The Meiji leaders, like Ataturk, used discussion in the assembly to assess the temper of traditional authorities. They also used it to educate them about the national need for a new form of government.[32]

As Ataturk built his bureaucratic party and the Meiji leaders consolidated their control over the Home Ministry and Financial Bureau, they were able to eliminate conservatives from the new government. It is important to note that neither Ataturk nor the Meiji revolutionaries based their power primarily on the army.

In Japan the government was reorganized and centralized a number of times in the first years of the Meiji regime. "The die-hard traditionalists, the court nobles and the feudal lords who appeared to dominate the bureaucracy in 1868 had nearly all disappeared by 1871."[33] The lower-status samurai who organized the Restoration moved up to openly hold political power in the centralized state, and then ousted the ex-daimyo from their positions as provincial governors. By this time, few daimyo had the will or power to resist. This was especially true since they were offered attractive alternatives. "There were no guillotines awaiting the dispossessed daimyo; rather they received generous financial settlements at the same time they were freed from the burdens of office."[34] Moreover, "their powers had come to be exercised, in fact, by officials who might trade for similar powers within a vastly larger organization."[35]

Likewise, Ataturk's party initiated governmental reorganization to exclude conservatives. In 1923 Ataturk and his ministers called for a new popular election. In the campaign, Ataturk's Republican People's party was the only organized force, and was thus able to elect a majority of its candidates to the second assembly. Less than one-third of the first assembly was reelected.[36] Both religious representatives and local notables were almost totally eliminated. The new assembly was even more urban and elitist with a higher percentage of army officers and bureaucrats.[37] Most moderates, who were primarily also military officers and civil bureaucrats, were reelected, but both the elimination of conservatives and the radical's control of the political party weakened their position. "The standard Kemalist attitude toward the role of the political party was to view it primarily as a mechanism for social control from above. The party was an organization for securing the necessary government and societal integration—a disciplined set of power and communication relations functioning mainly to implement certain decisions of top leadership."[38] Ataturk now used the party apparatus to force through the assembly the creation of the republic and abolition of the caliphate against the moderates' wishes. Despite resentment and muttered opposition,[39] they went along rather than resign and lose all political influence.

Unlike Japan, there were also revolutionaries in Turkey who were more radical than the bureaucratic leadership. Mainly intellectuals and independent professionals, they formed a leftist opposition by organizing a Communist party with direct ties to Moscow. Ataturk was constrained in dealing with them, partly because he received (and needed) Soviet military aid during the nationalist struggle,[40] and equally because a party with no mass base was not much of a threat. To counter it he used the same sort of bureaucratic manipulation that he devised to control his moderate and conservative supporters. Kemal organized his own "official" Turkish Communist party, led by bureaucrats loyal to him. "Its central committee included his top generals as well as some of the most prominent civilian leaders of the Kemalist regime . . . . The Ankara government combined the creation of the 'official' CP with an energetic propaganda campaign seeking to publicize the differences between Turkish (i.e., legitimate) communism and Soviet (i.e., illegitimate) Bolshevism. The newspaper of the official CP proclaimed: 'In the interests of the country we must counteract all the agitators and propagandists who have come on their own initiative, without consent of our ruling organs. Only Turks can introduce Bolshevism, and Bolshevism can be introduced only from above.'"[41] Later, after consolidating his own power in the Republican People's party, Ataturk outlawed and repressed the Soviet-linked CP. Yet instead of exiling or killing the CP leadership, Ataturk tried to reconcile them to his regime with inducements similar to those offered the conservative daimyo in Japan. He "boldly offered the intellectual elite of the CP the chance to enlist their energies in the Kemalist cause. Instead of casting them out as pariahs tainted for life for their involvement with communism, Ataturk provided them opportunities to use their talents in government service and indeed to play an important role in the ideological development of Kemalism."[42]

This generosity—as the consideration shown the daimyo—was the result both of a common aristocratic heritage and the fact that neither the Turkish radical intellectuals nor the conservative daimyo had an organized power base. It was only later with the introduction of social and economic reforms which abolished the Japanese samurai and the Turkish *ulema* (religious officials) that a counterrevolutionary force arose.

Organization and Tactics to Initiate Social and Economic Change   The most radical attempts at change began after Ataturk and the Meiji oligarchs had consolidated some degree of political control. It was at this point that these bureaucratic radicals passed beyond a political revolution by destroying the economic and social base of the traditional aristocracy. In neither case was this destruction motivated by class conflict or egalitarian ideals. The primary aim of the Meiji leaders was to strengthen the state. "Moves toward social equality were most often the result of measures taken for other more practical reasons."[43] Likewise, for Ataturk, "economic improvement and a bridging of class differences were practical requirements of national solidarity and international stature, rather than deeply felt needs of human justice and dignity. There is no reference in his speeches to inequalities of property."[44]

Their desire to use the state apparatus to foster economic development brought radical bureaucrats into direct conflict with the traditional aristocracy. The next chapter will demonstrate that the Japanese samurai and Turkish ulema were aristocracies created and sustained by the state. Samurai and ulema lived primarily off taxes collected by the state from the peasants. Unlike the Western feudal aristocracy, samurai had no direct economic control over the peasants, while the ulema only developed an independent economic base in the nineteenth century. Their status and power still derived primarily from the state.

Bureaucratic revolutionaries soon realized that continued government support of a large group of unproductive traditional officials made it impossible to support the military and industrial transformation necessary to regain national sovereignty. Not only did the stipends to samurai and the salaries of ulema drain government finances, but the maintenance of these artistocracies also reinforced traditional values which denigrated productive labor. Idle warriors and useless religious rituals became the epitomy of waste for the efficient bureaucratic reformers.

It was their ability to remove from power traditional social groups blocking modernization that differentiates the Ataturk and Meiji revolutionaries from earlier bureaucratic reformers in Japan and Turkey, and from many other leaders of national movements or military coups in Third World nations. It was not that Meiji oligarchs and Ataturk envisioned such destruction beforehand, but that when it became necessary within the logic of their radical action, they were willing and able to execute it. The degree of coercion and violence in this process was mitigated, however, by the continued use of the incremental and practical approach to change developed previously. Meiji leaders "moved forward in the economic sphere by solving immediate practical problems, such as balancing foreign payments, that had to be solved if they were to stay in power; and as they groped for solutions to these problems they hammered out an industrial policy that was successful, precisely because it was geared to present needs and not to distant and arbitrary objectives."[45] Ataturk said: "It is necessary to proceed by stages in implementing change, to prepare the feeling and spirit of the nation, and to try to reach our aims by degrees, profiting meanwhile in our experience."[46] The following pages will illustrate how the bureaucratic revolutionaries dismantled the traditional aristocracy while containing violent resistance.

DESTRUCTION OF THE ARISTOCRACY IN INCREMENTAL STEPS The abolition of status privileges and economic base of the samurai elite in Japan
was a gradual process cautiously engineered (often with reluctance) by the
samurai bureaucrats who led the revolution. The first measures taken to
stimulate economic growth and provide adequate revenue for the state
were not directly threatening to the samurai, for the new laws were aimed
at merchants and peasants and did not remove any of the samurai's status
or economic privileges. Guild and feudal restrictions on crops were
abolished as were restraints on trade. Both commoners and their produce
and goods were permitted to move freely across former feudal boundaries.
But most importantly, the land tax was revised in order to provide a tax that
"was easy to collect, difficult to evade, and one that would not fluctuate
according to the harvest."[47] Unlike the Tokugawa land tax, the new tax was
designed to stimulate production rather than to exercise control over land
and crops in the interests of security and stability.[48] Hence: (1) The Meiji
land tax was made payable to the central government in place of the han.
(2) It was levied directly on the landowner and not on the village collec-
tively. To make this possible, peasants were given title to the land and
permitted to transfer, buy, or sell land at will. Private property was thus
established not out of any ideological commitment, but to facilitate government collection of taxes. (3) Rather than a tax in kind levied on the crop
produced, the land tax was to be paid in money based on the value of the
land calculated on its average yield.[49] The tax rate set in this manner was
similar to the Tokugawa tax level, but small landowners had no cushion for
bad years, nor did they have the facilities to store part of their crop in
bumper years when the market value was low. The need to pay the land tax
in money swept many small cultivators into dependence on the market. As
a result huge numbers of peasants lost their land to debtors (mostly larger
landholders) in the 1870s and 1880s.[50] In an indirect and unpremeditated
way, a simplified method to collect a stable state tax consolidated large
landlords and led to increased class stratification of the countryside.[51]

A second set of government reforms challenged samurai prerogatives
more directly by breaking down status restrictions between samurai and
commoners. These new laws did not attack the economic base of the
samurai, however, nor did they force them to give up their habits and
lifestyle. One law permitted everyone to engage in any type of work:
samurai were allowed (not forced) to enter agriculture, commerce, and
industry. Other laws permitted commoners to have family names (formerly
restricted to samurai), to marry samurai and nobles, abolished dress and
hairstyle restrictions, and made the wearing of swords optional for samurai
(three years later the wearing of swords was forbidden). But it was the
conscription law of 1873 which most clearly threatened the samurai. This
law opened the officer corps to all men of talent and subjected both

commoners and samurai to conscription for army and navy service. The motivation for abolishing the exclusive military service of samurai was partly to encourage national identity among commoners.[52] More importantly, the government could not afford to equip, feed, and train a modern army of such a size that it would incorporate all the samurai.[53] (The new military and officer corps was considerably smaller than the number of samurai.)[54] This conscription law stimulated the first violent samurai opposition to the government.

The abolition of feudal domains and the promulgation of the new land tax and conscription laws still left the central government in a financial dilemma, for it had assumed the feudal obligation of paying daimyo and samurai stipends. These stipends, along with regular operational expenses of the bureaucracy, absorbed practically all government revenue. To raise funds for industrial investment, the revolutionary bureaucrats initiated a series of steps to reduce this financial obligation to the feudal class. (1) In 1873 all stipends were taxed on a sliding scale. (2) In 1874 all samurai were given the option of commuting their stipends to government bonds which would bear interest or could be sold for cash. (3) In 1876 all stipends were ordered so commuted.[55] Over the next few years, the commuted stipends cost the government one-tenth of what the yearly stipends had cost.[56] A small number of upper samurai received enough capital to invest in profitable enterprise. But lack of business experience, inflation in the 1870s, and the small settlement for most samurai wiped out ex-samurai capital.[57] The majority of samurai "went downward in the economic (and social) scale, ending up as common workers or even paupers."[58] But not before they attempted to revolt against the revolutionary bureaucrats who had sacrificed their own feudal class to the demands of economic development and national strength.

Economic development in Turkey necessitated the transformation of both external and internal constraints on the mobilization of resources. Prior to World War I, a large percentage of Turkish businesses and commercial enterprises were under direct foreign control. "Foreign groups administered the major ports, and owned many of the most important mines, all but 13% of the rail lines, and the greater share of the public utilities."[59] Much of the rest of productive and commercial enterprises was owned by Greeks, Armenians, and Jewish minorities. The latter problem was solved by an exchange of population with Greece after the War of Independence and by the free emigration of many other minority businessmen. The revolutionary regime quickly expropriated many foreign firms, and in March 1922 Ataturk put forth a six-point program for economic development. This plan sought: (1) to resuscitate and modernize agriculture and industry; (2) develop the forests; (3) nationalize economic enterprises most directly concerned with the general welfare; (4) exploit mineral wealth; (5) protect and invigorate existing and new industry; and (6) create a balanced state budget suited to the national economic structure.[60] As in Japan, this state initiative in economic matters "was an easy and familiar one, well in accord with the inherited traditions and habits of both the rulers and the ruled . . . . The idea of state direction and control in economic life came as a natural and obvious extension of the powers, prerogatives and functions of the governing elite."[61]

Internally, the Turkish bureaucrats soon saw the traditional religious elite as a barrier to economic development. Their concern was not only that this religious hierarchy drained state resources, but that their monopoly of legal and educational state resources[62] prevented creation of the legal infrastructure and human values necessary for the state to mobilize capital and foster the entrepreneurial and work values necessary for autonomous national industrialization. "The heavy residue of Ottoman mentality which tended to disparage business and industrial activity, the changeless and tradition-bound nature of Anatolian village society, and the small number of educated and technically skilled persons were all barriers to industrialization."[63] Even more than in Japan, the destruction of traditional barriers to economic development focused on alterations in the superstructure of society.

Ataturk first attacked the official religious hierarchy in order to eliminate the political power of religious officials. By abolishing the caliphate, confiscating the economic assets of the religious foundations (*wakfs*), closing all religious courts, substituting a secular legal code and courts, and outlawing all religious schools and instruction, Ataturk sought to create a new secular legitimacy for the state that would create acceptance of its right to foster economic development. He also sought to create a unified political elite committed to taking the lead in promoting a modern industrial society. To this end, he also substituted Latin for Arabic script in writing the Turkish language. Arabic script, "with its complexity of characters and accents, its paucity of vowels and its ambiguity of sounds in differing contexts, was hard for an ordinary person to read . . . . This led to the growth of two separate languages, that of the Ottoman mandarin class, which was written but largely unspoken, and that of the people, which was unwritten but spoken."[64] Thus, "language reform in Turkey was intimately connected with a renunciation of the cultural heritage of the educated class."[65] The radicalism of this change is seen when one realizes that educated youth today in Turkey find it difficult to read the 1924 Constitution and Ataturk's great speech of 1927. "Even when transcribed into the new script, they are as difficult for a Turkish schoolboy as Chaucer or even Langland for his English contemporary."[66] Because of the new script, and the purging of Arabic and Persian words from the Turkish language, the Turkish educated elite was culturally cut off from its Ottoman heritage.

In attacking religious officials and the culture of the traditional elite, Ataturk was also trying to undermine the possibility of political opposition from vested economic interests at the local level. "An important aspect of religion in the Ottoman Empire was that many of the most solid 'burghers' in the empire, owners of vineyards or even of farms and estates, were also persons who filled religious offices. This was so because the most stable institution in the empire was the Religious Institution, which was the most protected from imperial fiat."[67] Hence abolition of the political power of the ulema in Turkey—unlike elimination of the samurai in Japan—was also an attempt to undermine the potential political power of a landed class. It was an attempt by bureaucrats solely dependent on the state for their power, to eliminate the potential political opposition of those with economic power. It was this combined power of rural landowners and ulema which had provided the main opposition to the Young Turk reformers in the Ottoman parliaments in 1908-18. "Both these elements were traditional and conservative and in alliance, they formed a parliamentary group generally hostile to reforms."[68] The same combination had opposed Ataturk in the first Grand National Assembly. "To make language and territory the basis of nationhood violated the religious values which legitimized the local leaders. As a result, they fought vigorously to maintain the Islamic understanding of the nation by rejecting objective elements of nationhood and by stressing religious ties."[69]

Their opposition proved ineffective. By consolidating political power in the Republican party and by suppressing religious institutions, Ataturk broke the political authority of landlords and religious leaders.[70] But he never tried to combat or destroy the economic power of local notables. In Japan there was no powerful landed class, so no destruction was necessary. A nascent landlord class with traditional social status and political power at the local level did exist in Turkey. After the Ataturk Revolution, this landlord class consolidated its economic power, developed national organization and consciousness, and allied itself with a rising commercial bourgeoisie. Chapter 4 will document the counterrevolutionary activity of these economic classes. It was Ataturk's failure to destroy the economic power of local landlords with aristocratic status that later thwarted his revolution from above.

Response to Conservative Attempts at Counterrevolution and Moderate Opposition Movements The initiation of social and economic change by Meiji and Turkish bureaucratic revolutionaries provoked armed rebellion by conservative members of the displaced aristocracy and political opposition movements by moderate supporters of the revolution. Both the conservative and moderate opposition were led by traditional elites who lacked a mass base;

as a result their movements provided only a weak challenge to the bureaucratic revolutionaries. Moreover, the political controls consolidated by the revolutionaries' hold on the state bureaucracy permitted them to obliterate both types of opposition with a minimum of violence. The conservative counterrevolutionary rebellions were repressed with armed force, but there was no persecution or emigration of conservatives. The moderates were repressed politically, but without violence or the use of terror.

ARMED REPRESSION OF COUNTERREVOLUTION WITHOUT PERSECUTION OF CONSERVATIVES It was only after the abolition of those institutions in which a large segment of the traditional aristocracy had a vested interest—religious institutions in Turkey and the samurai in Japan—that armed resistance erupted. In Japan the gradual but complete termination of samurai privileges produced reactionary violence, including the assassination of several top revolutionary leaders, the attempted assassination of many others, and in 1873-78, four armed samurai uprisings. The Hizen Rebellion of 1874 sought to restore the daimyo, while the last and largest uprising, the Satsuma Rebellion of 1876, aimed at the restoration of the samurai. The feudal character of the samurai opposition to the Meiji regime is "clearly indicated by the fact that, except when they were able to utilize peasant discontent for their own ends as in the revolts between 1874-76, they helped the government in suppressing peasant uprisings."[71] The leaders of the Hizen and Satsuma rebellions in Japan were samurai who had held high office in the revolutionary government. The most famous case is that of Saigo, the leader of the Satsuma Rebellion, for Saigo had been a close friend of the revolutionary Okubo. They were both from Satsuma and early participants in the Loyalist movement; both had risen to highest office in the han government and had been primary leaders in the Restoration movement; both had been members of the early "Meiji triumvirate." The first serious split between Okubo and Saigo came in 1873 when Saigo resigned from the central government after being defeated on the Korea issue. It was in this controversy that Saigo clearly opted for traditionalism and Okubo for modernization. The explicit issue was whether the Japanese government should provoke a war with Korea. Implicitly, the question was whether Japan should concentrate on internal industrialization which would undermine the samurai class, or on immediate external expansion which would necessitate the mobilization of a large samurai army.[72] In the early years of the Restoration Saigo had supported industrialization, but he became increasingly disenchanted when he saw that such modernization meant the termination of samurai functions and privileges. He was especially opposed to the plan of recruiting commoners into the officer class of the new imperial army. For Saigo, then, a war with Korea necessitating the immediate mobilization of a large samurai army would avoid the issue of the samurai's future. After his defeat in council by Okubo and the modernizers, Saigo resigned from the government and returned to Satsuma, taking with him one-third of the imperial army. He briefly reentered the government in 1875; but in 1878, after the termination of samurai stipends, he led the rebellion. Okubo did not hesitate to crush it with federal troops. Saigo was killed in battle.

In Turkey, there was at least one high-level plot to assassinate Ataturk, but the conspirators were apprehended before its execution. The Kurdish Rebellion of 1925 was the most severe outbreak of armed counterrevolution; it was a reaction to attempts at central control and the secularism of the bureaucratic revolutionaries. The rebellion was fostered by an hereditary chieftain who wished to create an autonomous Kurdish state under the caliphate. "Rising beneath the green Islamic banner, in the name of the restoration of the Holy Law," he mobilized tribal forces to seize government offices in his province, imprison gendarmes, and march on several important cities.[73] The rebellion did not spread to other provinces, however, and was quickly put down by government troops.

These counterrevolutionary movements in the Japanese and Turkish revolutions did perpetuate some violence. In the Satsuma Rebellion over 13,000 were killed and 20,000 wounded.[74] The Kurdish Rebellion in Turkey was not very bloody, but afterward 40 rebels were executed. This violence, however, in no way compares with that in the French Revolution, when 400,000 perished in the Vendée reaction and 700,000 French soldiers were killed in foreign wars during 1792-1800.[75] Moreover, in neither Japan nor Turkey was there ever any movement to restore the shogunate or sultanate.

The most fundamental reason for the weakness of the conservative opposition and for the minimal use of government force against the conservatives derives from the bureaucratic character of radical and conservative elites. The revolutionaries could afford to use force only when they were faced with armed rebellion or attack, because they were so firmly in control of an efficient army and civil service. Bureaucratic control by the revolutionaries was especially enhanced by the fact that many of the top civil and military bureaucrats, who had remained neutral or loyal to the shogun and sultan before their defeat, were readily able to assume office in the new regime. An observer said of the Tokugawa bureaucrats: "With no apparent embarrassment . . . the former vengeful and anti-revolutionists, along with nearly everyone else in the empire, calmly presented themselves to the government headquarters and asked for employment."[76] Even more startling is the fact that 93 percent of the general staff officers of the

Ottoman Empire continued their service to the Turkish Republic, as did 85 percent of the trained civil servants.[77] Conversely, the conservatives' resources for resistance were greatly weakened by their bureaucratic heritage, for without office they lacked a base for opposition or for appeal to the masses. Because of the traditional separation and formality between bureaucrats and commoners, neither the displaced samurai nor the high ulema had much mass appeal.

It is significant that reactionary rebellions in Japan and Turkey occurred in localities where the conservative elite was least bureaucratized and least under control of the central government. Satsuma in Japan had a much larger percentage of *goshi* (rural-based samurai) than other provinces, and it was these rural samurai who were the basis of the Satsuma army and later of the Satsuma Rebellion.[78] Similarly, the conservative movement in Tosa "represented a combination of pre-Restoration loyalism with other elements of conservatism; its roots lay in the rural interests that had found earlier expression in the goshi and shoya movements."[79] The Kurdish Rebellion in Turkey also took place among a tribalized minority which was only nominally under control of the central government. It was aided by Islamic sects of dervishes who were traditionally distinct from the bureaucratized ulema and who had roots among the people.

A second reason for the lack of violent polarization between revolutionaries in power and the conservative aristocracy removed from authority was that the revolutionary governments were concerned with the personal fate of the conservatives and initiated various programs of compensation. This concern stemmed directly from the revolutionaries' past associations, and even friendships, with the conservatives. The deposition of the ulema in Turkey—removing them from their positions as judges, school teachers, and administrators of religious foundations (wakfs)—did not cause social and economic dislocation analogous to that resulting from the termination of samurai stipends in Japan. At the local level, ulema could still perform religious duties in the mosques with economic support from the local community. Many of these religious officials had also other sources of income as farmers or landowners. Many of the high religious bureaucrats who had been judges and administrators in the city were retained in secular positions in the new educational and judicial departments under the control of secular bureaucrats.[80]

In Japan the more severe economic dislocation of the samurai was met with a more comprehensive program of government compensation. We noted earlier that when the daimyo were displaced as governors of provinces, they were given a new aristocratic title and an extremely large financial payment. In many cases their financial position was improved. But the termination of samurai stipends affected a larger number of people and the terms of settlement were less generous. Many samurai—but still a minority—became bureaucrats, teachers, and policemen.[81] "Tokyo became a major attraction for the more capable of the han administrators and the prefectural governments provided employment for former han samurai and the more able of village headmen."[82] The warrior's monopoly of office holding was not "immediately in danger because no other class had yet the experience to compete."[83] But the majority of ex-samurai were plunged into poverty and unemployment. From 1870 to about 1889 the government directed to them a rehabilitation program which sought to involve the former warriors in economically productive enterprise. Not only would this mollify their resentment of the revolutionary regime, but it would also directly aid the state program of economic development. "The samurai were to provide a pool of uncommitted manpower from which financers, managers, and workers were to be recruited for the new Western style industries."[84] Many of these attempts at economic rehabilitation, such as the effort to resettle samurai as farmers and to start them in banking, were not very successful. Many samurai attempts at business and farming failed in the 1870s and 1880s. One program was more effective though. This was the issuing of government loans to associations of samurai and commoners—not to individual entrepreneurs—for the starting of businesses. "The samurai associations in little more than a decade (1876-1889) enlisted roughly 100,000 men or about 23% of the entire class."[85] This was enough to ally much discontent. Even after the huge Satsuma Rebellion by samurai in 1876 the government showed no resentment, but gave renewed effort to rehabilitation programs.[86] "By erasing the dangers of class rebellion and relocating a large social group with no apparent function in an industrialized society, the Meiji government did realize a measure of success. Although Meiji statesmen did not provide the class with a satisfactory financial settlement, the program did allow sufficient time and suitable means for the adjustment of the samurai to the new age. By the late 1880's the threat of class discontent had been removed, and the government could allow the program of rehabilitation to lapse."[87]

SELECTIVE POLITICAL REPRESSION OF MODERATE OPPOSITION WITHOUT A REIGN OF TERROR Revolution from above in Japan and Turkey did not necessitate a reign of terror for the radicals to pursue their programs of revolutionary change. In Japan there was no use of revolutionary tribunals and execution. In Turkey, special tribunals were organized after the Kurdish Rebellion to try "counterrevolutionaries," but less than fifty people were executed.[88] This is to be contrasted with the French terror where about 17,000 were guillotined (2,625 of these in Paris), or the Soviet terror where in 1918, 6,185 people were put to death and in 1919, 3,456.[89] The reign of terror in a mass revolution served functions which were precluded by bureaucratic revolution. Mass execution in a reign of terror created social atomization which both thwarted elite opposition and made the masses available for ideological mobilization.[90] In Japan and Turkey neither of these functions was considered necessary by the revolutionaries. The conservative aristocracy was easily removed from power and controlled by the superior organization of the revolutionaries. The masses were not an initial target or threat to the Japanese and Turkish revolutionaries; their main goal was to change the central institutions staffed and controlled by the elite. Thus in neither country did the revolutionaries attempt to change the life of the rural peasant. Even though Ataturk talked about changing the peasant, what has been said of Meiji Japan is also true of Republican Turkey: "The village remained predominantly a community of small peasants faced with similar problems of small-scale cultivation and marketing. Sentimental and organizational ties from an earlier period persisted with special force, and the authority of the village over its members remained exceedingly strong."[91] In chapter 4, I shall examine how the bureaucratic leaders created a repressive ideological and educational system to reinforce mass apathy.

Moderate supporters of the revolution were members of the traditional political elite that provided the most opposition to the bureaucratic revolutionaries and stimulated the use of some repressive measures by the regime. After elimination of the old regime and removal of conservative elites from power, cleavages developed between the revolutionary leadership and their more moderate supporters. The moderates were particularly alienated by the concentration of bureaucratic power in Ataturk's party and in the central executive in Japan, controlled by samurai bureaucrats from Satsuma and Choshu. In both countries a group of the most influential moderates voluntarily withdrew from the government and formed an opposition party. They did not seek to oust the revolutionary leadership from power, but only to increase their own participation in decision making and prevent personal autocracy. Their opposition, however, soon attracted other interests.

The Progressive party in Turkey was organized in 1925 by the four generals who, along with Ataturk, had initiated the revolutionary resistance. These generals had a higher status in the traditional Ottoman elite than did Ataturk. As a result they wished to reform, but retain, traditional Ottoman institutions, especially religion.[92] But at the same time they favored free enterprise and encouragement of foreign capital investment.[93] Hence they were less enthusiastic about an authentic revolution from above.

The split among Japanese revolutionary bureaucrats in 1873 over whether to send a military campaign to Korea (or to concentrate on internal industrialization) produced a moderate opposition movement in addition to the counterrevolutionary force in Satsuma. The Tosa bureaucrats who withdrew from the government formed a movement to agitate for a constitution, a national parliament, and the franchise for all ex-samurai, rich farmers, and merchants.[94] This movement for popular rights represented the Tosa samurai who reacted to their economic plight in a different way than their Satsuma counterparts. "Instead of rising in revolt, they endeavored to integrate themselves into the local economy."[95] Because Tosa was more commercialized than Satsuma, the samurai and peasant landlords were drawn closer. After the Satsuma Rebellion proved that armed resistance was futile, the movement for popular rights produced national organization and in 1881 initiated the first political parties. At the same time, leadership of the movement passed into the hands of the rural landlord-industrialists of peasant origin.[96] Ex-samurai remained the theorists and publicists in opposition parties, "but in the majority of the local affiliates which gave the democratic movement its momentum, the rural gentry were in command."[97] These landlords "resented the fact that much of the government revenue was derived from the land tax. Moreover, they looked with misgivings on the steady flow of taxes into the central treasury."[98]

In both Turkey and Japan, opposition parties became threatening to the bureaucratic revolutionaries when they began to attract mass support. The Turkish Progressive party, and its successor in 1930, the Liberal Party, drew widespread support from the urban lower class.[99] In Japan, small landowners, tenant farmers, and wage workers joined the popular rights movement between 1878 and 1881.[100] In neither case had the bureaucratic revolutionaries prepared to mobilize their own mass support or to control mass opposition. As a result, they used both repression and appeasement against the moderates. The Japanese and Turkish military were put under strict central control, and military officers were forbidden to participate in politics. Press censorship was initiated and more stringent laws of assembly were enforced.

The Progressive party in Turkey and its successor, the Liberal party, were completely suppressed. A number of the most prestigious leaders of the Progressive party were accused (without justification) of implication in the Kurdish Rebellion, and were arrested and brought to trial in special tribunals erected to try counterrevolutionaries. All of the moderates were acquitted, but six were sentenced to exile and a few others escaped overseas before being arrested.[101] However, all the exiles were soon granted amnesty. "'It was the people that I was afraid of.' Thus did Kemal in a remark to a friend seek to justify afterwards the liquidation of his opponents and his assumption of supreme powers."[102] But even Ataturk repented after the fact for his very limited foray into terroristic methods. "Though authoritarian practices were widely used to restrict the expression of dissent, no totalitarian terror ever stalked Kemalist Turkey . . . . Repressive measures were almost always regarded as temporary and unfortunate, even though of practical necessity, and they were productive of . . . a bad conscience. This bad conscience was eased periodically through attempts to live up to democratic norms by permitting the organization of opposition."[103]

The Meiji oligarchs used more subtle means to separate the samurai and landlord leaders of the opposition from its mass support. The cooptation of leaders into government office and the granting of a constitution and national parliament by the bureaucratic revolutionaries led to voluntary dissolution of opposition parties. The Meiji leaders had a remarkable ability to grant concessions at the proper moment. "Whenever popular pressure became too powerful to be suppressed, they would retreat without giving up the substance of power. They possessed the kind of suppleness which any regime wishing to remain in control must possess. Perhaps an explanation of this is to be found in the fact that these men were able to overthrow the Shogunate without having had to acquire a wide popular following. This left them unencumbered with commitments, thus enabling them to act freely as the occasion demanded."[104] But the landlord leaders of the opposition were also frightened by the spontaneous local revolts of tenants in the early 1880s.[105] They decided that working with the bureaucrats was less dangerous than mobilizing mass support.

In both Turkey and Japan the revolutionary bureaucrats consolidated political power in their own hands—in the single party in Turkey and in the executive bureaucracy free of parliamentary or party control in Japan. Yet because they had no base of mass support and feared continued political opposition from landlords and rural notables, bureaucratic revolutionaries made economic concessions to these local vested interests. In both countries they reinforced the landlords' social and economic control over local peasantry in return for rural support for the regime's program of urban industrialization. The bureaucrats used the army and public schools to indoctrinate peasants with traditional values legitimizing traditional structures in the countryside. Chapter 4 will document the social, economic, and political costs of these concessions to the rural middle classes, and the attempt to create a modern economy and polity without mass mobilization.

Notes

1. Dankwart Rustow, "Ataturk as Founder of a State," *Daedalus* 97 (1968): 797.

2. Ibid., 803.

3. Dankwart Rustow, "The Army and the Founding of the Republic," *World Politics* 11 (1959): 549.

4. Dankwart Rustow, "The Development of Parties in Turkey," in *Political Parties and Political Development*, eds. Joseph La Palombara and Myron Weiner (Princeton: Princeton University Press, 1966), p. 127.

5. Rustow, "The Army," p. 542.

6. Ibid., p. 524.

7. Elaine D. Smith, *Origins of the Kemalist Movement and the Government of the Grand National Assembly* (Washington, D.C.: Judd & Detweiler Press, 1959), p. 31.

8. Frederick Frey, *The Turkish Political Elite* (Cambridge, Mass.: MIT Press, 1965), p. 181.

9. Ibid., pp. 256-57.

10. Ibid., p. 208.

11. Rustow, "The Army," p. 545.

12. Albert Craig, *Choshu in the Meiji Restoration* (Cambridge, Mass.: Harvard University Press, 1961), p. 335.

13. Ibid., p. 358.

14. Neutralization of the masses would be more difficult in a more urbanized country.

15. Crane Brinton, *The Anatomy of Revolution* (New York: Vintage Books, 1938).

16. Lord Kinross, *Ataturk: The Rebirth of a Nation* (London: Weidenfeld & Nicolson, 1964), p. 44.

17. Masakazu Iwata, *Okubo Toshimichi: The Bismarch of Japan* (Berkeley: University of California Press, 1964), p. 115.

18. Ibid., p. 116.

19. William Beasley, *The Meiji Restoration* (Stanford: Stanford University Press, 1972), p. 320.

20. Ibid., p. 330.

21. Marius Jansen, "The Meiji State: 1868-1912," in *Modern East Asia: Essays in Interpretation*, ed. James Crowley (New York: Harcourt Brace, & World, 1970), p. 103.

22. Kemal Karpat, *Turkey's Politics* (Princeton: Princeton University Press, 1959), p. 38.

23. Kinross, p. 347.

24. Beasley, *The Meiji Restoration*, p. 284.

25. Ibid., p. 328.

26. Ibid., p. 331.

27. Ibid.

28. Ibid., p. 332.

29. Ibid., p. 347.

30. Huntington, p. 352.

31. Beasley, *The Meiji Restoration*, p. 291.

32. Robert Wilson, *Genesis of the Meiji Government in Japan: 1868-1871* (Berkeley: University of California Press, 1957), p. 83.

33. Sidney Brown, "Okubo Toshimichi and the First Home Ministry Bureaucracy: 1873-1878," in *Modern Japanese Leadership*, eds. Bernard Silberman and Harry Harootunian (Tucson: University of Arizona Press, 1966), p. 211.

34. John Hall, *Japan: From Prehistory to Modern Times* (New York: Dell, 1970), p. 272.

35. Smith, "Japan's Aristocratic Revolution," p. 138.

36. Frey, *The Turkish Political Elite*, p. 308.
37. Ibid., p. 183.
38. Ibid., p. 304.
39. Huntington, p. 353.
40. George Harris, *The Origins of Communism in Turkey* (Stanford: Hoover Institute Publications, 1967), p. 8.
41. Ibid., pp. 80-81.
42. Ibid., p. 141.
43. Hall, *Japan*, p. 281.
44. Rustow, "Ataturk as Founder of a State," p. 823.
45. Thomas Smith, *Political Change and Industrial Development in Japan* (Stanford: Stanford University Press, 1955), p. 102.
46. Kemal Ataturk, Speech (Leipzig: K.F. Koehler, 1929), p. 19.
47. E.H. Norman, *Japan's Emergence as a Modern State* (New York: Institute of Pacific Relations, 1940), p. 140.
48. Beasley, *The Meiji Restoration*, p. 394.
49. Henry Rosovsky, "Japan's Transition to Modern Economic Growth, 1868-1888," in *Industrialization in Two Systems*, ed. Henry Rosovsky (New York: Wiley, 1966), p. 117.
50. Norman, *Japan's Emergence*, pp. 143-45.
51. Beasley, *The Meiji Restoration*, p. 390.
52. Marius Jansen, *Sakamoto Ryoma and the Meiji Restoration* (Princeton: Princeton University Press, 1961), p. 365.
53. James Crowley, "From Closed Door to Empire," in *Modern Japanese Leadership*, eds. Silberman and Harootunian, p. 271.
54. Ibid., p. 268.
55. Beasley, *The Meiji Restoration*, p. 386.
56. Ibid., p. 389.
57. Rosovsky, p. 117.
58. Hall, *Japan*, p. 282.
59. Richard Robinson, *The First Turkish Republic* (Cambridge, Mass.: Harvard University Press, 1963), pp. 100-101.
60. Ibid., p. 104.
61. Bernard Lewis, *The Emergence of Modern Turkey* (London: Oxford University Press, 1961), p. 464.
62. Ibid., p. 259.
63. Robinson, p. 115.
64. Kinross, p. 441.
65. Uriel Heyd, *Language Reform in Modern Turkey* (Jerusalem: Israel Oriental Society, 1954), p. 109.
66. Lewis, *The Emergence of Modern Turkey*, p. 430.
67. Serif Mardin, "Ideology and Religion in the Turkish Revolution," *International Journal of Middle Eastern Studies* 2 (1971): 207.
68. Feroz Ahmad and Dankwart Rustow, "The Parliaments of the Second Constitutional Period, 1908-1918," unpublished paper, p. 9.
69. Karpat, *Turkey's Politics*, p. 53.
70. Ibid., p. 53.
71. Norman, *Japan's Emergence*, p. 90.
72. Crowley, "From Closed Door to Empire," p. 272.
73. Kinross, p. 396.
74. Iwata, p. 248.

75. Edwards, p. 180.
76. Fukuzawa Yukichi, *The Autobiography of Fukuzawa Yukichi* (Tokyo: Hokuseido Press, 1948), p. 312.
77. Rustow, "The Military," in Ward and Rustow, p. 338.
78. E.H. Norman, *Soldier and Peasant in Japan* (New York: Institute of Pacific Relations, 1943), p. 21.
79. Jansen, *Sakamoto Ryoma*, p. 373.
80. Lewis, *The Emergence of Modern Turkey*, p. 266.
81. Ex-samurai held almost a monopoly of police work in the new Meiji state, but they were not predominant in the Meiji military. Harry Harootunian, "Japan and the Samurai Class, 1868-1882," *Pacific Historical Review* 28 (1959): 261-63.
82. Hall, *Japan*, p. 277.
83. Smith, "Japan's Aristocratic Revolution," p. 138.
84. Harry Harootunian, "The Economic Rehabilitation of the Samurai in the Early Meiji Period," *Journal of Asian Studies* 2 (1958): 434.
85. Ibid., p. 436.
86. George Sansom, *The Western World and Japan* (New York: Knopf, 1950), p. 336.
87. Harootunian, "Economic Rehabilitation of the Samurai," p. 444.
88. Robinson, p. 88.
89. Edwards, pp. 180-82.
90. See Barrington Moore, *Terror and Progress USSR* (New York: Harper Torchbooks, 1966), ch. 6.
91. Thomas Smith, *Agrarian Origins of Modern Japan* (Stanford: Stanford University Press, 1959), p. 210.
92. Frey, *The Turkish Political Elite*, p. 324.
93. Kinross, p. 395.
94. Nobutaka Ike, *The Beginnings of Political Democracy in Japan* (Baltimore: Johns Hopkins Press, 1950), p. 59.
95. Ibid., p. 62.
96. George Beckman, *The Making of the Meiji Constitution* (Lawrence: University of Kansas Press, 1957), p. 41.
97. Ike, p. 70.
98. Ibid., p. 83.
99. Kinross, pp. 452-53.
100. Ike, p. 85.
101. Kinross, p. 435.
102. Ibid.
103. Frey, *The Turkish Political Elite*, p. 338.
104. Ike, p. 191.
105. Ibid., p. 159.

Chapter 3
The Genesis of Revolution from Above

Revolutions from above are possible only in a state where both the military and civilian administration have become highly bureaucratized. According to the classic Weberian definition, such bureaucratic administrations are based on technical specialization and hierarchical control. It was not the aristocratic or elitist nature of state functionaries in Japan and Turkey that was a precondition for revolution from above, but their bureaucratization.

Given a bureaucratic state, study of Japanese and Turkish history leads to the hypothesis that five conditions were necessary and sufficient to generate revolutionaries from within the top ranks of the military administration. Subsequent analysis of Egypt and Peru demonstrates that the fifth factor was historically specific to the relatively decentralized political system of Japan and Turkey. Military elites may stage coups and intervene in politics when one or more of these conditions are absent, but such political action will either maintain the given social and economic structure or attempt to restore a declining order.

·1. Military bureaucrats have the potential for leading a revolution from above when the officer class—or a significant segment of it—is independent of those classes which control the means of production.[1] Military bureaucrats are autonomous in this sense when they are not recruited from the dominant landed, commercial, or industrial classes, and when they do not form close personal and economic ties with these classes after their elevation to high office. Such bureaucratic autonomy is most likely to occur when there is no consolidated class of landlords or when such a class is in decline. In Japan and Turkey the creation of autonomous military bureaucrats derived from a distinctive development of the precapitalist state which bureaucratized the aristocracy and removed it from control over the land. The consolidation of an urban aristocracy whose power depended on holding bureaucratic office in the state retarded the growth of a consolidated class of landlords. When landlords did evolve in the nineteenth century, they had neither the aristocratic status, accumulated wealth, nor political hegemony that they did in the West. Urban merchants too were much weaker and politically subordinate in Japan and Turkey. At the same time, the Japanese and Turkish aristocracy never developed an independent base of economic power. Revolutions from above were led by socially mobile military officers who were drawn into the aristocracy and given high office because of their specialized skills. But the distinct character of the bureaucratized aristocracy in Japan and Turkey and its autonomy from the landed class provided the structural context within which military officers became radicals.

One cannot explain this historical development in Japan and Turkey by some concept like the "Asiatic mode of production," or "Oriental despotism,"[2] because China diverged from the pattern of Japan and Turkey. Chinese bureaucrats did become landowners and landlords, and organized themselves into an aristocratic estate (the gentry) with social privileges. Recent research suggests that precapitalist Europe and imperial China—unlike Togukawa Japan and Ottoman Turkey—developed private property in land.[3] Yet why land became privatized in China but not in Japan and Turkey, is still unclear.

Chapter 5 will demonstrate, however, that an autonomous military bureaucracy can be created in modern states with far different patterns of political evolution than those in Japan and Turkey. However attained, such class autonomy of military bureaucrats provides the potential for their radicalization. Because their status and power depends solely on the state, they do not suffer personally from abolition of existing economic structures. But such autonomy alone will not guarantee the precipitation of revolution from above.

2. As bureaucrats, military officers are trained to be specialized professionals working in a hierarchy and isolated from general poltical concerns. Autonomous military bureaucrats become revolutionaries only if they develop political cohesion. In late Tokugawa Japan and Ottoman Turkey this politicization was linked to the decay of traditional military functions and to military defeat by Western powers. National liberation through nation building became an alternative function for the military.

3. Autonomous miltary bureaucrats united around a nationalist ideology will act in a revolutionary manner only in response to movements within the country demanding an end to national degradation by foreign powers. Military leaders in Japan and Turkey became revolutionaries only when their own power was directly threatened by internal upheaval generated by foreign penetration. Military bureaucrats with ties to vested interests react to nationalist movements from below with conservative repression. It is

only bureaucrats without such vested interests who react positively to such nationalism by replacing movements from below by their own more rational revolutions from above.

4. Autonomous military bureaucrats can stage a successful revolution from above only when contradictions in the international constellation of power can be exploited to increase national autonomy. The ability of military leaders in Japan and Turkey to act in a radical way depended on the disinclination of Western powers to respond to their resistance. In the mid–nineteenth century the imperial powers were most interested in China. They were not ready to use massive force against Japan. Likewise, Western nations after the grueling course of World War I were not prepared to remobilize their armies to assure Turkish allegiance.

Under such conditions, military bureaucrats did not have the option of staging a coup with the limited aim of replacing the top personnel of government. The mere takeover of the existing regime would not have provided the requisite strength to stave off foreign intrustion and reestablish internal order. Like the classic French and Russian revolutionaries, bureaucratic revolutionaries have to build political power and forge a new legitimacy in order to rule. Without the Western threat there probably would have been no revolution in Japan and Turkey. But in the face of such threat and the rise of nationalist movements from below some of the highest officials of the state were willing and able to adopt revolutionary measures, for they believed such drastic action was the only way to bolster the power of a state bureaucracy which was the sole basis of their personal power and prestige.

5. In relatively decentralized states like Tokugawa Japan and Ottoman Turkey, dissident military bureaucrats must have a provincial base of power separate from the central government to stage a revolution from above. In both Tokugawa Japan and Ottoman Turkey movements led by radical bureaucrats in the lower echelons of state service arose in the 1860s. But the ethnic diversity of the Ottoman provinces prevented revolution from above in Turkey until the breakdown of the empire in World War I. In contrast, the Tokugawa polity—which created both a bureaucratic and a decentralized state with autonomous provincial administration and military forces—rapidly produced a revolution from above.

The following pages will trace in detail the historical maturation of autonomous, nationalistic, and finally revolutionary military bureaucrats in Japan and Turkey. Detailed exploration of this evolution of the traditional Japanese and Ottoman states not only supports the hypotheses advanced above but provides the categories and concepts for future comparative study of those states (China and Prussia) which did not create autonomous military bureaucrats in the course of their evolution to a modern polity.

Bureaucratization of the Traditional State and Aristocracy

Max Weber, in his *Economy and Society*, differentiates between two types of traditional authority—feudalism and patrimonialism—a distinction which helps to clarify the political and stratification systems of Ottoman Turkey and Tokugawa Japan. Whether or not these two societies were ever strictly feudal in Weber's terms, they were definitely patrimonial by the sixteenth century in Turkey and the seventeenth century in Japan.

Both a feudal and a patrimonial polity are traditional in that (1) all officials are recruited on the basis of personal loyalty to the ruler and not on impersonal and rational criteria; (2) the central political authority is weak and the sovereign does not have direct control over the population; and (3) political office is intertwined with personal property—there is no clear distinction between the private and the public.[4]

A patrimonial state develops when a patriarchal ruler extends his household administration over a wider political territory. This necessitates a military and administrative staff, recruited at first from the ruler's personal dependents—sons, servants, and slaves. At this stage, ruler and official remain tied by bonds of paternal authority and filial dependency, and official tasks are subsumed under that part of the original household administration to which they are most clearly related.[5] Officials, instead of being maintained in the king's household and at his board, however, are given land and sometimes equipment to sustain themselves in return for their military and administrative duties.

According to Weber, feudalism resulted from the breakdown of a patrimonial regime and hence was an extreme or marginal case of patrimonialism.[6] Feudalism triumphed when the land benefices granted to officials became not only hereditary fiefs but personal property over which the ruler had no control. In contrast, land under patrimonialism always remained a prebend, a nonhereditary form of support for officials which could be removed at the discretion of the ruler. Land and other benefices (fees or payment in kind for services) remained attached to the office and not to the incumbent.

A sovereign was most likely to maintain his patrimonial rule if he could control an independent military force by recruiting soldiers and officials from outside the landed stratum, such as from peasants, slaves, and foreigners.[7] "Patrimonialism stands opposed to the typical efforts of a landed aristocracy to prevent the transfer and fragmentation of landed property and to bar the social and economic ascent of individuals or groups outside the privileged stratum."[8]

Feudalism and partimonialism produced different kinds of social stratification. Feudal lords used their control over the land as a power base to win contractual rights from the king. In the struggle, the vassals developed organization independent of the state; they became an estate—a corporate aristocracy—with collective consciousness of their status interests. Patrimonial officials became a status group with honor and privileges vis-à-vis the general population, but their prestige remained tied to office, and hence they were personally dependent on the sovereign. Without an independent base of power (land), they failed to develop independent organization.[9]

Weber himself noted that patrimonial rule in the Ottoman Empire and Tokugawa Japan did not duplicate the feudal pattern characteristic of Western Europe.[10] Weber recognized that traditional Oriental monarchs retained more power than their counterparts in the West: in the Orient "the offices were indeed highly stereotyped, but the incumbent himself remained freely replaceable; this resulted from the absence of certain Occidental estate features and from the military power position of the Oriental ruler which had a different political and economic basis."[11] Weber said of Turkey: "The Turkish cavalry which held fief-like prebends existed next to the patrimonial Jannissaries (slave-troops) and therefore remained itself semi-prebendal."[12] Similarly, Weber noted that the great lords in Japan (daimyo) could be transferred from one district to another; hence their territory was a prebend and not a fief. Moreover, "these daimyos were forbidden to establish alliances, to enter into relations of vassalage with one another, to conclude treaties with foreign powers, to carry on feuds, or to build fortresses."[13] Likewise, the lords' vassals (samurai) were not granted land in return for military and civil services, but rice stipends.[14]

The creation of a patrimonial state in Turkey and Japan originated in the change from unstable military rule to a centralized and civil state—the Ottoman Empire (in the fifteenth century) and the Tokugawa Shogunate (in the seventeenth century). As Japanese and Turkish dynastic leaders gained power through military conquest, they began to create new and central institutions to consolidate their rule over semiautonomous provinces and over the warriors. To fill these new political roles, the rulers sought officials without access to resources (land and arms) independent of the ruler.

Until the nineteenth century, the Tokugawa and Ottoman states remained patrimonial and did not develop into a modern bureaucracy. Officials were most often appointed because of their personal connections or ability to pay for the office and not on the basis of merit or specialized knowledge. They were often compensated in irregular ways instead of a regular salary. Nor was their private property distinguished from the public domain. But the patrimonial state developed a hierarchy of semi-specialized officials which created the potential for rapid bureaucratization. It also developed an urban aristocracy whose status and power depended on the state and not on direct control over the land.

**Creation of Patrimonial
Institutions and a State Aristocracy
in Japan and Turkey**

OTTOMAN TURKEY In the fifteenth and sixteenth centuries, the emperor of the Turkish state—the sultan caliph—staffed central political institutions with slaves—a practice with roots in prior Islamic tradition. The sultan's slaves were recruited from three sources—from the sultan's dole of prisoners captured in battle, by royal purchase at the slave market, and through a tribute of Christian boys from peasant families in the Balkan provinces. The majority of royal slaves were converted to Islam, given a military education, and placed as soldiers in a central and salaried army—the famed janissary troops. The most promising slaves, however, were sent to select palace schools for education in languages, Islam, the humanities, and military arts. The highest civil and military officials of the state were recruited from these select slaves and given elite privileges and status. "The type of governing official which the Turkish sultans desired to produce through the medium of their palace system of education was the warrior-statesman and loyal Moslem, who should be a man of letters and a gentlemen of polished speech, profound courtesy and honest morals."[15] Besides staffing the central political institutions and leading the janissaries, these "slaves of the Porte" were made provincial governors with power to lead the regional troops in war and with civil authority over local elites.

Centralization of the Ottoman Empire did not completely displace the local aristocracy which had gained power through feudal military organization. The majority of Ottoman armed forces continued to be led by a territorial cavalry, the *sipahi*, who were granted fiefs (*timars*) by the sultan in return for their provision of troops for military campaigns. The sipahi had direct control over the peasantry on their lands and the right to collect taxes from them. These taxes were retained by the fief holders and not remitted to the central government. "This arrangement superficially resembled the feudal system of western Europe. In practice it was much more centralized and efficient when the empire was at its height. The sipahi were required to serve as long as they were needed in contrast to the 40 days per year limitation common in the West. The sipahi also paid allegiance to only one lord, their Sultan, and no subinfeudination was allowed to weaken this relationship. Furthermore, the sipahi were directly supervised by the Sultan's slaves sent out from Constantinople to administer the provinces."[16] The slaves of the Porte kept strict control over the timars (fiefs) through careful surveys of the land[17] and regulations as to how much the peasants could be taxed.[18] The sipahi were also required to live on the land and preserve its taxpaying potential through continued cultivation by the peasants.[19] If he failed to perform either his military or administrative duties, any sipahi could be dismissed. Although their position became hereditary, the state held title to the lands, which returned to the state if there was no heir. Even though the sipahi remained prebends under control of the state (and were not independent feudal lords), these local elites maintained the potential for developing an independent base of economic power.

The first step in the specialization of government functions in the Ottoman Empire was the separation of government from the sultan's household. In 1654, the sultan's chief lieutenant, the grand vezir, was given a separate residence, the Sublime Porte, which also housed the central administrative offices and became the seat of government.[20] The financial administration, subordinate to the grand vezir, was also given its own building. The sultan appointed the grand vezir, but he then had final authority over the appointment and control of all administrative and financial offices. In a similar manner, the sultan selected the grand judge of Istanbul (Sheyhual-Islam) from the highest religious officials. The grand judge had equal rank with the grand vezir, and he gained the authority to appoint all other legal and religious officials.[21] The highest janissary commanders remained more closely tied to the imperial household. Even though the janissary troops were quartered in cities throughout the empire, their leaders resided in the sultan's compound.[22] Yet the separation between the administrative, financial, and judicial bureaus and the sultan's household was never complete. He could always intervene to influence policy and to have his personal servants and slaves appointed to high office.

Functional specialization of the Ottoman central institutions also led to the separation of officials into four career lines—financial and administrative, judicial, military, and palace. Each of these divisions was further separated into a complex of offices. But even by the eighteenth century, there were still many overlapping jurisdictions. Several examples are these: (1) The grand vezir had his own law courts which handled some cases independent of the primary judicial system staffed through religious officials (ulema) and under the Sheyhual-Islam. There was no clear distinction as to what types of legal questions were handled by which court.[23] (2) Within the civil administration there was a ministry of the interior, ministry of justice and police, and a foreign ministry, but often their functions overlapped and each included a miscellaneous number of offices under their supervision. New offices were added, "not according to any rational plan, but rather by a process of accretion in response to the needs of the state as perceived and acted on over centuries. The absence of any concern for rationalization or separation of functions appears also in the way the staff of each office was organized."[24] The hierarchical ordering of offices within the four sections was further advanced than the specialization of function. However, this hierarchy was not a response to the need for efficiency or rational organization of work. Rather, it served to increase the power of top officials and to formalize (rather than rationalize) authority.[25]

The patrimonial character of the Ottoman state from the sixteenth to mid–nineteenth century is seen even more clearly in the manner in which officials were appointed and paid. The strength of the Ottoman Empire at its height in the sixteenth century rested on the creation of a slave army and administration which was completely loyal to the sultan and able to maintain central control over the feudal cavalry and provincial administration. But by the late sixteenth century the tally of Christian boys to fill military and civil offices was abolished and Moslem families came to constitute the chief source of recruitment for military, judicial, and administrative posts.[26] The highest officials were recruited from a group of important urban Moslem families. Janissary troops and lower religious and administrative office were filled by lower urban families. Here we will discuss only the high posts.

Future officials normally began their careers as boys at about age ten, just out of the elementary Mosque schools. To join the staff of a government office, the boys had to be brought before the appropriate officials to secure a warrant of authorization. This required an official patron—usually the boy's father—in a position to secure the document and make the proper payment.[27] Once appointed, the boys were trained as apprentices. In contrast to the training of ulema (religious officials) in Arabic and traditional religious sciences, civil officials were required to learn Arabic and Persian, and were also trained in accounting, geography, administrative law, or diplomatic procedure, depending on the office.[28] There was no set procedure for advancement in the state hierarchy; it depended on personal connections and often the payment of a fee to obtain appointment to a higher office.[29] Thus the procedure for appointment and advancement in the patrimonial state produced a tendency toward the monopoly of high offices by a stratum of urban families. This tendency was increased by the manner in which officials were reimbursed for their services.

Although the janissaries, standing cavalry, and the sultan's household were paid a salary in coin, all other officials were paid in a manner quite different from that of a modern bureaucrat. Most other officials were paid from the tax receipts of fiefs attached to their offices.[30] Unlike the fiefs granted to the feudal troops (sipahi), however, these administrative fiefs were connected to the office and not to the occupant of the office. Moreover, the official did not live on the land and had no contact with the peasants. Rather, "the administration of the fiefs was assigned to special agents appointed by the grand vezir so that the scribes themselves were entirely free to perform their duties."[31] In addition to the returns from fiefs, many officials were entitled to collect fees from the populace in return for issuing documents, hearing court cases, or performing whatever duty was required.[32] Some offices were recompensed solely through those fees. In fact, "in the imperial bureaucracy there were a number of assistants who served initially without any compensation in hopes of receiving after several years a share of the fees collected in the office and eventually being promoted into one of the higher classes and obtaining a fief income."[33] Another source of revenue for those in the highest offices was fees they collected for appointing particular persons to office. Often they themselves had to pay a large fee to obtain the high office, and they then tried to recoup their loss and make a profit by collecting from their subordinates.[34]

Because these high offices became a source of wealth, status, and power, they were eagerly sought after. The great increase in the number of candidates for office led to a system of short (one year) alternative tenures in office. Having obtained high office, the official not only had to recover the fees he had put out to obtain the post, but also enough to tide him over the period of unemployment, until his turn should come again for a one-year appointment.[35] It is not hard to see how this system of appointment and payment for office led to bribery, corruption, and also nepotism, which lasted until reforms in the nineteenth century sought to rationalize the Ottoman administration.

JAPAN In Japan a century of internal war between local lords preceded the decisive victory in 1600 which allowed the Tokugawa house to establish its hegemony over the great warriors (daimyo) and to found a quasi-centralized state. The Japanese emperor retained his ultimate legitimacy; but without power or support, he was forced to designate to Tokugawa Ieuasu the office of shogun (military commander of Japan) and authorize the creation of a "tent-government" (*Bakufu*) over the great military houses.[36] The shogun governed about one-fourth of the land directly, while the rest was divided between 280 daimyo who pledged personal loyalty to the shogun. Beneath these daimyo was the vast body of samurai warriors (about 6 percent of the population) who had been military retainers.

Although the shogun never created a truly centralized state—the daimyo retained final taxation and judicial power over the population on their land—he imposed indirect political controls over both the daimyo and their samurai retainers which deprived them of any independent base of power.

The 280 daimyo consisted of vassals whose landholdings yielded over 10,000 keku of rice. "The typical daimyo was one who had achieved his position by prowess on the battlefield and whose holding was a medium-size domain yielding 50,000-200,000 keku of rice."[37] There were three different types of daimyo in terms of their relationship to the shogun: (1) those related by blood to the Tokugawa house (*shimpan* daimyo); (2) those who had pledged their loyalty and became vassals of the Tokugawa before the great battle of 1600 (fudai or inside daimyo); and (3) those who had either fought against the Tokugawa in this battle or else pledged their loyalty afterward (tozama or outside daimyo).[38] The first measures adopted by the shogun to consolidate his authority was to reorganize the fiefs of all those great vassals—both to reward those who had been most loyal and to arrange the three types of lords geographically so that they would check each other's power. The tozama daimyo—the least loyal—were given land on the periphery of the island—hence the name of outside lords. The fudai—whose loyalty was more tried—were placed between the central lands of the Tokugawa and the outside lords. The shogun also claimed the right to confiscate or reduce any daimyo's domain when he lacked an heir, for mismanagement, or for infringement on shogunal rules.[39] The majority of those whose lands were reduced or extinguished in the first fifty years of the shogunate were among the one hundred or so outside daimyo.[40] All in all, by 1650 only ten or fifteen of the daimyo retained their original land,[41] 40 percent of the productive land had changed hands, and about one-third of the original daimyo had been deposed and other samurai raised to take their places.[42]

The shogun weakened the daimyo economically by requiring them to provide men and materials to build great castles and defensive fortifications.[43] He also promulgated a code to regulate daimyo conduct within their own fiefs. This code mandated each lord to destroy all but one castle on their lands and to limit their military forces. It prohibited the building of ships or contact with foreign countries. Each daimyo was to cooperate with inspectors from the shogunate who had the right to examine all their internal administration and finances. Rules were laid down to regulate the dress, marriages, and private conduct of all daimyo.[44] Most important of all was the imposition of the sankin-kotai (alternative residence) system for daimyo. This regulation required that each lord establish a permanent residence at the shogun's court in Edo (Tokyo). The lord's family was to live there permanently, and each daimyo and his chief retainers was required to spend every other year at the shogunal court. Collecting the daimyo in Edo—where they spent much of their income—"transformed them from independent territorial rulers into what amounted to a species of bureaucratic agents of a powerful national government."[45]

Just as the shogun controlled his retainers and drew them into the city, so too did the daimyo regulate their samurai by removing them from the land into their castle towns and compensating them through a rice stipend from the daimyo's granary. The size of the samurai's stipend could be increased, decreased, or taken away at the will of his lord.[46] By 1700, nearly 90 percent of the daimyo had forced their entire samurai elite off the land. This meant that the samurai lost all powers of interference in the affairs of the villages, which once comprised their fiefs.[47] Since the lords were allowed to maintain only a small military establishment, about one-half of the samurai warriors became local officials engaged in the government of the castle town, the collection of taxes, financial administration, and the supervision of public works.[48] These official samurai were also given a new style of education and inculcated with new values. In the fief schools, established to train samurai for office, traditional military training was combined with education in Confucian classics and philosophy borrowed from China. The civil Confucian ethics did not completely abrogate traditional military values but combined with them to form a distinct ethic called "Bushido." Education in morality and in principles of government soon became more important than training in military skills.[49] "Though as a class they nostalgically clung to the concept that they were a landed aristocracy, they had been converted, in reality, to little more than salaried officials of the daimyo. As their bureaucratic functions multiplied, their security became increasingly identified, not with the land, but with government service. Separated from the duties of actual management, they became a thoroughly urbanized group living increasingly in sedentary style."[50]

The centralization and urbanization of those samurai who were direct retainers of the shogun was achieved somewhat differently. There were some 22,500 of these warriors of whom 20,000 were drawn into the castle-city of Edo or other major shogunal cities, and given stipends instead of land. However, 2,500 of the highest-ranking samurai were given their own fiefs to govern, much like the daimyo. But like the daimyo, they too were required to participate in the sankin-kotai system, to build a permanent residence in Edo and spend every other year in the city. Moreover, they had even less independence in governing their fiefs. The Bakufu administered justice on their lands, and set the policy toward commerce, tax rates, and collection procedures.[51] Any inclination for these samurai to become territorial rulers was completely negated by the redistribution of their estates in the late seventeenth century. The shogun's goal was to "redistribute land so that each enfeoffed samurai would have a combination of dry fields, paddies, and uplands and thus be spared extreme tax fluctuations resulting from the failure of a specific crop. In the process, most fiefs were broken up and dispersed."[52] Many of the landed samurai ceased all visits to their fiefs and some even turned their land over to the shogunate in return for a stipend. "In short, the fiefs of most samurai were sources of income, different in nature but the same in function as the stipends of other large liege vassals. Like these others, fief holders mostly spent their lives in Edo; like them they resembled urbanized, stipended bureaucrats, more than the hardy, land-based yeoman warriors who had been their ancestors."[53]

In Tokugawa Japan a number of parallel and autonomous urban governments were formed. The "central" Bakufu apparatus directly controlled the shogun's land (one-fourth of Japan) and had a great deal of influence over the small fiefs of approximately 150 (out of 280) lords. It also presented a model which all the independent daimyo followed in setting up their domain governments.[54] The proliferation of a number of patrimonial governments in Japan meant that the provinces were much more controlled than in Ottoman Turkey, and the gap between governing elite and masses was never as great. "By the end of the seventeenth century, Japan was probably one of the most thoroughly governed countries in the world."[55] While I will focus the discussion here on the organization of the shogunal government, it must be kept in mind that this process was duplicated all over Japan on a smaller scale.

As in Ottoman Turkey, the Bakufu officials originated in the shogun's household and gradually gained autonomy. But the division was never complete. The early shogun merely appointed favored vassals to handle Tokugawa house affairs. Theirs was government by a group of close, personal subordinates who lived in the shogun's castle and served at his personal direction.[56] As the government stabilized, specific offices were formed and it became traditional to appoint only specific ranks of the warrior elite to each post. The offices and households of these officials were established in the exterior castle grounds. After 1684, the shogun no longer personally directed the government, but met with his officials only on formal occasions.[57] To influence government policy, the shogun now had to rely on trusted intermediaries chosen from samurai who served as his personal attendants (chamberlains). If the shogun was weak or uninterested in government, the chamberlains themselves often assumed a powerful role, since the shogun's seal was required on all government edicts and financial outlays. "One may compare the grand chamberlain to the continental eunuch, who functioned as a tool for controlling bureaucratic officialdom."[58] Thus, during the eighteenth century, Bakufu government encompassed a battle for power between the shogun's personal retainers and samurai officials. It was not until the nineteenth century that the officials finally won control over the appointment of the shogun's attendants and could thus subordinate them.[59] In the daimyo domains, samurai officials became dominant more quickly. Because their lord had his mansion and family in Edo and spent half his time there, the samurai were left in the castle town to govern their province without much dynastic interference.

At the top of the Bakufu state apparatus were the five senior councillors. They shared control over the appointment and supervision of lower officials with four to five junior councillors. Below the councillors there were 275 different types of offices, almost all concerned with civil administration. "The only clearly military officials were the guard unit captains and the keeper of the Osaka castle. All other officials were civil, even though in theory they retained military duties."[60] Some of the most important offices were superintendent of temples and shrines, master of shogunal ceremony, Edo city magistrate, superintendent of finance, financial comptrollers, inspector general, etc.[61] Other offices included public works, irrigation, and education.[62] All these bureaus had numerous officials and clerks working for them: 17,000 samurai in all worked in the shogunate apparatus.

The senior councillors kept control over this vast officialdom, not through formal rules and regulations, but through a hierarchy of personal ties and obligations. Officials were managed through the formation of competing vertical cliques[63] (this was also the case in the daimyo regimes). This meant that the administration was politicized. "In the bakufu there was no conceptual distinction between administrators and politicians."[64] As in Ottoman Turkey, an official had to be political to survive. Politics did not revolve primarily around issues but on personal rivalry. As in Ottoman Turkey, this rivalry was fanned by the fact that there were more aspirants to office than posts available.

All daimyo and samurai in Japan inherited military rank and a base stipend, but not office. However, the practice became traditional that particular posts had to be filled from particular military grades.[65] The top sixty or so offices in the shogun's apparatus were reserved for daimyo—but not any of the 280 daimyo. Not only were the outside lords and those related to the Tokugawa house barred from office in the central state, but so too were those "loyal" inside daimyo who themselves possessed a large domain of contiguous and defensible land. Rather, the senior councillor posts were reserved for the fudai (inside) daimyo who had medium-sized fiefs, which often lacked extensive and contiguous land. Daimyo with small fiefs could rise as high as junior councillor. Hence it was the medium-sized inside daimyo who dominated the government, through the senior councillors who appointed all other officials.[66] Thus the highest officials in Japan—and those beneath them—had no reliable base of private power. "It was as bakufu officials, not as daimyo, that they were of political consequence."[67]

Not all medium-fiefed fudai daimyo obtained office. An individual aspirant had to establish personal contacts with a ruling clique. Hereditary ties were always the most effective—but not the only—type of personal entry to a clique. It was this personal tie that enabled a fudai daimyo to be appointed to a Bakufu office and to rise through the official hierarchy to the post of senior councillor. Most likely to reach this peak was an aspirant who was the offspring of daimyo families who had risen to high office during the reign of the third shogun when the shogunal government was first consolidated.[68]

The majority of offices in the Bakufu—and all posts in the provincial governments—were reserved for samurai. In the Bakufu 17,000 samurai attained office, but there was a great difference in the opportunities open to these warriors of high hereditary rank compared to those born into families with a lowly military status and small hereditary stipend. These lower samurai were assigned routine duties—guards, messengers, attendants, cleaners, porters—with small office stipends attached. They had little choice of job and little chance of significant promotion. Their positions were mostly paternally hereditary. These officials were not political and Bakufu politics did not involve them.[69] The significant offices were reserved for those samurai of higher military rank, but many of these officials could be selected from within a relatively broad spectrum of ranks.[70] This promoted competition for office, especially since "the acquisition and retention of Bakufu office was a crucial matter in a samurai's life. It gave him extra income, but more important, it gave him something to do."[71] Such competition did not lead to the selection of officials on the basis of merit or special ability. Personal and political considerations were always predominant—at least until the reforms of the nineteenth century.

Competition for office in Japan promoted gift-giving in the process of obtaining office. "In a political system where official preferment depended so often on the whim or favor of a superior, the practice of gift-giving had been developed to a fine art. Under such circumstances the dividing line between protocol and bribery was hard to define. By custom, presents went with each request for nomination to office or upon receipt of office, and as regular tokens of appreciation."[72] As in Turkey, these gifts became a circulating capital passing between officials. Still, the practice of selling offices never arose in Japan and corruption in political spoils never reached the height that it did in Ottoman Turkey. Perhaps this was because regular salaries (adequate at the upper levels) were paid, in addition to hereditary stipends. Perhaps the sheer number of officials in the Bakufu and daimyo governments made any concentration of wealth impossible. Certainly the density of government in a small, culturally homogeneous nation made supervision of officials much more effective than in the vast Ottoman Empire.

In summary: The growth of patrimonial government in Japan and Turkey created a group of autonomous officials whose wealth and status were based on office and not on land. These officials were not modern bureaucrats for their positions depended on personal status and political connections and not on merit, skill, or specialized knowledge. But the growth of a social group with aristocratic status and power based on patrimonial office prevented the creation of an estate of landlords in Japan and Turkey with autonomous political and legal rights. We must analyze more concretely why political officials in Japan and Turkey did not consolidate control over the land and why landlords and merchants did not gain political power.

Separation of Political and Economic Power

OTTOMAN EMPIRE Turkish bureaucrats who became wealthy, both through legitimate and extralegal benefits of office, attempted to acquire property.[73] However, a number of developments blocked them from consolidating large land estates or other forms of wealth. These deterrents were four: (1) the rapid turnover in high office; (2) the sultan's right to confiscate the wealth of officials when they died or were dismissed; (3) Islamic inheritance laws; and (4) the particular character of religious estates (*wakfs*).

1. Previously we considered how the opening up of lucrative government offices once filled solely by non-Moslem slaves of the sultan created a surplus of candidates for office and hence an annual turnover in top posts. The competition among officials for a relatively small number of positions prevented bureaucratic office from becoming hereditary and also hindered political consolidation among the bureaucratic elite. Rapid rotation in office limited the amount of wealth that an official could accumulate. "The rewards which went with the most lucrative posts were amassed in part at the expense of other officials, including those who held less advantages, but still eminent positions.... The rewards of high position were thus distributed in large part by a process of circulation and redistribution among those who were eligible for them.... Far from being recognized as the more or less legitimate fruits of individual enterprise, the fortunes together constituted a sort of circulating capital, belonging fundamentally to the state and passing about in much the same way as the offices themselves."[74]

2. The ability of officials to accumulate property was further thwarted by the sultan's legitimate right to confiscate fortunes. This right stemmed from the tradition of government officials as slaves completely subordinate to the ruler. "While an ordinary scribe might pass a life of relative stability, sheltered by his own obscurity, his superior would be in constant danger, not just of loss of position, but also of exile, death, and expropriation."[75] In the eighteenth century when the empire ceased to expand militarily, while the janissaries cost more and more, the government was always in desperate need of revenue, and hence confiscation of officials' property increased.[76]

3. If the fortune of a bureaucrat escaped confiscation at his death, the Islamic law of inheritance broke up his estate. "A large proportion of the deceased's estate went in gifts and bequests to religion, wives and slave girls; then there were the various dues, which amounted to a twentieth of

the estate; and the balance had to be divided among the heirs in the proportions prescribed by the religious law. Thus, accumulated wealth was destined to be dispersed in every generation." [77]

4. There was one way that state officials managed to escape confiscation of their estates or their distribution at death. This was to endow a religious wakf while the official lived. A wakf was land or a business whose yearly income was to pay for a religious or charitable establishment, such as a mosque, convent, hospital, or school. Such property could not be sold, nor could it be taken over by the government. [78] It was possible to make a provision that any surplus over expenditures needed to maintain the charity could revert to the founder's family. Although the owner might thus make some profit, the organization of a wakf prevented the aristocracy from expanding their wealth and property. "Because wakfs were fundamentally consuming institutions, they never assumed the characteristics of a really capitalistic enterprise." [79] Moreover, during the nineteenth-century reform movement, the state extended its control over wakfs and found means to divert superfluous income into the state treasury.

Nor were landholders successful in either consolidating autonomous economic power or winning political influence. The Ottoman state in the seventeenth and eighteenth centuries reclaimed land granted in fiefs. Because the state did not have the personnel to collect taxes from peasants who farmed this land, they leased it to tax farmers. A tax farmer contracted to pay the treasury a fixed sum in advance (determined in relation to the normal yield of the lands concerned) in return for the right to collect for their own benefit, all the tithes and taxes legally due from the inhabitants. [80] At first such tax farms were leased for only one year, but this proved to be so exploitative of the peasants that many fled their lands disrupting agricultural production. In the eighteenth century land was leased to a tax farmer for his lifetime. This regularized government finances but also created a new group of powerful landholders, called ayan—local notables.

These new landholders came from diverse and often humble origins— urban merchants, former sipahi, former janissaries, or even a few peasants. [81] Unlike the former feudal sipahi, ayans were primarily urban residents who had no direct control over peasants. [82] Like the sipahi, they gained political autonomy through providing provincial armies at the request of the central government. In the late eighteenth century after the janissaries decayed, the government was completely dependent on these local troops to fight its continuing wars with European powers. [83] "Thus, in the eighteenth century the ground work had been laid for the rise of a powerful semi-feudal aristocracy in the provinces of Anatolia and in the Balkans. Many of the ayan families were able to maintain their position for several generations and founded local dynasties." [84] By 1800, the ayan with their armies ruled many areas of the central empire. Some historians maintain that only a few provinces in Rumealia and Anatolia (the Turkish heartland) were still under the direct administration of the sultan.[85]

In 1808 a provincial ayan army even marched into the capital, seized Istanbul, suppressed a janissary uprising, deposed the new sultan (seated by the janissaries) and installed a third one. The leader of the ayan army made himself grand vezir and forced the sultan to sign a formal agreement with the ayan. This document pledged local respect for the sultan, grand vezir, and central government, but it forced the sultan to promise respect and security for the authority of the provincial dynasties. Thus, it promulgated a formal limitation on the power of the central administration in favor of the ayan landed class.[86] A few years later this "Magna Carta" was abolished and the armies of the ayans were destroyed by a group of bureaucratic reformers. In the next section we shall study how these reformers arose and why they were successful.

If the ayan landholders had consolidated their control over local administration—and eventually attained offices in the central administration—subsequent political history in the Ottoman Empire would have been very different (probably more like China). As it was, the ayans managed to keep sizeable estates, but "the bulk of the land seems to have passed into the hands of the peasants, small holdings which took 75% of all cleared land in Asia Minor."[87] The ayans then became the backbone of a Muslim middle class composed of artisans, landowners, and other groups engaged in economic occupations. But this class never again exercised decisive political influence in Ottoman Turkey.[88] With the destruction of native handicrafts and industry in the nineteenth century—due to the influx of European manufactured goods—indigenous economic power was concentrated in the hands of non-Muslim urban merchants— Greeks, Armenians, and Christians—who had no control over the countryside and little political influence.[89]

TOKUGAWA JAPAN We have seen how both sectors of the warrior elite in Japan—the daimyo and the samurai—were withdrawn from the land and urbanized. We also discussed how those daimyo who continued to rule over large domains with contiguous and defensible lands—a base from which the lord could build peasant identification and support for his family house—were barred from office in the central Bakufu administration. The sankin-kotai system which kept the daimyo's family in Edo and required the lord to live every other year in the capital also destroyed the economic independence of the daimyo. Life in Edo—as life at the French court of the old regime—fostered conspicuous consumption—the maintenance of elaborate mansions, fine clothiers, large banquets, etc. The journey back and forth to the provinces with a large number of retainers was also very costly. All this had to be paid for out of that part of his rice taxes that was left over after paying samurai stipends, payments in kind for han services, and consumption by his own household.[90] "The basic dilemma of the daimyo lay in the fact that the greater part of their money income was derived from that portion of the han rice tax they could convert into cash. Only a few exceptional han had other sources of cash revenue extensive enough to make a difference. Since total rice production could be increased very little, the cash income of the daimyo tended to be fixed, while their cash requirements grew."[91] This financial weakness of the daimyo—and also of the shogun—implicated the whole warrior stratum: "The Chinese gentry could be financially secure even though his dynasty was bankrupt, because his family usually owned land, and independently of his authorized salary he was able to squeeze a good living out of his local gentry functions. The Japanese warrior of the Tokugawa period, however, had no such freedom, for his entire income, regardless of its form, was usually derived directly from his lord's tax sources. The lord's poverty was equally the vassal's."[92]

From 1700 on, the excess of expenditures over income led the daimyo and many samurai into continuous debt to the large merchants of Osaka and Edo (and later to wealthy provincial merchants) who acted both as rice brokers and bankers for them. The warrior elite never themselves performed commercial functions, for both the warrior ethic and Tokugawa law forbade it. In Confucian ethics, which the warriors adopted, commerce was degraded and merchants given a lower status in society than peasants. Thus high political office in Tokugawa Japan never became a stepping stone for a man or his sons to commercial wealth. Nor could the large merchants who became exceedingly wealthy through Tokugawa commerce ever hope to enter high political office. A few of them gained samurai status (the right to wear two swords, use a family name, and receive an hereditary stipend), often as a reward for their financial services to the daimyo, but they never obtained the high rank which would qualify them for important state offices. Nor did merchants attain political autonomy in the cities. "Unlike Western Europe, Japan did not develop self-governing towns with charters that expressed in concrete terms their political and legal independence of the surrounding feudal authority."[93]

The increasing economic power of the merchant class in Japan was never translated into political power. On the contrary, the wealthy merchants became politically more dependent as their economic power increased. They continued to be tied to the feudal system, for their wealth derived from the commercial and banking functions they performed for the ruling elite. As the warriors' economic position declined they used their political power against the merchants. Merchants could not be eliminated for they performed essential economic services which the warrior officials (felt they) could not perform for themselves. But the Bakufu and han governments did periodically confiscate large commercial fortunes, extract forced loans from the merchants, refuse to pay debts or cancel them outright, and refuse to hear litigation brought by merchants against daimyo or samurai who refused to repay loans.[94] Merchants not only lacked political power, but they were denied legal or political security in their economic enterprises. "The complete subjection of the merchants to the political power of the Bakufu and their impotence in the face of confiscation emphasizes the separation between political and economic power. The separation becomes more striking with the increase in merchant wealth and the attendant impoverishment of the ruling classes."[95]

This "symbiotic antagonism"[96] between merchants and warrior-bureaucrats explains why the powerful merchant class in Japan never became a revolutionary force. It is significant that it was not those daimyo and samurai who were most economically in debt and dependent on the merchants who rose in revolt, but rather those from several of the outside han who through successful reforms managed to revive the financial position of their domains and remain solvent vis-à-vis the moneylenders and merchants.

While the merchants in Japan were much more of a threat to the political viability of the state aristocracy than the commercial sector in Turkey, rural notables in Japan never became as powerful as the ayans in the Ottoman Empire. However, independent landlords did evolve in Japan. The shogun and daimyo theoretically remained the landholders, but their "ownership" was restricted to the political right to survey the land and collect taxes. From the earliest days of the Tokugawa regime, warriors were removed from any supervision over division of the land between individual peasants or their methods of cultivation. Nor did the warriors as they became urbanized impose or collect taxes directly from individual peasants. Rather, the peasant villages themselves selected a headman who was responsible for collecting taxes and interceding with the samurai officials. Samurai intendants who collected taxes from the village headmen never developed the characteristics of the tax farmer in Turkey. At times they engaged in petty corruption vis-à-vis their superiors, but they never developed any hold over the land or the peasants. Samurai tax collectors remained "appointive, paid, revocable, subordinate and accountable to the central authorities."[97]

Village headmen—who were in the peasant stratum—developed into independent landlords. Even in the seventeenth century at the beginning of the Tokugawa regime, the peasants were highly stratified in terms of their landholdings. Many of the larger landholding peasant families could trace their ancestors back to petty warriors, even though their samurai status had been lost in the consolidation of the Tokugawa regime. It was the large landholders, whatever their origins, who became village headmen and exercised political authority at the local level.[98] Historically there was a group of local notables in Japan with a base of economic power on the land. As the market penetrated agriculture in the eighteenth century, many of these peasant notables increased their landholdings at the expense of poorer peasants who became their workers or tenants. They also used the surplus gained from cash crops to develop manufacturing concerns (e.g., saki brewers, soy sauce firms, silk textiles). Some merchants in the rural castle towns also became landlords, when some of the han in the eighteenth century sought to increase their revenues by reclaiming land for agriculture. The merchants often financed and carried out the reclamation and then managed the land.[99] Unlike the cities, where merchant capital was tied up in usury and purely commercial ventures, provincial businessmen-landlords used their capital in production. By the nineteenth century a large percentage of the increasing production in Japan in both luxury and everyday goods was carried on in agricultural communities.[100] Many peasant-landlords became quite wealthy. "They took concubines, frequented inns and hot springs, collected books and art objects, built fine houses, studied poetry, painting, and even the military arts."[101]

Although these provincial landlords and businessmen were far less dependent on the daimyo and samurai than the city merchants, they never became an independent political or military force in the way the ayans did in Turkey. Some village headmen were granted samurai status, but like the merchants who gained the right to wear two swords, this did not mean access to high bureaucratic office. The landlords remained tied to their local domain with no access to their peers in the other han. Merchants and landlords (much more than samurai) were limited by commercial restrictions between the han and by Tokugawa edicts which limited freedom of movement for commoners across domain boundaries. Landlords and rural merchants had no way to consolidate their economic power in order to win political or legal rights from the state.

Tokugawa Japan and Ottoman Turkey as patrimonial states were thus structurally distinct from the feudal states of Western Europe. The power of patrimonial aristocracies in Japan and Turkey was based on office, not on land. Even during the decline of feudalism in Europe, the landed nobility "continued to own the bulk of the fundamental means of production in the economy, and to occupy the great majority of positions within the total apparatus of political power."[102] Because of this congruence of economic and political power, the absolute monarchies in Europe acted to protect and stabilize the social and economic power of the landed nobility. In Europe "the increase in the political sway of the royal state was accompanied, not by a decrease in the economic security of noble landownership, but by a corresponding increase in the general right of private property. The age in which 'absolutist' public authority was imposed was also simultaneously the age in which absolute private property was progressively consolidated. It was this momentous social difference which separated the Bourbon, Hapsburg, Tudor, or Vasa monarchies from any sultanate, empire, or shogunate outside Europe."[103]

Decay of the Military Base of Aristocratic Status and Power Dependence on state office as the basis of aristocratic status and power was further consolidated by the decay of the feudal and military base of the aristocracy in Ottoman Turkey and Tokugawa Japan.

THE OTTOMAN MILITARY In the seventeenth and eighteenth centuries both the feudal army and the janissaries decayed as a military force in the Ottoman Empire. Scholars agree that the sipahi (feudal forces) became militarily ineffective and lost control over their fiefs beginning in the late sixteenth century, as a result of government initiative. There is some disagreement as to whether financial or military needs of the government were primary in prompting policies which were antithetical to the maintenance of the feudal cavalry. One theory stresses that the central government's need for revenue—increased by an influx of American silver which caused prices to rise—led them to take back fiefs when a sipahi died.[104] This meant that taxes paid by peasants now went to the central treasury rather than for the support of these military forces. Another theory emphasizes that changes in European military technology made the sipahi cavalry obsolete. "The real reason why the sipahis came to be neglected was that this light cavalry was no match for the heavily armed German fusiliers. The sipahi cavalry failed to adapt itself to modern warfare, in respect not only of its equipment, but also of its organization. Its campaigning season was between March and October. Outside these months, the sipahis wished to return to their villages and collect the revenue of their timars."[105] As a result the number of janissaries was greatly increased and they were trained in the use of firearms.[106] This required a greatly increased central treasury to pay them and hence the government had to repossess fiefs.[107]

Ironically, the manner in which the government recruited increasing numbers of janissaries also led to their disorganization and decay. Already in 1582, the sultan indiscriminantly recruited thousands of nonslaves without providing the special janissary training. In the seventeenth and eighteenth centuries many new janissary recruits were drawn from the artisan classes in towns where the troops were stationed. Because of inadequate resources for the building of barracks and maintenance of troops, janissaries married, lived in the town, and continued their occupations. These conditions made it increasingly difficult to subject the troops to discipline and training. To overcome these deficiencies, the janissary corps began to affiliate even larger numbers of men, attracted to service by the privileges of the janissaries (e.g., emblems of elite status and immunity from the regular courts). This expedient further degraded standards. Up until 1740, the numerous campaigns against the enemy, even when unsuccessful, supplied the army with military training and maintained their identity as soldiers. In the thirty years of peace after 1740, disorganization became complete, for the janissary officers initiated the corrupt practice of selling the certificates used to draw military pay. The janissary certificates were thus transferred to wholly private persons, usually urban artisans and merchants.[108] In Sulieman's time, at the height of the empire in the sixteenth century, there had been 12,000 janissaries. By 1683 there were 100,000.[109] In 1800 there were still about 100,000 janissaries, but only about 2,000 were trained soldiers. The rest enjoyed janissary privileges, but no longer upheld professional or ethical standards, nor thought of themselves as an elite with special social duties.[110]

Janissaries were still legally part of the ruling aristocracy, but socially and economically they were distinct from those who held high administrative and judicial posts. This division was reinforced by cultural differences. While the administrative and judicial officials adhered to orthodox Islamic teachings and doctrines (Sunni Islam), janissaries became members of the heterodox sects (Suffi Islam). Orthodox and heterodox Islam propagated different values and lifestyles. "There have always been two levels to Islam: first, the rational, abstract, unemotional devotion to God of the learned ulema, and second, the immediate, warm, emotional ritualistic pattern of the sects and brotherhoods. The first is a religion without intermediaries, without music or dancing, with a minimum of ritual, and no priests and no helpers to approach the all powerful, but distant God. The second is full of Seyhs (mystics) and dervishes, rituals varying with particular sects, tombs of saints, sacred intermediaries, secret orders and brotherhoods."[111] The heterodox sects allowed drinking, dancing, and the unveiling of women in public; orthodox Islam did not.

There were thus many reasons for the state to abolish janissaries. They were a military and financial liability. They no longer had social, economic, or cultural ties to the ruling elite. However, the holders of janissary certificates, backed by well-organized trade guilds, prevented successive attempts by the civil administration to abolish the troops or their privileges. Urban janissary-artisans became the organizers of uprisings against the sultan and his government. In the late eighteenth and early nineteenth centuries, numerous janissary uprisings, supported by the urban masses, forced the resignation of high officials and compelled the abdication of sultans.[112] In 1807 the janissaries of Istanbul, with popular support, even took over the central government for a time and severely limited the political control of the sultan and ruling elite. The cause of this revolt was the sultan's attempt to create a new army under his direct command. This uprising forced the deposition of the sultan, put a conservative ally of the janissaries in the office of grand vezir, and led to the purge of officials supporting reform. The janissaries' power was soon checked, not by the sultan or the state officials, but by the intervention of newly formed and rebellious provincial armies. It was the threat to the state by these uncontrolled military forces with a mass base that prompted the reform movement of the nineteenth century—a reform that bureaucratized the state.

THE TOKUGAWA MILITARY The two centuries of peace following the founding of the Tokugawa regime in 1600 left large numbers of samurai warriors who could not be absorbed into useful occupations. Most of the samurai were drawn into the cities and about half of them were given bureaucratic and civil posts. But the half who remained in purely military service performed only minimal police, guard, and ceremonial duties, while military organization and technology deteriorated. The status and pay of these warriors was much less than that of the samurai who held administrative posts. The result for many of the elite was a life of hypocrisy and indolence. A Tokugawa writer in the late eighteenth century said: "On looking at the condition of the present day military class, I observe that the members have grown up in a most fortunate age of prosperity which has continued for nearly two hundred years. For five or six generations they have not had the slightest battlefield experience. The martial arts have steadily deteriorated. Were an emergency to occur, among the bannermen and horsemen who must come to the Shogun's support, seven or eight out of ten would be as weak as women and their morale as mean as merchants. True martial spirit has disappeared completely."[113]

The economic growth which resulted from the urbanization of the samurai undermined the economic basis of the samurai code of ethics, especially for those remaining in warrior posts. The centralization of Tokugawa political organization—both the drawing of the samurai into castle towns and the required attendance of the lords at court—promoted commercialization of the economy. Both lords and samurai received their incomes in rice, but an urban existence necessitated a more transportable medium of exchange. Lords, who received their rice taxes in the provinces but needed money for their residences and expenses in Edo, began to establish large warehouses in the port city of Osaka and to require the services of merchants and money exchanges. The concentration of elites in towns also stimulated the growth of urban artisans and merchants to serve their consumption needs. Both this commercialization and the measures adopted by state officials to meet their growing financial needs undermined the economic position of the samurai in military posts. The Tokugawa and domain governments often cut samurai stipends and extracted forced loans from them. They also attempted periodic debasement of the currency, which devalued the samurai's fixed salary and meant that the stipends of lower samurai often became inadequate for a livelihood. Tokugawa literature is filled with examples of samurai who ran up huge debts, were unable to pay for schooling, pawned their swords, and resorted to infanticide.[114] Many warriors were also forced to take up part-time business and handicrafts, marry their daughters to merchants, adopt (for money) commoners' sons, and even to renounce samurai status and privileges for commercial or agricultural occupations.[115] Some unemployed samurai (ronin) engaged in rowdy and criminal conspiracies in the cities and made a cult of their warrior heritage. While many samurai were thus degraded to commoner occupations, many successful merchants and wealthy peasants were able to buy samurai status, including the privilege of wearing two swords and using a family name. "Not even a pretense was made that the purchaser had aristocratic origins; a man had only to make sufficient contribution to his lord's perennially straitened finances to qualify."[116]

As in Turkey, the economic and occupational differentiation between civil officials and those who held military office produced social and cultural segregation. In Japan, the samurai eligible for high office were educated in fief schools where they became accomplished in Chinese language and Confucian ethics. The lower samurai, who held only military posts, were educated in private schools where they learned only writing, arithmetic, and swordsmanship. The social separation between upper and lower samurai gradually became complete. "The two groups almost never intermarried; they used different styles of speech and writing; and they built their houses differently. The telling difference, of course, was the size of their rice stipends."[117] The upper samurai could often afford luxuries, but the lowly warrior could barely subsist with the most careful economy and frugality. To reinforce these social and cultural distinctions, a great deal of deferential behavior was required from lower samurai toward administrative officials.[118]

In Japan and Turkey the decay of feudal institutions, urbanization of standing troops, and infiltration of urban artisans and merchants into the military hastened the decline of military skills and segregated those who held military positions from the political elite. A military occupation still carried aristocratic status, but in reality prestige and power came to reside in the civil administration. Although the lower samurai never became a military threat to the Japanese power structure (as the janissaries were in Turkey), their economic decline threatened both the economic viability of the state and the legitimacy of the elite. Samurai status could not be abolished in Japan for it was hereditary military rank which qualified one for high political office and legitimized the privilege of officials vis-à-vis peasants, merchants, artisans, and lower-ranking samurai. As in Turkey, military decay became a prod to reform and rationalization of the bureaucratic elite.

Transition from a Patrimonial to a Bureaucratic State As in Western Europe, patrimonial administrations in Tokugawa Japan and Ottoman Turkey were rationalized into modern bureaucracies in the nineteenth century under both internal and external challenges to state power. As in Europe, rationalization in Japan and Turkey was "most often forced on the monarchy by some domestic or international catastrophe."[119] The series of prerevolutionary reforms that rationalized state administration in nineteenth-century Japan and Turkey also increased and solidified the class autonomy of the state apparatus in a manner quite distinct from European bureaucratization.[120]

Reform in the Ottoman and Tokugawa political systems was initiated to check internal challenges to state authority—the military and political rebellion of janissary and ayan armies in Turkey and the economic threat of wealthy merchants and peasant landlords in Japan. Reformers sought to suppress autonomous sources of power outside the state. While strengthening and rationalizing the state apparatus, reforms culminating in the 1840s in Japan and Turkey precluded the future possibility of either a bourgeois or peasant revolution, for they destroyed any organizational base for revolution from below.

The second stage of reform in these two countries was in response to Western intervention (or increased Western pressure in the Turkish case) in the mid–nineteenth century. In reaction to Western demands for economic concessions backed by military threats, reformers accelerated the measures began earlier. All these reform measures accelerated the transition from a patrimonial state to a modern rational-legal bureaucracy in Tokugawa Japan and Ottoman Turkey. As Max Weber outlined it, this process involves: (a) a clear division of tasks between different offices, eliminating overlapping jurisdictions and separating military and civil administration; (b) recruitment of officials on the basis of specialized knowledge and skills and not because of hereditary status or personal connections; and (c) separation of private and official property, so that offices and equipment cannot be appropriated by officials, and their salaries are clearly distinct from tax and other government revenue.[121]

What was distinctive of Japan and Turkey was that rationalization of patrimonial officials created bureaucrats who were both politicized and autonomous from vested economic interests. Both developments created the potential for innovative action. Officials who were recruited on merit (often from lower-status urban families) with new (often Western) types of technical knowledge, were not as committed to the traditional status structure nor the personal cliques within the state apparatus. These same bureaucrats became politicized because reforms could not prevent further encroachment from the West. Continued Western pressure produced bureaucrats who developed and propagated nationalist ideologies.

BUREAUCRATIZATION AS A RESPONSE TO INTERNAL CHALLENGES TO STATE POWER Although the military and political power of the janissaries was curbed by traditional means—as was the economic power of merchants and wealthy peasants in Japan—the existence of these threats motivated high officials to undertake reforms to rationalize and strengthen their only base of power—the state apparatus. In both countries reform was justified by an appeal to traditional values. Reformers saw the need for utilitarian innovations that clashed with tradition. But they also looked back to a prior age of a vital polity and cohesive aristocracy. They needed the support of the dynastic heads of state. The sultan and shogun wished to check the decay of state power, but they were threatened by the increasing independence of their officials. They were willing to support reforms presented as an attempt to revitalize the state and to reinstate an earlier and purer age, but not reforms that would overtly weaken their own personal control. In fact, the reforms did exactly that.

Ottoman Turkey. The most concerted and successful set of early reforms in Turkey was executed under the leadership of Sultan Mahmud II during 1826-39. Mahmud destroyed the janissaries by force—at least 6,000 were slain—and replaced them with new military units under central control. Mahmud's original intention was not to exterminate the janissaries, but to again attempt to create an army under civil control—a reform that was directly responsible for the janissary uprising that deposed the previous sultan in 1808. Aware of this history, the reformers made careful preparations over several years, obtaining the pledged support of high ulema (religious and judicial), civil, and military officials.[122]

The religious hierarchy supported reforms to replace the janissaries because orthodoxy was threatened by the heterodox Islamic sects allied to the janissaries, and opposed the religious officialdom.[123] The reformers also used a populistic appeal to traditional religious values to turn the religious students and lower ulema against the janissaries, their traditional allies. Although the new troops were to be trained with Western weapons, the sultan presented their formation as a return to the great military forces which had won the empire. He named the new army the "victorious Muhammedan troops," required religious instruction and services in the army, and vowed they would be instructed only by Muslim officers and not by Christians or foreigners. He also obtained a decree from the highest Islamic official authorizing formation of the new army.[124]

Both the creation of a personal clique of elite support and the appeal to traditional values guaranteed a counterforce to the expected janissary reaction. When the janissary rebellion erupted it was violently suppressed by loyal military units, with the support of previously mobilized elites. The new army was placed under the control of a civilian Ministry of War, which was able to prevent the recurrence of anything like the janissary uprisings.[125]

With the support of the new army and by playing the ayan landlords off against each other, the sultan and his advisors also disbanded the provincial armies and destroyed the independent military and political power of provincial notables. They did not succeed in eliminating the economic power of the ayans. The remaining feudal lands (timars) were abolished in 1831, and the state created a new bureaucratic apparatus to centralize the collection and expenditure of revenues from lands held in religious trusts (wakfs). But the attempt to abolish tax farming was unsuccessful and the ayans were left in full control of large tracts of land in various parts of the empire (including the Turkish heartland). A later attempt to reassert state control over the land (in the land code of 1858) in fact helped extend the scope of private landownership.[126] "The large landed estates seen during the last year of the Empire did not originate in the old timars and crown estates but in the new land system instituted during the Tanzimat [reforms]."[127]

The reformers tried to insure the political loyalty of the landed notables by granting them seats in new provincial councils set up to advise the governor and other officials sent to the provinces from Istanbul. When these councils in some areas began to gain control over centrally appointed officials, a new law was promulgated to give the Porte (seat of bureaucratic government in Istanbul) final say over the choice of notables for provincial councils.[128]

One other bureaucratic reform in the early nineteenth century checked the remaining source of autonomous political power in the central Turkish lands—the religious hierarchy. The ulema were removed from their base of popular support, bureaucratized, and brought under the control of the civil administration.[129] To mitigate religious opposition to making the religious-judicial officials part of the state bureaucracy—a clear deviation from tradition—the government renewed its support of the religious establishment by building new mosques and issuing repeated orders for Muslims to perform their religious duties.

These reforms removed most of the traditional checks (except the sultan) on the power of the bureaucratic elite. "The old and well-tried checks of despotism had all gone; the corps of janissaries with its ancient privileges and its deep convictions of corporate identity and prerogatives; the feudal sipahis; the local dynasties of the valley lords and the provincial magistry of the ayan; the separate power of the ulema, controllers of the law, religion and education, buttressed by an independent hierarchy of dignitaries and underpined by vast independent revenues. These, and all other intermediate powers had been abrogated or enfeebled."[130]

Still, the continued and increasing economic autonomy of the ayan, the existence of large numbers of lower ulema and religious students who could not be brought completely under bureaucratic control, and the need to build a new military machine (with the potential for independent power), all signified the need for Ottoman reformers to strengthen their own base of power. This entailed: (1) centralization of control over bureaucrats sent to govern the provinces; (2) a new central fiscal apparatus to collect tax revenue from the peasants in place of older sipahi authorities and more recent tax farming methods;[131] and (3) elimination of one-year appointments for top bureaucrats and the establishment of regular and sufficient salaries in place of the system of financial corruption and payoffs.[132] It also depended on a reduction in the power of the sultan to arbitrarily interfere in government and appoint his favorites to office whether qualified or not. To so curtail the sultan's power it was necessary to advance the legitimacy of general laws which would bind him as well as other officials.[133]

All the above reforms in the organization and operation of the state depended on the suppression of personal connections and factors in government and the systematization and codification of the bureaucratic role.[134] Even though many of these early reforms initiated under Sultan Mahumud II were ineffective (they failed, for example, to abolish bribery and pay salaries regularly), still they paved "the way for a system of government based on malleable and interchangeable groups instead of powerful and entrenched individuals."[135] Mahmud's reforms established the respectability of change.[136]

Tokugawa Japan. From the mid–eighteenth century on, the Tokugawa and domain governments in Japan initiated periodic attempts to suppress and control the commercial wealth of merchants and peasant landlords and revitalize the economic position of the samurai. At first, all attempts at reform sought a return to a more traditional economy and society. To bolster the samurai's economic position, the shogun issued continual decrees demanding a life of frugality and forbidding bourgeois amusements and conspicuous consumption. To control the power of the merchants, the shogunal bureaucracy periodically broke up merchant guilds, regulated the rate of interest, cancelled samurai and government debts to merchants, and forced loans from them. They also tried to revive the traditional agricultural economy by repressing the commercialization of agriculture and forbidding peasants to enter merchant occupations, engage in rural handicrafts, or migrate to the city. These measures reinforced the political subordination of the merchants and rich peasants, but did not resolve the economic contradictions in the Tokugawa system.

These traditionalizing reforms had least impact in the central Tokugawa lands because commercialization was too advanced and too complex to be reversed. Especially disastrous was the shogun's attempt to dissolve merchant guilds. This produced economic chaos and higher prices and soon was revoked.[137] Because the Tokugawa government could meet its immediate financial needs by ad hoc coercive measures against merchants, it failed to look for drastic administrative innovations that would eliminate the contradition between the political power of the samurai officials, the social status of the samurai group as a whole, and the economic power of the merchants and peasant landlords.

In contrast, reformers in several of the large autonomous han—where commercialization was less advanced and han finances could not so easily be bolstered by ad hoc "loans" from merchants—succeeded in revitalizing their samurai and producing financial solvency for their governments. Reformers in these provinces sought to bolster the traditional order through utilitarian innovations. They "saw the solution to society's ills in a more efficient exploitation of the commercial economy by the feudal class, not its restriction or abolition in the name of an agrarian ideal."[138] It was these reforms in Satsuma and Choshu which laid the basis for revolution from above against the Tokugawa regime..

Reforms in Satsuma channeled the wealth produced by peasants and merchants into government coffers. For example, Satsuma officials established a government sugar monopoly where peasants were forced to increase production and sell to the han government at a stipulated price. The han then sold the sugar all over Japan for a profit.[139] The peasant landlords were unable to oppose this and other han monopolies because they were faced by increasing discontent and revolt from poor peasants who had been expropriated from the land. Since the landlords lacked military, police, or political power they had to seek an entente with the feudal elite in order to retain their hegemony in the countryside.[140] By 1848, the sugar monopoly and others like it produced a surplus for the han treasury in spite of rising expenses. These financial resources were later used to introduce Western industry under han sponsorship into Satsuma.[141]

Choshu han, in contrast to Satsuma, never tried to establish han monopolies or industries. Choshu, like the Tokugawa, favored economic retrenchment—it opposed commercialization, curtailed government expenses, and imposed frugality on its samurai. As in the Tokugawa domains, these reforms were not very effective.[142] However, Choshu created an innovative han bureau of savings and investment which produced financial solvency and even a surplus. The original funds for the bureau were obtained by a new land survey to find and tax previously unrecorded cultivated land. These funds, once set aside in the bureau, could not be used for regular han expenses even when the han was in debt. They could only be used for unexpected emergencies; meanwhile the funds were increased through investment in land, harbor development, and commerce which also bolstered the domain economy.[143] It was this monetary reservoir which was later used to buy rifles, cannons, and ships after Japan was opened up by the West—military weapons, which were then used against the Tokugawa regime.[144]

Fiscal reforms in Choshu and Satsuma further rationalized the government bureaucracy and improved the moral and economic position of the samurai elite. As in the Ottoman Empire, attempts at bureaucratic reform in Tokugawa Japan, whether successful or not, paved the way for further reforms as a reaction to the threat of Western domination.

BUREAUCRATIZATION AS A RESPONSE TO WESTERN IMPERIALISM In the mid–nineteenth century, Japan and Turkey faced a new and immediate challenge of Western economic and military penetration which threatened the autonomous existence of the two states.

In the 1840s, Russia, the Austrian Empire, and England began to interfere directly in the Ottoman Empire in order to advance their own economic interests vis-à-vis each other. For example, by 1850, the Ottoman Empire had become the third most important outlet for British manufactures.[145] All three powers put direct diplomatic and military pressure on the Ottoman regime with demands for economic concessions, attempts at political control of the Arab provinces, and agitation among Christian minority groups of the empire to arouse anti-Turkish nationalism and separatist drives. At the same time, the Europeans demanded reforms in the Ottoman government which would improve the status of Christian minorities and increase their participation in the central government. This meant indirect imperialistic political control, for "the growth of European trade gave wealth and economic power to Ottoman Christian and Jewish merchants who were for the most part either formal protégés of one or other foreign consultate or morally attached to it."[146] England also urged rationalization of the Ottoman regime to remain strong enough to ward off interference or annexation by Russia and Austria.[147] The British further demanded an agricultural revolution which would give the empire increased purchasing power to buy more extensively from Europe.[148] In all, Western pressure on the Ottoman Empire was directly a result of capitalist expansion. England as the most advanced economic power had the greatest influence.

Japan in the 1840s in contrast to Turkey, had had far less contact with Western nations. The first three Tokugawa shoguns, in order to entrench their own power vis-à-vis the dissident daimyo, closed Japan to all foreign contact and trade and excluded all Christian missionaries. The only exception was a small group of Dutch traders who were restricted to the port of Nagasaki. Japanese subjects were prohibited from going abroad and forbidden to build ocean-going ships. Throughout the seventeenth and eighteenth centuries, some trade (mostly illicit) with Korea and China continued, and the importation of a few Chinese and Dutch books acquainted a small group of Japanese scholars with Western military and scientific advancement. But in general, the exclusion policy was very effective in preventing both Western economic and cultural penetration.

Increasingly in the early 1900s Russia and British ships entered Japanese harbors with requests for services and trade. When they were rebuffed, however, they retreated without protest. Both Britain and Russia were interested in economic expansion in the Far East, but they were preoccupied with European problems and then with commercial expansion in East India and China.[149] Yet when the Japanese learned of the Anglo-Chinese war of the 1840s, and of how British naval strength enabled the English squadron to destroy Chinese warships, they became disturbed by a new perception of their own military weakness. As a result, the shogun proclaimed a more conciliatory policy toward foreigners. In 1842, he ordered coastal officials to furnish food and fuel to foreign ships, while firmly rejecting any overtures for trade.[150] It was only when faced with direct military threat that the shogun retreated from the exclusion policy. In 1853, Commander Perry arrived in Tokyo Bay with four American gunboats. Perry had a letter from President Fillmore demanding the opening of Japanese ports to American trade. If these concessions were not granted he avowed to use force. This threat was followed by similar demands from Russia, England, and Holland. Within a few years, the Tokugawa regime was forced to open selective ports to foreign trade, set a low tariff, and grant foreign businessmen exemption from Japanese law.

As in Turkey, the main objective of foreign intervention was to open new markets for Western manufactured goods. Because of Japan's long isolation from the West and its complete military backwardness, Western penetration was also seen as an immediate threat to Japan's independence. "If the demands of trade were to disrupt her economy, then a hostile political reaction among the Japanese, or simply chaos within the country, could provoke intervention in defense of the West's economic 'rights.' From this it was but a short step to becoming a European colony or protectorate. Alternatively, if Japan's economy were to adjust smoothly to the new situation, she might, as the weaker partner in an outwardly symbiotic relationship, become so subordinated to external control as to acquire a 'semicolonial' status. Foreign economic superiority, in other words, buttressed by such devices as extraterritoriality and a regulated tariff, could gradually undermine the country's political independence as well as its economic independence."[151] Moreover, the hegemony of the central Tokugawa regime, like that of the Ottomans, was menaced by independent European contacts with its semiautonomous provinces.

The Western threat provoked an immediate and common response from the governing elites in both countries. All agreed to the necessity of strengthening the power and effectiveness of the state in order to stave off European domination. The decision to prevent Western domination meant in practice, however, selective and defensive Westernization. As the reforming daimyo of Satsuma put it in 1856: "At this time when defense against the foreign barbarians is of crucial importance it is the urgent duty of all samurai both high and low to cooperate in learning of conditions in foreign lands so that we may adopt their good points and supplement our deficiencies, reinforce the military might of our nation, and keep the barbarian nations under control."[152] The rapid acceptance of Western technology stemmed directly from the aristocracy's dependence on the state and their lack of an autonomous base of power. They were not at this time nationalists, but were traditionalists with a desire to maintain their own power and position. As power elites, reformers readily discerned that the selective use of Western techniques to buttress the state vis-à-vis Western powers would also increase their own power vis-à-vis internal competitors.

The period of concerted defensive Westernization was 1839-76 in Turkey (called the Tanzimat, "reform" period) and 1853-68 in Japan. The Westernizing reforms centered around (a) importation and adaptation of technology and science in educational institutions to train modern bureaucrats; and (b) recruitment of government officials on the basis of merit and technical ability.

Innovations in Educational Institutions. From the early nineteenth century on (but especially in the 1850s), schools of science, medicine, military technology, and Western languages were established in Japan and Turkey. Besides the official schools, private colleges of Western learning also emerged. All these schools, official and private, were oriented primarily to technical and practical education for the Ottoman and samurai governing elite. They did not emphasize theoretical or humanistic learning. Both the Ottoman and Tokugawa regimes also established new translation and military offices for the importation and copying of modern weapons and technical innovations. Because study, scholarship, military training, and administration were traditional values and occupations of the samurai and Ottoman patrimonial aristocracy, some of them were able to assimilate Western learning and technology to transform themselves into modern bureaucrats.

Recruitment of Officials on the Basis of Merit and Technical Ability. Recruitment on the basis of merit was sanctified by traditional elite values in the two countries, but in fact offices in the late eighteenth and early nineteenth century were obtained mainly on the basis of social status and personal ties.[153] Yet in the crises created by Western encroachment, these values could now be used to legitimize the advancement of men with new skills. Reformers of the highest status and power inititated the establishment of new schools and bureaus for training members of the bureaucratic aristocracy in Western languages and skills. But it was primarily the sons of middle and lower Ottoman and samurai families who entered these schools and bureaus and then sought mobility into higher offices. "It was the products of the Western academies and schools who received the promotions at the end of the Tokugawa-period, carried out the reforms in their own fiefs, and eventually brought about the political revolution of the 1860's"[154] Likewise, in Ottoman Turkey from the mid–nineteenth century on, the bureaucracy was "transformed from one in which promotion was based mainly on such descriptive considerations as patronage to one in which merit was at least one of the main determinants of advancement."[155] "A new elite was in fact created in the Mulkiye (the Civil Service School established in 1859) from the ranks of middle and lower level administrative and military families ... many of them located in provincial and district centers."[156]

The recruitment of some officials on the basis of specialized skills and technical knowledge created new sources of conflict and cleavage within the aristocracy—between those officials recruited by status and those by merit, between those who upheld traditional values exclusively and those who wished to augment these with aspects of Western culture. For example, Westernization increased mobility by merit into the Ottoman civil and military bureaucracy, but much less so into the religious-judiciary official-dom. In Japan, Westernizing reforms increased the recruitment of top officials on the basis of technical competence in the large Western provinces, but less so in the Tokugawa hierarchy. The Bakufu government was as active as the largest autonomous han in sponsoring Western education and technical innovations, but in its government, officials with new skills staffed advisory bureaus, and did not have access to the traditional offices.[157] The most powerful posts in the Bakufu continued to be monopolized by daimyo and the highest grades of samurai. In Satsuma, Choshu, and Tosa, in contrast, men with new and Western skills—most often of lower samurai origins—did rise to the highest offices in han government.[158]

An even more important cleavage arose between those in high offices and a large number of officials in minor posts who had acquired modern skills, but for whom there was little possibility of mobility into positions of power. It was some of these bureaucrats who created the first radical nationalist movements in Ottoman Turkey and Tokugawa Japan.

The Rise of Nationalist Movements

Organized movements arose in the 1860s to agitate for basic changes in the political structure of Tokugawa feudalism and the Ottoman Empire. The Loyalist movement in Japan, the Young Ottoman movement, and the subsequent Young Turk movement were organized and led by minor military and civil bureaucrats who were highly educated in both traditional and Western culture. These dissidents differed from the reformers and Westernizers who held high bureaucratic office in that they were less pragmatic, more intellectual, and committed primarily to cultural reform. While not opposed to many of the rationalizing reforms of their superiors, they criticized the autocracy and arbitrariness of these bureaucrats in internal reforms, and their weakness, vacillation, and concessions in confronting the West. In Japan and Turkey some of these minor bureaucratic intellectuals, frustrated by their failure to gain influence or high office, resigned their posts to devote full time to political agitation, journalism, and organization. Removed from the exigencies of power, committed to traditional values, but also attracted to Western strength, they were most interested in the restoration and reform of traditional values and culture. To this end they propounded nationalistic doctrines which tried to revitalize traditional values while integrating them with a committment to Western innovations in technology and organization. Neither the Loyalist movement in Japan nor the Young Ottomans and Young Turks ever became revolutionary, and all failed to meet their more limited objectives of reform. But they were indispensable in creating the initiative and ideologicai foundations for later revolutions led by higher-placed bureaucratic officials.

Before looking at the specific characteristics of these nationalist movements and why they failed, let us anticipate our argument by enumerating the continuities and disjunctions between these first radical movements and subsequent revolutionary movements, both led by bureaucrats.

Radical nationalist movements in Tokugawa Japan and Ottoman Turkey were initiated by lower-level bureaucrats who felt blocked from mobility into higher office. Revolutionary movements were led by military bureaucrats who had gained office through social mobility. Some of these revolutionary leaders had been active in the radical nationalist movements and were subsequently drawn into high office. A second continuity between the two types of movements was that the doctrines of nationalism created by radical movements of lower bureaucrats were used to legitimize revolutions from above. A third continuity was that some rural landlords and preindustrial entrepreneurs (of nonaristocratic status) were drawn in to support nationalist and later revolutionary movements, but they never had any control or a decisive voice in the movements. The fact that these bourgeois (and potentially bourgeois) groups participated in radical and revolutionary movements controlled by bureaucrats with aristocratic status prevented them from organizing an independent movement or providing leadership for a peasant revolution from below. As we shall see in chapter 4, the participation of rural landlords did have an impact on the results of revolution from above.

In contrast to the above continuities between radical nationalist and revolutionary movements led by bureaucrats, there were also ways in which the earlier nationalist movements were antithetical to revolution from above. The predominance of traditional (and reactionary) interests and values in these early movements is the most important reason why revolutionary bureaucrats could evolve only after the radical nationalist movements were repressed. Most of the support for the nationalist movements came from downwardly mobile traditional elites which had not gained bureaucratic office. In Turkey, unemployed religious students (many of whom were displaced urban craftsmen) idealized the janissary spirit; in Japan, many poorer and unemployed samurai (ronin) idealized the spirit of the independent feudal warrior. Both groups supported nationalist movements because they sought a return to an idealized traditional society. Their lack of vested economic interests led downwardly mobile aristocrats and bureaucrats thwarted in their upward mobility, to take radical (but individualistic) terrorist action against both foreigners and bureaucratic officials. Yet the use of radical means was not revolutionary. These downwardly mobile aristocrats and aspiring bureaucrats had no base of power, no control of political resources, and did not see themselves as a new ruling class. Rather they sought the return to power of the Japanese emperor and an effective sultan caliph, further opening up of the bureaucracy, and partial transfer of power from bureaucrats to parliamentary institutions representative of traditional interests.

Let us look more closely at the social bases, program, and reasons for failure of radical nationalist movements in Tokugawa Japan and Ottoman Turkey.

The Social Base of the Loyalist, Young Ottoman, and Young Turk Movements   All three movements had a diverse social base. They were led and controlled by upwardly mobile bureaucrats with relatively high traditional status, and all three movements were at times aided by members of the royal family (nobles of the Imperial Court and disaffected members of the Tokugawa clan in Japan; relatives of the sultan in Turkey). But the main body of activist supporters were downwardly mobile members of the traditional aristocracy who did not qualify for bureaucratic office, and commoners with an independent base of economic power.[159] What united these groups in protest was that their traditional base of power (whether political or economic) was being undermined by bureaucratic reforms and increasing Western encroachment. We will consider the social characteristics and motivation of (1) upwardly mobile bureaucrats, (2) downwardly mobile traditional elites, and (3) commoners with an economic base.

UPWARDLY MOBILE BUREAUCRATS The most prominent leader and prime ideologue of the Loyalist and the Young Ottoman movements in the 1860s, Yoshida Shoin and Namik Kemal respectively, illustrate the social and educational attributes of the bureaucratic leaders of these movements.

Yoshida Shoin was born in 1830 in a lower samurai family in Choshu, one of the large autonomous han in Western Japan. He was adopted by an uncle who taught traditional military science in the fief school. Shoin was trained in this school and became a teacher there. In 1850, when he was sent by the han administration to study military science in another part of Japan, Shoin came in contact with Western technology and military science. He also studied at the famous Mito school, which stressed the study of Japanese traditions and the importance of the emperor as a unique Japanese institution. This training in traditional military science, Western technology, and Mito philosophy, formed the basis of Shoin's ideas. In 1854 Shoin was imprisoned for his attempt to board one of Captain Perry's ships in order to go to the West. While in prison he started to formulate his ideas on how Japan could meet the Western threat and began to write books of opinion and poetry. After being released from prison, he instituted his own private school which combined classical, national, and Western studies, and trained many future revolutionaries and Meiji leaders. As he became increasingly concerned with the inadequate politics of the shogun in dealing with the West, Shoin organized a local Loyalist movement to agitate and take violent action against provincial and Tokugawa bureaucrats. In 1859 the shogun ordered Choshu han to send Shoin to Edo for trial. Loyal to his lord, Shoin obeyed, and in 1859 was executed by the Tokugawa government.[160] But his students carried on his ideas and spread them to bands of Loyalists in many han.

Namik Kemal was born in 1840 into a highly traditional elite family, but one which had not obtained high bureaucratic office and had thus lost status and power.[161] Kemal's grandfather had been chamberlain to the sultan and his father was the court astrologer. Kemal received a traditional Ottoman-Islamic education, became learned in Persian and Arabic literature, and in 1857 was given a position in the Ottoman bureaucracy in the newly-created translation bureau. In this position he learned French, began to read Western literature, engaged in a part-time career in journalism, and started to form his ideas on the problems and needs of the Ottoman state. Along with friends from the Translation Bureau and from journalism, he founded the first Young Ottoman society in 1865, during a picnic in an Istanbul forest, which was "prepared by a cook and two servants who had been sent on ahead."[162] The six young aristocrats pledged to seek constitutional reform in the Ottoman state through public agitation. For these activities Kemal and many of his friends were forced into exile in 1867. They then founded an exile Young Ottoman group in Paris. For the next twenty years, Kemal continued to propagate his ideas on reform through journalistic and creative writing, attempting their implementation through repeated acceptance of public office and periodic agitation from exile. Although he came to revolutionary conclusions in theory (e.g., for the founding of a republic), in practice Kemal never advocated or made a revolutionary break with the sultan caliph. He died in exile imposed by that sultan.[163]

After suppression of the Young Ottomans in the 1870s, the ideas of Kemal were kept alive through the reading of forbidden Young Ottoman writings in all the elite schools of higher education in Ottoman Turkey. A new and secret organization for revolutionary activity was formed in 1889 in the imperial military-medical school, and soon spread to other students, intellectuals, and minor officials. The discovery of this movement by the sultan's spies produced another wave of exiles and the reorganization of an exile movement in Europe. The exiles were limited to journalistic agitation, but in 1906 secret revolutionary cells were independently organized in the army, especially in the divisions of the army in the European provinces of the Empire in Macedonia. This movement, called the Committee of Union and Progress, was initiated by lower army officers, all of whom had been trained in the Westernized war college.[164] These Young Turk officers were less intellectual than their Young Ottoman predecessors or than the revolutionaries in exile, but they were motivated by similar frustrations.

The Loyalists, the Young Ottomans, and the Young Turks were led by intellectuals with relatively high status, with practical experience in civil or military bureaucratic offices, and with some Western training. They were all led to revolt against high bureaucratic reformers because of frustrated personal ambition.

"A group of young samurai who met on the morrow of Perry's first alarming visit to Japan to consider what they might do for their country were exhorted by their leader to do what they could even though none held high office. One cried out: 'But what can we do without office?' No one, it seems, complained of the lack of age, wealth, or high rank in the group."[165] The Loyalists in Japan used the antiforeign movement to express hostility toward feudal superiors. For example, Yoshida Shoin said of his bureaucratic superiors: "To wear silk, eat dainty food, hug beautiful women, and fondle darling children are the only things hereditary officials care about. To revere the emperor and expel the barbarian is no concern of theirs."[166] Many of these samurai with low bureaucratic offices sought to acquire Western knowledge in order "to gain access to power via new positions in the civil bureaucracy.[167] Likewise, many low-ranking officials left their provinces to become ronin (masterless samurai) in Kyoto. It was more exciting to join a movement to restore the emperor than to be stuck in a meaningless job with no prospects of advancement.[168]

The motivation of the Ottoman bureaucrats who joined the Young Ottoman and Young Turk movements was very similar. The Tanzimat reforms made it more difficult for the sultan to arbitrarily remove high bureaucrats from office. But this reform brought to a sudden stop the circulation of bureaucratic officials described earlier. As a result in the 1860s "within the ranks of the Ottoman state servants a deep chasm had formed separating the functionaries who came from families which had been able to maintain their status for one or more generations from those who depend only on their own ability for advancement."[169] In contrast, the new Ottoman army was not "anchored down by tradition since it had been created anew after the destruction of the Janissaries."[170] But ambitious young officers were also outside the Ottoman bureaucratic establishment; they were controlled by the civil bureaucrats and had no hope of gaining these high offices. Thus they too resented the high bureaucratic reformers.

By the early twentieth century, conditions in the Ottoman army were even more frustrating for young army officers. The army recruited their officers from a wide social background, but "promotion was rarely accorded on the basis of ability. The intolerable espionage system was extended to the army and the surest way to earn preferment was to submit reports on fellow officers."[171] A contemporary observer said of the younger officers from the military schools: "The more thoroughly they were devoted to their career and the more keen was their professional ambition, the longer was their list of grievances."[172]

While the personal ambition of lower-level bureaucrats was blocked by status restrictions on high office, these dissidents were still completely dependent on the state apparatus for any possibility of personal success. Thus their revolt against high bureaucrats always aimed to save and revitalize a centralized state.

These radical nationalists in Japan and Turkey were not too different in social background and motivation from those who became revolutionary leaders in the French, Russian, and Chinese revolutions. Skocpol notes that in France, Russia and China "nationalist radicals tended to 'precipitate out' of the ranks of those who possessed specialized skills and were oriented to state activities or employements, but either lacked traditionally prestigious attributes such as nobility, landed wealth, or general humanist education, or else found themselves in situations where such attributes were no longer personally or nationally functional . . . . The primary orientation of these marginal elites was toward a broad goal that they shared with all those, including traditionally prestigious bureaucrats, whose career, livelihoods, and identities were intertwined with state activities: the goal of extension and rationalization of state powers in the name of national welfare and prestige."[173] As we shall see, it was primarily the response from above to these nationalists that differentiates the Tokugawa and Ottoman states from the old regimes in France, Russia, and China.

DOWNWARDLY MOBILE TRADITIONAL ELITES In both Tokugawa Japan and Ottoman Turkey members of the traditional aristocracy who had not gained bureaucratic office joined the anti-Western nationalist movement with the vision of restoring a more traditional and decentralized society and polity.[174] The lower-ranking religious elites (ulema) in Turkey and the lower samurai in Japan had lost status, power, and function to the secular bureaucrats. Those who held religious positions in the Ottoman state, and purely military positions in the Tokugawa system, also suffered financially from Western economic penetration. The destruction of native handicrafts in Turkey, through the competition of Western manufactured imports, swelled the ranks of religious students and ulema as many former craftsmen sought religious careers. (Traditionally there were close social ties between local religious officials, craftsmens guilds, and the janissaries. With the demise of the latter two, the former grew.) Although manufactured goods did not enter Japan in any significant amount in the late Tokugawa years, contact with the West did precipitate an economic crisis in Japan which hit the lower-level samurai without office the hardest.[175] The increasing export of Japanese goods and monetary exchange with the West led to "a growing shortage of goods, badly debased money, and a great increase in the normal amount of currency in circulation. Prices therefore rose. Between 1854 and 1968 prices increased by more than 800 percent, including essentials like rice and salt."[176] Many han cut samurai stipends in order to pay for new defense works, import ships and guns, send embassies overseas, and pay indemnities for attacks by the Loyalists on foreigners.[177] The increasing poverty of the lowly samurai focused his anger against both the han bureaucrats and foreigners.[178]

In Japan and Turkey these downwardly mobile elites lacked the qualifications (education and rank) for bureaucratic office and were most prone to use terrorism and violence against foreigners and bureaucratic officials alike.[179] The use of individual terrorism (modeled after traditional heroes) was most predominant in the early stages of the nationalist movements when bureaucratic control was weak: it was almost completely absent in subsequent revolutionary movements. Some of the xenophobic and traditional values favored by these downwardly mobile elites were incorporated into the nationalist doctrines propagated by the bureaucratic revolutionaries. Hence many of the lowly ulema and samurai sympathized with the revolutionary movements and some of them participated (under strict control) in the revolutionary armies. It was this sector of nonbureaucratized aristocracy that lost out after the revolution. Their interests and values were sacrificed to foster economic development and build a strong and more centralized state.

COMMONERS WITH AN INDEPENDENT ECONOMIC BASE Those nonaristocrats who participated in the nationalist movements represented traditional and precapitalist economic interests which had been thwarted by bureaucratic reforms and were threatened by Western economic penetration. What is important is that those who joined the radical movements from these groups identified with traditional aristocratic values. They sought economic independence from bureaucratic controls, but also personal opportunity to gain mobility into the state bureaucracy and aristocracy. They did not represent a capitalist or bourgeois force against the traditional elite. Hence they were content to accept subordinate roles in a nationalist movement. Their role became more subordinate as nationalist movements evolved into revolutionary ones.

In Japan, it was not the rich urban merchants nor those who worked for the han bureaucrats who identified with the Loyalist movement, but rural peasant landlords and entrepreneurs, some of whom held the office of village headman (*shoya*, a peasant office subordinate to samurai bureaucrats), and some of whom had gained the status of rural samurai (*goshi*— with the right to wear a sword and use a surname, but not eligible for office) through land reclamation.[180] Representatives of these rural economic interests participated in the Loyalist movement as financial supporters, terrorists, and soldiers in new irregular army units which were initiated in Choshu and Tosa han. These troops which mixed commoners and samurai were organized officially by han bureaucrats and unofficially by extremist samurai, in both cases with the financial backing of rich peasants and rural merchants.

The economic interests of rich farmers and rural entrepreneurs were in opposition to the majority of Japanese peasants, but they had also come into conflict with the interests of upper bureaucratic reformers, especially those successful reformers in the large, autonomous han in Western Japan. Conflict between peasant landlords and samurai bureaucrats grew out of a struggle for the surplus of the countryside.[181] "The village leaders were bitterly resentful of efforts to limit their wealth and authority in the interests of the new han monopolies and projects, and the old order which they sought to resurrect was one in which no feudal middlemen would interpose between the honorific (Imperial) court and the powerful rural leaders."[182] Thus, the ideology and values of the wealthy peasant Loyalists "were distinctly non- (and really pre-) commercial, and they would have been irate indeed had they been told they were a nascent bourgeoisie."[183]

While the rural wealthy saw their economic interests threatened by bureaucratic reformers, they did not see themselves in conflict with the samurai caste. For example, the following story is told of one of Japan's leading post-Restoration industrialists: "Shibusawa Eiichi, the eldest son of a wealthy village headman, tells how as a boy he was insulted by a Tokugawa official whom he considered in every way his inferior, and how then and there he determined to overthrow a system which put good men at the mercy of bad. Significantly, Shibusawa did not set about organizing a commoners' movement against warrior government; instead he joined warriors conspiring against the Bakufu, and even became a warrior himself."[184] He, like most other nonsamurai Loyalists had a samurai education, accepted samurai values, and adopted a samurai way of life.[185] For all that the Loyalists in Choshu and Tosa "represented the interests of the rural well-to-do against the interests of their urban and bureaucratic superiors, they expressed their views once the treaties had polarized politics in terms that were virtually indistinguishable from those used by the Satsuma middle samurai; a nationalist sentiment that condemned both Bakufu and domain for their weakness toward the foreigner."[186]

The desire of commoners who joined the Loyalist movement to identify with and join the feudal aristocracy is evidenced by the different behavior of peasants who did not join the Loyalist movement. In Choshu, local guard units—composed solely of peasants and under peasant officials—remained neutral during the civil war between Loyalists and the han government. The only peasants—mostly wealthy—who fought for the Loyalist cause in Choshu were those that were under the command of samurai.[187] Even in the Loyalist uprising at Yamato in 1863, where leaders representing rural interests outweighed urban samurai, the rebels "gave themselves high sounding feudal titles, calling on the farmers in the area to follow them in terms that sound more like commands from lords to subjects than an appeal for popular support."[188]

The Loyalist samurai were very wary of the status drives of wealthy peasants. They used peasants in their armies and accepted merchant financial support out of necessity; they did not see it as an alliance based on mutual economic interest.[189] "The care taken by the Loyalist leaders not to disturb the economic or social base of the han was reflected in the regulations concerning the preservation of traditional class and rank within the shotai irregular armies."[190] Sharp distinctions were maintained between samurai and commoners, even in the ceremonies for those who died in battle. Few commoners in the Loyalist armies were ever granted samurai status. "It is not unnatural for military organization to preserve sharp distinction in rank, but it is significant that the distinctions in the shotai were based on feudal status."[191]

In Ottoman Turkey, the repression of ayan landlords and the ruin of urban handicraft guilds meant that commoners with an independent economic base played a much lesser role in the Young Ottoman than in the Japanese Loyalist movement. However, one of the six or seven leading Young Ottomans, Ali Suavi, was an ulema, the son of a paper merchant, before joining the dissidents and becoming an activist journalist. He "expressed the hostility of small tradesmen in the capital who had been ruined by the Western economic impact."[192] Support for independent economic groups was expressed in all the Young Ottoman writings. Nemik Kemal and other Young Ottoman ideologists criticized the earlier suppression of provincial gentry.[193] They also wrote of the need for a Muslim bank and corporations, and they sought protection for Turkish merchants.[194] Even though most Young Ottomans were not personally linked to urban handicraft and merchant interests or to rural notables—and supported these groups mainly to advance their own interests in the bureaucracy vis-à-vis those who held high office—their agitation did force the sultan to promul-. gate an imperial legislative assembly in 1876. About one-third to one-half of the deputies represented merchant, landowner, and religious interests, and during the brief life of the parliament these deputies clashed sharply with those representing high-level civil and military bureaucrats.[195]

The subsequent Young Turk movement had more of a base among rural landlords and notables.[196] The new intellectuals of the late nineteenth and early twentieth century "came from the provincial towns. They were often the sons of local notables, scions of agricultural families, or even of the rising local Muslim-Turkish merchants."[197] It is significant that none of the five founders of the first Young Turk organization in 1889 came from Istanbul, and by 1908 many of the Young Turk leaders were of provincial or lower-class origins.[198] Moreover, "the rebellion of the officers in Salonica in 1908 was supported by widespread popular meetings in the area. These meetings were led mostly by the local Muslim notables of the Balkan towns."[199] After the parliament was reestablished in 1908, many rural notables joined the new political parties. The dominant party of the Young Turks, The Committee of Union and Progress, selected its nominees for parliament "from among the professional men in the town and the landed proprietors."[200]

Yet notables representing landlord and merchant interests in the Young Turk movement were always subordinate to leaders representing the interests of civil and military bureaucrats. Some of these bureaucratic leaders came from rural or lower-class families, but they had gone to elite schools and become urban intellectuals or military officers. The few ulema leaders in the Young Turk movement were also liberal and urbane.[201] When at times representatives of rural notables or urban merchants clashed with the bureaucratic leadership of the movement, the bureaucrats always won.[202]

The Program of the Loyalist, Young Ottoman, and Young Turk Movements None of these movements had a clear vision of alternative political institutions; rather they sought limited reforms in the existing polity—more mobility into the top civil and military offices, and consultative (not legislative) parliaments which would integrate the provincial leaders into central decision making. Powerful bureaucrats in Japan and Turkey did attempt these reforms in order to undermine the nationalist movements. But in so doing, they also further eroded the viability of the old regimes. Consultation with previously excluded provincial leaders undermined the hegemony of the existing polity, while increased mobility into high office put radicals in positions of control over bureaucratic and military resources.

The creation and propagation of doctrines of nationalism was the special contribution of these early radicals to subsequent revolutionary movements. Their nationalism revitalized traditional values, adapted them to changed conditions, and spread political consciousness to groups (but not the mass of peasants) who had not previously had a voice in national politics.

Nationalist doctrines formulated by intellectuals with ties to lower bureaucratic office in Tokugawa Japan and Ottoman Turkey aimed at the destruction of old and particularistic loyalties to dynastic leaders, loyalties that had been manipulated by bureaucratic elites to their own advantage. Nationalism substituted for these ancient fealties a new and more general allegiance to the state. The nationalistic intellectual-bureaucrat recognized that his status (like that of the high bureaucrats) depended on the state, and that the stability of the traditional state in the face of Western interference necessitated more political integration—a new and more vital commitment of all "leading" citizens to the central polity. Nationalism as anti-Westernism sought to fight the demoralizing and destructive aspects of Western penetration, while facilitating the acceptance of the positive aspects of Western civilization.[203] The doctrines of Japanese, Ottoman, and later, Turkish nationalism are summarized here.

Yoshida Shoin created a neotraditional Japanese nationalism by propagating the political theory of *sonno-joi* (honor the emperor—expel the barbarian) developed in the 1830s by scholars in the Mito school, and infusing its concepts with new meaning. He changed the ethical duty of honoring the emperor from a duty subordinate to loyalty to the feudal lord, to one preceding feudal loyalty. He changed the means of "expelling the barbarian" from a policy of excluding all foreign influence to one of adopting Western technology in order to prevent Western domination.[204]

During more than two centuries of Tokugawa feudalism, the Japanese imperial system had declined as an institution. Although in theory the Tokugawa shogun received his power to rule by delegation from the emperor, in practice the emperor had no power, and there was no actual contact between shogun and emperor. The emperor was not even a symbolic or public figure, and many Japanese hardly knew of his existence. It was only in the 1830s that a political theory giving increased importance to the emperor was developed by the Mito school (an official school in one of the Tokugawa fiefs) and began to spread through other fief schools. The Mito theory was based on the concept of *kokutai*, which expressed the idea that every country had an ideal and national essence based on its unique history. The emperor was the historical basis of Japan's national essence, and "kokutai" pictured the Japanese as one great family with the emperor as father and lord. This theory was formed from a synthesis of Confucian ideas with traditional Shintoism, an indigenous Japanese religion founded on a belief that the Japanese emperor was descended from the gods. The Mito theory was given expression in the slogan "sonno-joi," which was designed to promote moral regeneration of the samurai, but was in no way intended to be antishogunal or to alter existent political procedure.

Shoin, as he propagated the theory, added the idea that loyalty to the emperor should be superior to loyalty to the lord. "In Shoin's view, duty to the nation was not the special prerogative of any one group, but transcended class divisions and local loyalties of the han system."[205] By thus substituting loyalty to the emperor for loyalty to the lord, Shoin was attempting to generalize and nationalize the ethic of samurai loyalty. Shoin further advocated that loyalty to the shogun was only obligatory if the latter acted according to imperial instructions. Although no action was taken in his lifetime, the resort to arms against the shogun in 1868 was justified in Shoin's terms. Yoshida Shoin, too, was the first to popularize the idea that foreigners were barbarians only in regard to their ethical and moral values, not in their science and technology. He argued that for Japan to defeat these barbarians it must adopt Western industrial and military technology. Many early activists in the Loyalist movement—especially samurai without office and without any Western education—sought to literally expel Westerners by force (assassinating their representatives and shelling their ships). When they came face to face with Western military might (as in the retalitory attacks by Western gunboats on Satsuma and Choshu in 1864 and 1865), however, they quickly accepted Shoin's formulation which they had overlooked earlier. They dropped the slogan, "expel the barbarian," for a new one: "enrich the country, strengthen the army."

Namik Kemal was also committed to the national integration of the Ottoman Empire. He believed that Westernizing reforms of the bureaucratic elite had decreased, rather than increased, structural and cultural integration of the empire by increasing separatist communal organization of minority groups while destroying much of the base (the ayans, janissaries, and guilds) of Muslims and weakening the Islamic basis of the state. He charged that the new concept of Ottoman citizenship formulated by the upper bureaucrats had no symbolic or popular appeal. Namik Kemal created new and emotional ideas of patriotism through reformulation of traditional concepts. He publicized his patriotic ideals through poetry, romantic historical novels, and plays. Particularly popular were his concepts of fatherland and nation, through which he attempted to promote a new Ottoman patriotism. Kemal spoke of the fatherland, "as being not only a geographical unit, but also an emotional bond in which the memories of ancestors, the recollection of one's own youth and earliest experiences all had a place."[206]

Kemal's ideas of the fatherland and the nation came originally from the West, especially from his reading of Rousseau and Montesquieu, but he attempted to infuse Western concepts with Islamic and Turkish meanings. *Vatan*, popularized by Kemal to inspire patriotism to the fatherland, was a Turkicized form of *watan*, a classical Arabic word meaning place of birth or residence. For the vast number of minority groups (one-half the Ottoman population), their vatan was their religious and ethnic community with its autonomous legal and administrative organization. But Kemal sought to apply the word to the empire as a whole and transfer commitment from the local community to the larger state. Likewise, *millet*, the term which Kemal coined to refer to the Ottoman nation, originally meant "religious community," and has been used to refer to the organized minority religions in the empire, but not to Islam. In applying it to the Ottoman state, the Young Ottomans were attempting to create an Islamic community and Muslim identification with the state. Traditionally, the state had been the only basis of Islamic community, but "the more the state lost its traditional features, that is, the more the state's religious and political features became separated, and the more the state was portrayed as a political association of millets, the more the Muslims found themselves in a vacuum."[207] Thus Namik Kemal and the Young Ottomans simultaneously tried to create a secular patriotism (vatan) for the minority groups, and an Islamic patriotism (millet) for the Muslims. They purposely never really distinguished what was Ottoman and what was Islamic, for to have done so would have alienated one-half of the population or the order.

Like his Japanese counterparts, Namik Kemal was committed both to the retention of traditional values and the adoption of Western science and technology. Unlike the Japanese, he believed that some aspects of Islamic culture limited its ability to promote material progress. He thus suggested that the fatalism inherent in Islam be replaced by Western values of progress and liberty—values which he believed were responsible for Western economic progress. The ideas of freedom and progress became an integral part of his doctrine of patriotism.

The failure of Ottoman nationalism to integrate an empire of such diverse religious and ethnic groups led to the formulation of a specifically Turkish nationalism. The first signs of this Turkish (as opposed to Ottoman) national consciousness appeared in the late nineteenth century, but it did not become widespread until after 1908.[208] It was an intellectual, Ziya Gokalp, who was the most influential in formulating a doctrine of Turkish nationalism that became the basis of Ataturk's revolution and was then used to legitimize a homogeneous (and nonimperial) Turkish nation-state. Gokalp was born into a family of lower-level provincial bureaucrats in southeastern Anatolia. He attended a local religious school, a military elementary school, and then the Veterinary College of Istanbul, where he read the Islamic classics, Young Ottoman works, and Western thinkers, especially the French sociologist Durkheim. Later Gokalp was made a professor at the University of Istanbul, and was also a key member of the Young Turk Committee of Union and Progress, first in Salonika and then in Istanbul.[209] Gokalp was ahead of other Young Turks in seeing the impossibility of maintaining an empire of diverse nationalities, and he began to formulate an alternative vision that became more popular as the Young Turks failed to hold the empire together.

Like Nemik Kemal and the Young Ottoman intellectuals, Gokalp advocated the acceptance and use of Western science and technology.[210] But in contrast to them, he believed that technical, economic, and organizational modernization would succeed only if national integration was based on specifically Turkish values and on the rejection of both Western and Islamic culture as a basis for political loyalty.[211] Gokalp advocated a secular state, but refuted those who feared that secularization meant Westernization. He began to make conscious, systematize, and propagate Anatolian traditions from their pre-Islamic past along with current popular customs and folklore.[212] In advocating a nationalism that appealed to popular values, Gokalp explicitly excluded the formalism and the use of Persian and Arabic language and customs which had marked the Ottoman elite and cut them off from popular culture. He called the aristocratic culture "artifical, in contrast to the literature, morality, law, economics, and organization of the folk."[213] Gokalp said: "we must look for the sources of our literature on the stone engravings of deer skins, on the one hand, and in the folk poems, folk tales and epics, on the other. Our national language must be based on Turkish grammar. Our national literature must take its themes, its symbols, from Turkish social life, for Turkish social organization, and from Turkish mythology and epics. We must discard foreign rules from our grammar, foreign metre from our poetry, foreign symbolism from our literature . . . . We must revive the history of Turkish laws by studying Turkish folkways, mores, and tribal laws."[214]

As we shall see in later chapters this populist nationalism (like the Japanese appeal to ancient and popular imperial myths) was very effective in legitimizing a revolution that was essentially elitist and antithetical to the interests of the common people. But creative nationalism was not enough to make the Loyalist, Young Ottoman, or Young Turk movements a success.

Reasons for Failure of the Loyalist, Young Ottoman, and Young Turk Movements By 1863 the Loyalist movement had been crushed and many of its leaders killed. Most of the Loyalists were either arrested by the han government, crushed by the military force of han armies, or assimilated into these armies where they were controlled by officials of the han. In 1868 the sultan's spies discovered a coup plot by the Young Ottomans and ordered the leaders arrested. Many of the Young Ottomans escaped to Europe and continued propaganda from exile, but the exile movement was fraught with constant quarrels and defections and never succeeded in reorganizing within Turkey. The Young Turk movement had a somewhat different history, but also ended in failure. Their military revolt in 1908 forced the sultan to establish an Ottoman parliament. The Young Turks formed a political party, but when they were unable to control the Assembly in 1913, they staged a coup which concentrated power in a triumvirate of two young officers and a former telegraph clerk. But even this attempt at dictatorial control failed to quell the revolts by the non-Turkish provinces for national independence. It was this Young Turk dictatorship that also precipitated the Ottoman's disastrous entry into World War I, which decisively destroyed the empire. As one commentator said: "There are very few movements in the world that have given rise to such great hopes as the Ottoman Constitutional Revolution (of 1908); there are likewise very few movements where hopes have been so swiftly and finally disappointed."[215]

The failure of these movements organized by radical minor bureaucrats was caused by three main weaknesses: conflicts and ambivalence in goals; ineffective organization; and lack of a power base. But their demise was also—and more importantly—the result of the way top bureaucrats responded to the challenge from below.

CONFLICTING AND AMBIVALENT GOALS None of these radical nationalist movements ever proclaimed revolutionary goals. No Loyalist "envisioned the abolition of the domains or the dismantling of feudal society."[216] Likewise, the Young Turk revolt was essentially conservative: "There was no ideology, no program behind it, no understanding of the fundamental problems which confronted the Ottoman state. Imperialist in essence, blind to the new nationalist forces now at work in the modern world, the Young Turks aspired merely to conserve, if in a more liberal form, the Ottoman Empire of their forebearers."[217]

Yet the personal ambition of the minor bureaucrats who led the Loyalist, Young Ottoman, and Young Turk movements prevented them from even becoming serious reformers. For example, the Young Ottomans in exile have been compared to their Russian counterparts: "In contrast to the Russians who turned into sworn enemies of the Czarist regime, the Middle Eastern intellectuals never seem to have lost their sense of identification with the State . . . . They always cherished hopes of assuming high office as soon as a new ruler came to the throne or a new vezir to the divan."[218] The result was that Loyalists, Young Ottomans, and Young Turks time and again sacrificed their immediate objectives, and often their ideal goals, upon appeal from their rulers. Yoshida Shoin, obedient to his lord, did not resist execution by the shogun. Namik Kemal often returned from exile on assurances of reforms by the sultan, only to find later that he had completely compromised his goals. Moreover, few of the Loyalists, Young Ottomans, or Young Turks were immune to the attractions of high office; leaders of both movements were often coopted into the bureaucratic elites. What has been said of the Loyalists is also true of Young Ottomans and Young Turks: "The shishi when close to power tended to utilize more and more of the ideas and techniques of the upper bureaucratic reformers, men whom they had revolted against and often tried to murder, while the upper classes later remembered that the thing that had kept them from espousing full loyalism earlier was that it seemed to be associated with lower samurai."[219]

The goals of these movements also reflected the conflict between the leadership with knowledge of the West and their completely traditional supporters. All three movements left their goals consciously ambivalent and open to conflicting interpretations by progressives and restorationists. "Honor the emperor—expel the barbarian," the slogan of the Loyalists, could be interpreted as completely anti-Western and consistent with feudal loyalty to the lord, or as advocating the imitation of Western techniques to prevent "barbarian" control, and the replacement of feudal loyalty by national commitment to the emperor. The nationalism of the Young Ottomans and Young Turks proposed simultaneously the return to Islamic principles of state and the creation of a parliament based on secular representation. This ambivalence was at first effective in attracting both progressive and reactionary elites to the movement, but in the end the contradictions were exposed by the dynastic leaders and conservative bureaucrats. They were able to undermine these movements led by lower bureaucrats by appealing more directly to the traditional values of the samurai and ulema. The bureaucratic elites could unmask the "Western" and "heretical" attitudes of the Loyalist, Young Ottoman, and Young Turk leaders to their conservative followers.[220]

INEFFECTIVE ORGANIZATION Whatever the inadequacies of their goals, the Loyalists, Young Ottomans, and Young Turks were much more effective at devising and propagating ideas for radical reforms than at developing methods to achieve them. All three groups were composed of militants with an inclination to individual acts of heroism—assassination and secret coups—rather than to pragmatic and tactical planning or to the mobilization of organized strength. The Loyalists were "children of the storm, bravos and toughs, revolutionaries without a program and followers in search of a leader."[221] Kemal said with pride that the Young Ottomans had no individual leaders, but were held together by "a brotherhood of opinion and kinship of the heart."[222] Enver Pasha, the young military officer who was the hero of the Young Turk revolt of 1908 and the Young Turk dictator of 1913-18 was "the flamboyant, diminutive hero of the revolution who spellbound Istanbul theatre audiences by jumping on stage in the grand finale of a patriotic melodrama to mete out justice to the villians; the parvenu who married the Sultan's niece and promoted his brother from major to lieutenant general; the easy prey to flattery who returned from festive dinners in Berlin, a lifelong Germanophile; the opportunist who left his assigned battle station to be the first to march into Edirne, but fled the country in the dark of night after leading it into ruinous defeat; the quixotic dreamer, who concluded among Turkestani bandits the meteoric career begun among Balkan Komitadjis."[223]

This lack of rational organization and experienced leadership doomed these movements. It is said of the demise of the Loyalists: "It . . . demonstrated the impossibility of building a successful revolution around Court nobles and ill-organized samurai bands. Too many leaders, too little discipline, a lack of economic resources . . . nullified the advantage of courage and fanaticism when the conspirators found themselves confronting a coherent military force."[224]

The Young Turk movement had more organization, in the Committee of Union and Progress, than either the Young Ottomans or the Loyalists, but it too was inadequate. The original organization of the Committee of Union and Progress was a series of secret five-man cells. Members were initiated by secret rituals patterned after Turkish religious sects. There was a central committee to coordinate the cells, but the leadership was multiple, changing, and secret. After 1908, the committee remained a private and secret society. Even though it established branches in all of the country, it attempted to govern by manipulation from behind the scenes. This secret and manipulative organization had multiple disadvantages for consolidating political support. "The committee of Union and Progress . . . was simply a series of decentralized committees scattered over the various provinces of the Empire, and only loosely linked together, without proper coordination or central control. It had no leader, only a changing series of leaders. Moreover, it was saturated with the Oriental spirit of secrecy and intrigue. It was still an underground organization, which took its decisions behind closed doors with all the abracadabra of the secret society, in which conspiracy flourished, rivalry was rife in the paying off of personal scores, and power was abused through the informer, the plotter and the political assassin."[225] This organizational inadequacy was compounded by the administrative inexperience of the leaders. "Few of the Young Turks had ever had practical experience in governing, and there was not a sufficient number of officials to do the work, while the energy of many of the leading men were absorbed in the struggle for power."[226] As a result, the major government offices were left to bureaucratic officials of the old regime, most of them unsympathetic to the Young Turk ideals.

LACK OF A POWER BASE Since all of the radical nationalist movements based their support on aristocrats, the notable, or the wealthy—and showed little inclination to reach the masses—it is unlikely that rational organization and experienced leadership would have been enough to insure their success as reform or revolutionary movements. In earlier pages we discussed how the development of an independent and politically conscious bourgeoisie was suppressed in Tokugawa Japan and Ottoman Turkey, while the bureaucratic elite had no base of economic power. Without an independent social and economic base, bureaucratic radicals could only become effective if they had a political base of power. Since they were removed from the "people," the only source of political power was the civil and military bureaucracy. Thus it was only when the ideals of radical nationalism were taken up and expanded by those who controlled bureaucratic and military resources that were (or could be) detached from the central control of dynastic leaders and conservative bureaucrats that these movements became revolutionary.

It was the existence of semifeudal, provincial bureaucratic and military forces in Tokugawa Japan that made a revolution from above possible five years after the demise of the Loyalist movement. Because the semiautonomous provinces in the Ottoman Empire were controlled by non-Turks, it took fifty years and the destruction of the empire by war before an autonomous military force could form. A coalition of high-level civil and military bureaucrats who sympathized with the Young Ottomans staged a military coup in Istanbul in 1876. They forced the sultan to promulgate a constitution and establish a national consultative assembly. Some of the original Young Ottomans actually sat on the committee to draft the constitution. But the first Ottoman Constitutional Assembly lasted less than a year: as soon as it began to take independent action, the sultan disbanded it. The small number of high-level bureaucrats who supported the Young Ottomans could do nothing for they had no independent power base. The majority of central bureaucrats and officers were loyal to the sultan, and there was little real support for the constitution in provincial cities.[227] In contrast, the Ataturk movement took advantage of the fact that the Young Turk Committee of Union and Progress had gained control of the provincial administration in a number of Turkish districts.[228]

The Rise of Revolutionary Leadership in the Military Bureaucracy

Radical nationalist movements arose in many countries in response to Western encroachment, organized and led by intellectuals closely connected to state service, with support from traditional groups economically and socially displaced by modernization. The reaction of high civil and military bureaucrats to these movements determined whether nationalist leaders turned upward or downward for support. The thesis developed and supported in this chapter is that bureaucrats who depended solely on the state for their power, status, and wealth—and did not themselves have vested economic interests outside the state nor dependent ties to landlords or industrialists—gave more support to radical nationalists, accepting many of their leaders,and ideas, while bringing their own greater organizational experience and resources to the leadership of the movement. In contrast, bureaucrats with vested economic interests reacted to the combination of foreign pressure and internal dissonance with primarily repressive and conservative responses (in Prussia in 1848, China in the nineteenth century, and Russia in the early twentieth century). In these latter countries, nationalist intellectuals and lower bureaucrats had to turn outside the state—to peasants or the urban working class—for support.

The preceding chapter demonstrated how revolutions from above in Japan and Turkey began with the establishment of an alternative center of authority controlled by some of the highest officials of the old regime, mobilized around traditional organs of the government, and claiming legitimacy on the basis of traditional symbols and values. In both countries military bureaucrats took the initiative in forming an alternative center of power.[229] The rise of military leadership was partially the result of the greater social mobility possible in the military as compared to the civil bureaucracy.[230] Men with marginal aristocratic status, but with technical skills and innovative ideas, rose to high military office, many of them already radicalized by the Loyalist and Young Turk movements which arose among the lower military officers. The nationalist ideologies of these earlier movements provided a coherent ideology to mobilize bureaucrats for political action.[231] Like Ataturk, the radical military bureaucrats in Choshu "could lay claim to a legitimacy at least equal to that of the government. They represented the principles for which the entire han had fought in the recent past; they upheld the martial pride of the samurai creed, which found repugnant Choshu's abject submission to the Bakufu army; and by involving the han in national politics they sought to regain the glory that had belonged to the house of Mori before the Tokugawa victory in 1600."[232]

Without the threat from the West, it is unlikely that high-level military officers would have risked their official status by engaging in illegal revolutionary action. For example, when Ataturk was removed from his title of general and his military command because of his defiance of the Istanbul government, he "became nervous, depressed, and uneasy.... His military rank had meant everything to him. It had given him a sense of security and purpose which, with his (low) family background he had previously lacked."[233]

Support for my thesis on the genesis of radicals from within the Japanese and Turkish military bureaucracy is provided by a comparison with the Prussian state bureaucracy in the 1840s.

Junior officials in the elaborate state bureaucracy of Prussia in the 1840s became frustrated with their lack of opportunity for mobility. These bureaucratic dissidents challenged seniority in appointments to high office, advocated merit appointment and advancement, and protested bureaucratic absolutism. Like their counterparts in Japan and Turkey, some of these officials dropped out of state service to devote full time to radical journalism and organizing.[234] Along with professionals and intellectuals, they took the most active leadership in the attempt at revolution in Prussia in 1848. "In 1848 it was not the businessmen or the laboring poor but the young professional men, most of whom were in the service of the state who demanded the most radical political changes."[235] This helps explain why the initial programs of the Prussian revolutionaries "were so little concerned with the problems of the businessmen and laboring poor ... but placed such great emphasis on a strong unified state as the first step toward the solution of other problems."[236]

In contrast to the high bureaucratic officials in Japan and Turkey, their counterparts in Prussia reacted to dissident lower bureaucrats and intellectuals "with a combination of fear and hostility.... As a result the progressive image of the Prussian state, an inheritance from the earlier Reform Era (1806-1819) faded."[237] Instead of becoming more adaptable as problems began to pile up, "the older generation of Prussian bureaucrats seems to have clung ever more closely to the traditional symbols of status. In the 1840s these men enforced the seniority customs of their profession with unyielding stubborness, refusing to make way for younger men who might be able to handle problems more effectively."[238]

This conservatism of top bureaucrats in Prussia was the result of their close ties with the Junkers, and hence their vested interest in maintaining the economic status quo. These ties between bureaucrats and landed aristocrats were strengthened in the 1840s as the Prussian bureaucracy changed "from a privileged body, proud of its cultural and social leadership in a corporate society, into a dependent element of the new upper class."[239] As a result, dissident minor officials were not drafted into high office, nor was the bureaucratic elite responsive to their programs and

ideology. Rather than contributing to a revolution from above, "a significant minority of the bureaucrats, mainly younger, lower-ranking members,
defected temporarily or permanently to the liberal and radical opposition
movements."[240] Here they joined independent professionals, journeymen,
storekeepers, and workers in a mass revolutionary movement.

Once the popular uprising of 1848 in Prussia had overthrown the old
regime, the Junker landed aristocracy—in contrast to conservative aristocrats in Japan and Turkey—organized an effective counterrevolutionary
movement.[241] But even before the mobilization of this opposition, liberal
revolutionaries in Germany who had worked for the state were less radical
than bureaucratic revolutionaries in Japan and Turkey. The former were
constantly in fear of their mass support taking over to the detriment of their
own interests.[242] In contrast, bureaucratic revolutionaries in Japan and
Turkey had no fear of the masses, for they did not depend on their support
and they controlled military and bureaucratic force sufficiently to suppress
any opposition.

The thesis presented here also offers an alternative to many of the
hypotheses developed by Western scholars as to why the Japanese re-
pulsed the threat of Western economic domination by building a centralized state and sponsoring successful industrialization (after the Meiji
Restoration), while China for one hundred years (from the 1840s to 1945)
was exploited by foreign capitalists as its own economy stagnated and
centralized political control disintegrated.

In the mid–nineteenth century opposition to both the Chinese traditional
polity and Western penetration arose from among lower bureaucratic
officials (or those who aspired to office but had not received appointment).
In contrast to similar radical nationalists in Japan and Turkey, this opposition "mainly dissipated itself in fruitless revolts and insurrections within the
prevailing framework."[243] Chinese bureaucratic reformers also arose
within the high officialdom in response to internal dissidence and external
threat, but their attempt to revitalize the polity failed. "To gain adequate
revenue to put down internal rebellion and face foreign enemies after
1830, the Manchu government would have had to destroy the whole
system of gentry [aristocratic] privilege."[244] This they could not do, for
Chinese bureaucrats, in contrast to the Tokugawa and Ottoman officialdom, were drawn from—or used their offices to enter—a landholding
aristocracy. "The link between office and wealth through lineage was one
of the most important features of Chinese society."[245] In the nineteenth
century the upper gentry (with the highest aristocratic status) held most
high offices and also received the most income from landholding.[246] As a
result bureaucratic reformers in nineteenth-century China sought to
strengthen the social and economic position of the landholding gentry,

which in turn weakened centralized bureaucratic control.[247] Repeatedly, "new officials and functions were absorbed into pre-existing local and especially regional cliques of gentry."[248] After 1911 centralized bureaucratic control broke down completely into rule by landlords who became provincial warlords.[249] Even under the attempt at recentralization after 1927 the landed aristocracy retained the substance of political control.[250]

The close ties between political and economic power in China, along with the intensity of Western pressure, prevented the Chinese state bureaucrats from either initiating effective bureaucratic reforms or undertaking a bureaucratic revolution. This explanation contradicts those offered by a variety of sociologists, historians, and Asian specialists. Let us briefly consider three propositions offered by these scholars to explain the distinct reactions of Chinese and Japanese bureaucrats to the Western challenge:

1. The most prominent explanation stresses the distinct value attributes of Japanese Confucianism as it became culturally distinct from the original Chinese religion.[251] Special emphasis is often given to the tradition of cultural borrowing in Japan[252] and to the precedence of group loyalty (to han or daimyo) over family loyalty.[253] These cultural traits are seen as facilitating both a nationalistic and an adaptive response to the West in Japan as compared to the Chinese propensity to capitulate to Western demands, while resisting technical innovations developed by Western science. Even a recent Marxist analysis of Japanese development falls back on a cultural explanation. Jon Halliday asserts: "Part of the reason why Japan was not turned into a colony was the organized resistance of the Japanese ruling class. It had a long and uninterrupted tradition of rule behind it and enjoyed a very high level of literacy and education. Japan's population was also unusually well-educated; its culture was relatively homogeneous."[254] In contrast, the thesis presented here argues that cultural differences between China and Japan are secondary and derivative from the distinct relationship between political and economic power in the two countries. "The organized resistance of the Japanese ruling class" was based on the existence of autonomous bureaucrats and not on their cultural "tradition of rule." My analysis sees values as based on socioeconomic reality. A cultural explanation by itself is inadequate and misleading.

2. A second interpretation of the different modern histories of Japan and China emphasizes the feudal and decentralized character of Japan as the most important factor structuring its creative response to foreign pressure. Reischauer and Fairbanks, for example, argue that China was so politically centralized and bureaucratized that only men in the capital could make innovations. This inhibited a creative response to the West. In contrast they

say: "Japan's feudal experience had been similar to that of Europe, and the nation was already evolving along a course not far different from the one Europe had taken . . . . A class structure rather like that of feudal Europe was breaking down in somewhat the same way as it had broken down in the West."[255] The data presented in this chapter contradicts this analysis for it demonstrates that Japanese feudalism and its class structure were very different from the European case. The proliferation of provincial bureaucracies and the sankin-kotai system meant that traditional Japan was probably more politically centralized than China. In China, political power was continually devolving onto large numbers of local gentry landlords; in Japan political power was concentrated in a relatively small number of castle town bureaucrats.

3. Barrington Moore in *The Social Origins of Dictatorship and Democracy* presents another explanation for the divergence of Japanese and Chinese modern history. He incorrectly identifies the daimyo and highest samurai in Japan as a landed aristocracy and sees them as playing an historical role similar to that of Chinese gentry. As a result, he attributes the different revolutionary histories of China and Japan to distinctions in peasant organization which gave Chinese peasants a greater potential for revolution.[256] While there may be variations in the potential of peasants to be mobilized for radical action, these differences will only become operative when the state apparatus has lost effective social control. Differences in peasant organization cannot explain why Japan undertook a bureaucratic revolution from above almost one hundred years prior to the triumph of a mass peasant-based revolution in China. Rather, a thesis which explains why Japanese bureaucrats could respond to the West in a more radical and nationalistic manner than their Chinese counterparts seems to be a more productive first step in elucidating the historical development of divergent revolutionary histories.

Notes

1. I deliberately refrain from talking about ownership of the means of production in order to stress control. In Tokugawa Japan and Ottoman Turkey the dynastic head of state owned much of the land, but this did not mean that state bureaucrats controlled production on the land or distribution of its product.

2. Perry Anderson in an excellent comparative study of the development of the absolutist state in Europe presents a long appendix criticizing the Marxist concepts of an Asiatic mode of production and Oriental despotism. Anderson points out both contradictions in Marx's original concepts and the great differences in economic and political structures in the "Oriental" Islamic and Chinese societies. Anderson says: "The similarity which Marx and Engels perceived between all the states they deemed Asian was a deceptive one, to a large extent the product of their own

inevitable lack of information, at a time when historical study of the Orient was only just starting in Europe. Indeed, nothing is more striking than the extent to which they inherited virtually en bloc a traditional European discourse on Asia, and reproduced it with few variations." *Lineages of the Absolutist State*. (London: New Left Books, 1974), pp. 491-92.

3. Ibid., pp. 424, 543.

4. Max Weber discusses these two types of traditional society in chapters 7 and 8 of *Economy and Society*, eds. Guenther Roth and Claus Wittich (New York: Bedminster Press, 1968).

5. Ibid., p. 1026.

6. Ibid., p. 1069.

7. Ibid., p. 1015.

8. Reinhard Bendix, *Max Weber: An Intellectual Portrait* (New York: Doubleday, 1960), p. 365.

9. Weber, *Economy and Society*, p. 1081.

10. For an excellent critique of the indiscriminate use of the term *feudalism* as a worldwide phenomenon by current scholars see Anderson, pp. 401-03. For a critique of those Marxists, including Anderson, who designate Tokugawa Japan as feudal see my article, "State Power and Modes of Production: Implications of the Japanese Transition to Capitalism," *The Insurgent Sociologist* 8 (Spring 1977).

11. Weber, *Economy and Society*, p. 1028.

12. Ibid., p. 1073.

13. Ibid., p. 1075.

14. Ibid.

15. Barnett Miller, *The Palace School of Mohammed the Conqueror* (Cambridge, Mass.: Harvard University Press, 1941), p. 45.

16. John Saunders, *The Muslim World on the Eve of Europe's Expansion* (Englewood Cliffs, N.J.: Prentice-Hall, 1966), p. 17.

17. Charles Issawi ed., *The Economic History of the Middle East* (Chicago: University of Chicago Press, 1966), p. 71.

18. Rosat Aktan, "Agricultural Policy of Turkey," Ph.D. dissertation, University of California, Berkeley, 1950, p. 80.

19. Kemal Karpat, "The Land Regime, Social Structure, and Modernization in the Ottoman Empire," in *Beginnings of Modernization in the Middle East*, eds. William Polk and Richard Chambers (Chicago: University of Chicago Press, 1968), p. 76.

20. H.A.R. Gibb and Harold Bowen, *Islamic Society and the West* (London: Oxford University Press, 1967), vol. 1, p. 113.

21. Islam had no autonomous church organization; the highest religious officials were judges holding political office by appointment from the government.

22. Gibb and Bowen, vol. 1, p. 61.

23. Ibid., p. 149.

24. Carter Findley, "Legacy of Tradition to Reform: Origins of the Ottoman Foreign Ministry," *International Journal of Middle Eastern Studies* 1 (1970): 338.

25. Ibid., p. 342.

26. There is disagreement among scholars as to exactly when the slave system declined, and when and how Islamic families gained access to high office. See Norman Itzkowitz, "Eighteenth Century Ottoman Realities," *Studia Islamica* 16 (1962): 73-94.

27. Findley, p. 345.

28. Ibid., p. 346.

29. Ibid., p. 348.
30. Saunders, p. 17.
31. Stanford Shaw, *Between Old and New: The Ottoman Empire Under Sultan Selim III, 1789-1807* (Cambridge, Mass.: Harvard University Press, 1971), p. 173.
32. Findley, p. 353.
33. Ibid., p. 340.
34. Ibid., p. 353.
35. Gibb and Bowen vol. 1., p. 196.
36. John Hall, "The Nature of Traditional Society," in Ward and Rustow, pp. 14-41.
37. Peter Duus, *Feudalism in Japan* (New York: Knopf, 1969), p. 88.
38. John Hall, *Government and Local Power in Japan: 500-1700* (Princeton: Princeton University Press, 1966), p. 353.
39. Ibid., p. 362.
40. Duus, *Feudalism in Japan*, p. 90.
41. Hall, *Government and Local Power*, p. 355.
42. Duus, *Feudalism in Japan*, p. 90.
43. Ibid., p. 91.
44. Hall, *Government and Local Power*, p. 368.
45. Toshie Tsukahira, *Feudal Control in Tokugawa Japan: The Sankin-Kotai System* (Harvard University: East Asian Research Center Monographs, 1967), p. 2.
46. Duus, *Feudalism in Japan*, p. 90.
47. John Hall, "Feudalism in Japan," in *Studies in the Institutional History of Early Modern Japan*, eds. John Hall and Marius Jansen (Princeton: Princeton University Press, 1968), p. 47.
48. John Hall, "The Nature of Traditional Society," p. 22.
49. Ronald Dore, *Education in Tokugawa Japan* (Berkeley: University of California Press, 1965), chs. 1, 2.
50. John Hall, "The Castle Town and Japan's Modern Urbanization," *Far Eastern Quarterly* 15 (1955): 52.
51. Conrad Totman, *Politics in the Tokugawa Bakufu* (Cambridge, Mass.: Harvard University Press, 1967), p. 137.
52. Ibid., p. 137.
53. Ibid., p. 139.
54. Hall, *Government and Local Power in Japan*, p. 369.
55. Duus, *Feudalism in Japan*, p. 1.
56. Totman, p. 239.
57. Ibid., p. 231.
58. Ibid., p. 245.
59. Ibid., p. 231.
60. Ibid., p. 40.
61. Ibid., pp. 193-95.
62. Hall, *Government and Local Power in Japan*, p. 413.
63. Totman, p. 256.
64. Ibid., p. 256.
65. Hall, "The Nature of Traditional Society," p. 28.
66. Totman, p. 154.
67. Ibid., p. 162.
68. Ibid., pp. 168-69.
69. Ibid., p. 145.
70. Ibid., p. 147.

71. Ibid., p. 142.
72. John Hall, *Tanama Okitsugu: Forerunner of Modern Japan* (Cambridge, Mass.: Harvard University Press, 1955), p. 54.
73. Gibb and Bowen vol. 2, p. 169.
74. Findley, pp. 354-55.
75. Ibid., p. 354.
76. Gibb and Bowen vol. 2, p. 169.
77. Halil Inalcik, "Capital Formation in the Ottoman Empire," *Journal of Economic History* 29 (1969): 138.
78. Gibb and Bowen vol. 2, p. 165.
79. Inalcik, "Capital Formation in the Ottoman Empire," p. 21.
80. Gibb and Bowen vol. 2, p. 21.
81. See Inalcik, "The Nature of Traditional Society," p. 47; and Karpat, "The Land Regime," p. 28.
82. A.H. Hourani, "The Fertile Crescent in the Eighteenth Century," in Issawi, p.28.
83. See *ayan* in the *Encyclopedia of Islam*, new edition, 1960.
84. Inalcik, "The Nature of Traditional Society," p. 48.
85. Karpat, "The Land Regime," p. 78.
86. Inalcik, "The Nature of Traditional Society," p. 52.
87. Issawi, p. 19.
88. It was only in the postrevolutionary republic that the bourgeoisie became politically significant.
89. Kemal Karpat, "The Transformation of the Ottoman State, 1789-1908," *International Journal of Middle Eastern Studies* 3 (1972), p. 256.
90. Tsukahira, pp. 81-83.
91. Ibid., pp. 101-2.
92. Totman, p. 83.
93. Moore, *Social Origins of Dictatorship and Democracy*, p. 238.
94. Charles Sheldon, *The Rise of the Merchant Class in Tokugawa Japan* (Locust Valley, New York: Association for Asian Studies, 1958), p. 122.
95. Ibid., p. 104.
96. Moore, *Social Origins of Dictatorship and Democracy*, p. 237.
97. Totman, p. 69.
98. Thomas Smith, "The Japanese Village in the Seventeenth Century," in Hall and Jansen, p. 268.
99. E.S. Crawcour, "Changes in Japanese Commerce in the Tokugawa Period," in Hall and Jansen, p. 196.
100. Sheldon, p. 150.
101. Smith, *The Agrarian Origins of Modern Japan*, p. 127.
102. Anderson, p. 429.
103. Ibid.
104. Issawi, p. 71.
105. Halil Inalcik, "The Heyday and Decline of the Ottoman Empire," in *The Cambridge History of Islam*, vol. 1 (Cambridge: Cambridge University Press, 1970), p. 345.
106. Issawi, p. 71.
107. Gibb and Bowen, vol. 2, p. 25.
108. Ibid., vol. 1, pp. 173-99.
109. L.S. Stavrianos, *The Balkans since 1453* (New York: Holt, Rinehart, & Winston, 1961), p. 122.

110. Gibb and Bowen, vol. 1, pp. 181-85.

111. Nur Yalman, "Westernized Reformers and Reactionary Conservatives: The Major Cleavage in the Turkish Polity," unpublished paper, p. 38.

112. Gibb and Bowen, vol. 1, p. 181.

113. Quoted in Hall, *Tanama Okitsugu,*p. 112.

114. Jansen, *Sakamoto Ryoma*, p. 12.

115. Hall, *Tanuma Okitsugu*, ch. 6.

116. Smith, *The Agrarian Origins of Modern Japan*, p. 177.

117. Robert Bellah, *Tokugawa Religion* (Glencoe, Ill.: Free Press, 1957), p. 44.

118. Johannes Hirschmeier, *The Origins of Entrepreneurship in Meiji Japan* (Cambridge, Mass.: Harvard University Press, 1964), p. 50.

119. John Moffett in an unpublished dissertation makes an incisive analysis of the rise and effects of bureaucratic states in Europe. "Bureaucratization and Social Control: A Study of the Progressive Regimentation of the Western Social Order," Columbia University, Department of Sociology, 1971, p. 45.

120. In contrast, reform and rationalization of the Prussian bureaucracy in 1800-1850 allied the bureaucracy even more closely with the other powerful interest groups, the Junker landed aristocracy and the rising capitalist class. See John Gillis, *The Prussian Bureaucracy in Crisis, 1840-1860*. (Stanford: Stanford University Press, 1971), p. 212.

121. Weber, *Economy and Society*, chs. 12, 13.

122. Roderic Davison, *Reform in the Ottoman Empire, 1856-76* (Princeton: Princeton University Press, 1963), p. 26.

123. Uriel Heyd, "The Ottoman Ulema and Westernization in the Time of Selim III and Mahmud II," *Scripta Hierosolymitana* 9 (1961), p. 75.

124. Ibid., p. 91; Lewis, *The Emergence of Modern Turkey*, p. 77.

125. Lewis, *The Emergence of Modern Turkey*, p. 95.

126. Karpat, "The Land Regime," p. 86.

127. Ibid., p. 88.

128. Davison, p. 141.

129. Lewis, *The Emergence of Modern Turkey*, p. 95.

130. Ibid., p. 131.

131. Karpat, "The Transformation of the Ottoman State," p. 253.

132. Serif Mardin, *The Genesis of Young Ottoman Thought* (Princeton: Princeton University Press, 1962), p. 150.

133. Ibid., p. 157.

134. Stanford Shaw, "Some Aspects of the Aims and Achievements of the 19th Century Ottoman Reformers," in Polk and Chambers, p. 33.

135. Lewis, *The Emergence of Modern Turkey*, p. 97.

136. Mardin, *The Genesis of Young Ottoman Thought*, p. 171.

137. Jansen, *Sakamoto Ryoma*, p. 14.

138. Beasley, *The Meiji Restoration*, p. 60.

139. Ibid., p. 41.

140. See Eiji Yutaimi, "Peasantry and Revolution in Pre-industrial Japan," University of California, Berkeley, Center for Japanese and Korean Studies, unpublished paper, 1972.

141. Craig, *Choshu in the Meiji Restoration*, p. 72.

142. Ibid., p. 49.

143. Ibid., p. 44.

144. Ibid., p. 26.

145. Frank Bailey, *British Policy and the Turkish Reform Movement* (Cam-

bridge, Mass.: Harvard University Press, 1942), p. 82.

146. Albert Hourani, "Ottoman Reform and the Politics of Notables," in Polk and Chambers, p. 67.

147. Bailey, p. 129.

148. Allan Cunningham, "Stratford Canning and the Tanzimat," in Polk and Chambers, p. 254.

149. Sansom, *The Western World and Japan*, p. 275.

150. Grace Fox, *Britain and Japan, 1853-1883* (New York: Oxford University Press, 1969), p. 34.

151. Beasley, *The Meiji Restoration*, pp. 108-9.

152. Ibid., p. 121.

153. See Thomas Smith, "Merit as Ideology in the Tokugawa Period," in *Aspects of Social Change in Modern Japan*, ed. Ronald Dore (Princeton: Princeton University Press, 1967), p. 75.

154. Dore, *Education in Tokugawa Japan*, p. 208.

155. Joseph Szyliowicz, "Elite Recruitment in Turkey: The Role of the Mulkiye," *World Politics* 23 (April 1971): 390.

156. Ibid., p. 397.

157. Beasley, *The Meiji Restoration*, p. 69.

158. Craig, *Choshu in the Meiji Restoration*, pp. 110-11.

159. The Loyalist party in one domain in Japan, Tosa, in the early 1860s was composed of 51 lower-ranking samurai, 54 goshi (rural samurai farmers), 14 peasant village heads, 3 farmers, 2 upper samurai, 1 doctor, 1 artisan, and 1 priest. Jansen, *Sakamoto Ryoma*, p. 110. Of the 75 leading conspirators in a Loyalist uprising at Yamota in 1863 which attacked and tried to destroy the Tokugawa district magistrate's office, 24 were samurai, 18 were goshi, 10 were peasants, and there was one doctor and a few priests. Smith, *Political Change and Industrial Development in Japan*, p. 17. The Young Ottomans "represented an alliance of bureaucrats, ulema and soldiers." Mardin, *The Genesis of Young Ottoman Thought*, p. 121. The Salonika Committee of Union and Progress which began the Young Turk revolution in 1908 was composed of "young officers in the army, civil servants of different departments, land-owning Macedonian beys, professors, lawyers, doctors, and some of the ulema. Of officers of high rank and of the heads of the civil service there were none." E.F. Knight, *Turkey* (Boston: J.P. Millet, 1910), p. 103.

160. See David Earl, *Emperor and Nation in Japan* (Seattle: University of Washington Press, 1964), pt. 2.

161. Many of the other Young Ottoman leaders came from bureaucratic families of varying prestige. For example, Mehmad Bey came from one of the highest bureaucratic families, Sinasi's father was an officer in the army, and Ziya Pasa's father was a minor customs official. See Mardin, *The Genesis of Young Ottoman Thought*.

162. Davison, p. 187.

163. Mardin, *The Genesis of Young Ottoman Thought*, ch. 10.

164. E.E. Ramsaur, *The Young Turks* (Princeton: Princeton University Press, 1967).

165. Smith, "Japan's Aristocratic Revolution," p. 137.

166. Beasley, *The Meiji Restoration*, p. 150.

167. Silberman and Harootunian, p. 419.

168. Jansen, *Sakamoto Ryoma*, p. 110.

169. Mardin, *The Genesis of Young Ottoman Thought*, p. 122.

170. Ibid., p. 130.
171. Ramsaur, p. 116.
172. Charles Buxton, *Turkey in Revolution* (London: T. Fisher Unwin, 1909), p. 51.
173. Skocpol, "France, Russia, China: A Structural Analysis of Social Revolution," p. 202.
174. Downwardly mobile traditional elites were not very important by the time of the Young Turk movement in the early twentieth century. The military and civil officials had become so Westernized that religious students and officials could not identify with them.
175. Beasley, *The Modern History of Japan*, p. 49.
176. Peter Frost, *The Bakumatsu Currency Crisis* (Harvard University, East Asian Monograph Series, 1970), p. 41.
177. Beasley, *The Modern History of Japan*, p. 49.
178. Jansen, *Sakamoto Ryoma*, p. 124.
179. Beasley, *The Meiji Restoration*, p. 171.
180. Jansen, *Sakamoto Ryoma*, pp. 27-31.
181. Ibid., p. 32.
182. Ibid., p. 369.
183. Ibid., p. 370.
184. Thomas Smith, "The Discontented," *Journal of Asian Studies* 21 (1961): 219.
185. Beasley, *The Meiji Restoration*, p. 159.
186. Ibid., p. 160.
187. Craig, *Choshu in the Meiji Restoration*, p. 277.
188. Beasley, *The Meiji Restoration*, p. 169.
189. Craig, *Choshu in the Meiji Restoration*, p. 358.
190. Ibid., p. 279.
191. Ibid.
192. Mardin, *The Genesis of Young Ottoman Thought*, p. 79.
193. Ibid., p. 169.
194. Karpat, "The Transformation of the Ottoman State," p. 264.
195. Robert Devereaux, *The First Ottoman Constitutional Period* (Baltimore: Johns Hopkins University Press, 1963), appendix.
196. Karpat, "The Transformation of the Ottoman State," p. 276.
197. Ibid.
198. Mardin, "Power, Civil Society and Culture in the Ottoman Empire," p. 277.
199. Karpat, "The Transformation of the Ottoman State," p. 280.
200. Feroz Ahmad, *The Young Turks* (London: Oxford University Press, 1969), p. 28.
201. Ibid., biographical appendix.
202. During the Young Turk parliaments in 1908-18, landlord interests stood for administrative decentralization, while the bureaucrats favored more centralized control. Also some Turks who had become linked to foreign business interests opposed plans by the Young Turk bureaucrats for state monopolies. Ibid., p. 59.
203. Japanese and Ottoman nationalism differed in its relationship to Western culture. Yoshia Shoin created a Japanese nationalism synthesized from only traditional values, while the Ottoman nationalism of Namik Kemal combined Islamic values with concepts drawn from the West. Furthermore, Shoin advocated only the importation of Western technology and the exclusion of Western culture, while

Kemal believed that the strengthening of the Ottoman state depended on the adoption of certain Western values.

204. See Earl, pt. 2.

205. Ibid., p. 169.

206. Mardin, *The Genesis of Young Ottoman Thought*, p. 327.

207. Niyazi Berkes, *The Development of Secularism in Turkey* (Montreal: McGill University Press, 1964), p. 321.

208. Lewis, *The Emergence of Modern Turkey*, p. 341.

209. Andreas Kazamias, *Education and the Quest for Modernity in Turkey* (Chicago: University of Chicago Press, 1966), pp. 108, 112.

210. Ibid., p. 110.

211. Berkes, *The Development of Secularism in Turkey*, p. 365.

212. Heyd, *Foundations of Turkish Nationalism*, p. 112.

213. Niyazi Berkes, ed., *Turkish Nationalism and Western Civilization: Selected Essays of Ziya Gokalp* (New York: Columbia University Press, 1954), p. 89.

214. Ibid., p. 91.

215. Y.H. Bayur as quoted by Lewis, *The Emergence of Modern Turkey*, p. 207.

216. Beasley, *The Meiji Restoration*, p. 152.

217. Kinross, p. 30.

218. Dankwart Rustow, "The Appeal of Communism to Islamic Peoples," in *Islam and International Relations*, ed. J. Harris Proctor (New York: Frederick Praeger, 1965), p. 44.

219. Jansen, *Sakamoto Ryoma*, p. 152.

220. For example the conservative bureaucrats used religious appeals to stimulate an army revolt against the Young Turks in 1913.

221. Jansen, *Sakamoto Ryoma*, p. 136.

222. Quoted in Davison, p. 195.

223. Rustow, "The Military," p. 374.

224. Beasley, *The Modern History of Japan*, p. 90.

225. Kinross, p. 45.

226. Sir William Ramsey, *The Revolution in Constantinople and Turkey* (London: Hodder & Stoughton, 1911), p. 29.

227. Davison, p. 383.

228. Ahmad, *The Young Turks*, p. 101.

229. Twelve of the seventeen Turkish army generals of World War I supported the cause of Turkish nationalism; only two served the sultan until the end. Rustow, "The Army and the Founding of the Republic," p. 533. "In many ways the leadership of one of the shotai provided a better channel for future eminence than did minor bureaucratic positions in the han; many who rose through ordinary channels to become bureaucrats at this time remained obscure officials after the Restoration." Craig, *Choshu in the Meiji Restoration*, p. 267.

230. Craig, *Choshu in the Meiji Restoration*, p. 255; Rustow, "The Army and the Founding of the Republic," p. 515. In contrast to the Ottoman army and the han armies in Japan, the Prussian army in the nineteenth century was always closely allied with the Junker landholding aristocracy, while the civil bureaucracy was more open to mobility.

231. Under other circumstances, nationalism can also politicize bureaucrats in a counterrevolutionary or fascist direction. This is especially likely when bureaucrats have vested economic interests and feel threatened by a mass movement from below.

232. Craig, *Choshu in the Meiji Restoration*, p. 252.

233. Kinross, p. 176.

234. Gillis, *The Prussian Bureaucracy in Crisis*, p. 77.

235. John Gillis, "Political Decay and the European Revolutions, 1789-1848," *World Politics* (April 1970): 357.

236. Ibid., p. 362.

237. Ibid., p. 356.

238. Ibid., pp. 358-59.

239. Gillis, *The Prussian Bureaucracy in Crisis*, p. 214.

240. Gillis, "Political Decay and the European Revolutions," p. 359.

241. Theodore Hamerow, *Restoration, Revolution, Reaction: Economics and Politics in Germany, 1815-1871* (Princeton: Princeton University Press, 1958), ch. 10.

242. Ibid.

243. Moore, *The Social Origins of Dictatorship and Democracy*, p. 174.

244. Ibid., p. 182.

245. Ibid., p. 165.

246. Franz Michael, "State and Society in Nineteenth Century China," *World Politics* 7 (1955): 426.

247. Moore, *The Social Origins of Dictatorship and Democracy*, p. 183.

248. Skocpol, "France, Russia, China: A Structural Analysis of Social Revolution," p. 191.

249. Further research is needed into why the close ties between bureaucrats and landlords in Prussia never led to such bureaucratic breakdown. It can be suggested that the degree of centralized bureaucratic control was greater in the early nineteenth century in compact Prussia than in the diffuse Chinese empire, and that the degree of economic penetration by more highly developed capitalist countries was less severe in Prussia.

250. Moore, *Social Origins of Dictatorship and Democracy*, p. 196.

251. Robert Bellah expounds this thesis in *Tokugawa Religion*. Samuel Huntington (*Political Order in Changing Societies*, p. 170) says: "In China, Confucian values and attitudes delayed the conversion of the political elite to the cause of reform."

252. John Fairbanks, Edwin Reischauer, and Albert Craig, *East Asia: The Great Tradition*, vol. 1 (Boston: Houghton Mifflin, 1962), p. 672; William Lockwood, "Japan's Response to the West: The Contrast with China," *World Politics* 2 (1956): 41-42.

253. Marion Levy, "Contrasting Factors in the Modernization of China and Japan," *Economic Development and Cultural Change* 2 (1953): 161-97; Beasley, *The Meiji Restoration*, ch. 10.

254. Halliday, *A Political History of Japanese Capitalism*, p. 17.

255. Fairbanks, Reischauer, and Craig, pp. 673-74.

256. Moore, *Social Origins of Dictatorship and Democracy*, p. 475.

Chapter 4
The Results of Revolution from Above

The important long-range results of revolution from above in Japan and Turkey stem from the lack of mass involvement and mass mobilization in these revolutions. Rather than actively involve the mass of the population in attempts at economic, social, and political change, military bureaucrats sought to control and depoliticize the Japanese and Turkish people. This factor was ultimately responsible for the failure of these two revolutions from above to achieve even their technical aims—a stable and powerful nation-state based on an autonomous capitalist economy. The following pages will document the early success of the Meiji and Ataturk regimes in: (1) consolidating an authoritarian political regime with none of the instability associated with military coups; and (2) using the state apparatus to mobilize resources for economic development. I will then demonstrate how compromise with the anticapitalist landed and commercial classes undermined both economic development and political stability, in the context of increasing imperialist pressure on both Japan and Turkey.

Consolidation of Military Supremacy in an Authoritarian-Bureaucratic State

Unlike leaders of a coup d'etat, military men who lead a revolution from above do not establish a military government. Rather, they seek to create a bureaucratic state structure based on civil institutions. Ataturk and the Meiji oligarchs were successful in consolidating political power because they themselves took on civilian duties and quickly brought large numbers of civil bureaucrats into prominent positions in the regime. Prior reform and rationalization of the bureaucracy and its autonomy from class forces facilitated this process. Both Ataturk and the Meiji bureaucrats also sought to remove the military from politics. But their own charisma and example as revolutionaries who became consummate politicians set a precedent for the Japanese and Turkish military. Even though military and political functions were clearly distinguished, a military career became an important (but not the only) channel to political office. Military officers studied, read, and discussed politics and saw themselves as guardians of the revolution.[1] In both Japan and Turkey it was the military—and not the bureaucratic and party organs created by the revolutionaries—that institutionalized an ideological commitment to revolution from above. Ataturk and the Meiji leaders sought to consolidate new organs of government that would carry out the functions they had performed as extraordinary individuals.

The leaders of the Meiji Restoration—all of whom performed both military and civil bureaucratic functions in the Tokugawa regime—at first acted informally (as the power behind the throne) to coordinate the political institutions they created. Their immediate successors (a group of nine men) became institutionalized around 1890 as the *genro*—elder statesmen. Those who became genro were all from Satsuma or Choshu han, all from moderate-status samurai families, and all were active in the Restoration movement.[2] They were also all "intimately connected with the birth and early growth of the modern bureaucracy; as ministers during the period of radical political innovation, they had accumulated years of experience at the highest level of the government. They were a talented elite, conscious of their role as leaders, with the capacity to meet the requirements national survival seemed to them to demand."[3] Until the 1920s, these nine men chose the prime ministers, made the most important foreign and domestic policy decisions, and coordinated the expanding military and bureaucratic machine. The genro "functioned as a free-floating decision-making body, informed, independent, and non-partisan, attempting to determine issues in a detached manner from the perspective of long-range goals; on the other hand, it was a structural unit at the top of the political hierarchy, which was manipulated by the senior leaders of the Sat-Cho coalition to preserve their dominance."[4]

But the power of the genro waned over time. From 1890 to 1900, the genro headed the cabinet. During 1901-12, the genro withdrew from top administrative posts, but they continued to control the important decisions of government from behind the scenes. In 1912-24, the remaining genro selected the prime minister, but they could only influence the long-range policies of government and not its day-to-day operations. After 1924, there was only one genro left and his power and influence rapidly deteriorated. The most fundamental weakness of the genro as an institution was that as an informal body, based on individual ability and personal ties, it could not perpetuate itself. "The very personal nature of their power meant they could not bequeath it to their proteges."[5] This autonomous body had no social, economic, or even political base outside the individuals who composed it.

Ataturk also sought a civilian base for his power by founding the Republican People's party. But the party remained Ataturk's personal vehicle and did not acquire independent prestige or power. It was Ataturk personally who held the government together, and his prestige was military. "The body of men who seized and shaped the new Republican power was essentially a military body. The loyalty of this elite, as of the larger populace, was given to Kemal—the triumphant military commander. It was the military corps that named and military prestige that sustained the leader."[6] After Ataturk's death, his trusted military aid in the War of Independence, General Inonu, was made head of the party and prime minister of the country. But in spite of his greater administrative and political skill, Inonu could not hold the party together, use it as a base of power, nor increase its popular prestige.[7] It was the military and not the party that became "the fountainhead of progressive practices; an organ for the spread of the reforms considered vital. Further, it was the ultimate base of power for the regime, 'the guardian of its ideals'"[8]

The leaders of the Ataturk and Meiji revolutions failed to consolidate new organs of government that would carry out the functions they had performed as extraordinary individuals. The autonomous and elitist political institutions they created—the genro and the party—soon atrophied. They were more successful in consolidating a ruling bureaucratic structure based on a coalition of military and civil organs. Many military officers resigned to join the civil bureaucracy and the top military officers worked closely with politicians in this bureaucracy.

During 1923-50 ex–military officers served as presidents of the Turkish Republic for all twenty-seven years, sixteen and one-half years as prime ministers, and sixteen and one-half years as ministers of defense. The first cabinet with no ex–military officers in it was in 1948. Many of the provincial governors during these years were also professional military officers by training.[9] In the Grand National Assembly, ex–military officers and ex–civil bureaucrats worked together in the single party to control legislation. Officials were the largest occupational grouping in the assembly during the entire single-party period. "The higher one goes in the political system, the greater the Kemalist reliance on the official group. The peak of official power obtained from 1935-1939 when fully 61% of the cabinet members were former bureaucrats or officers."[10] The minister of national defense (a civilian who was often an ex-officer) did not act to control the military, but served "principally as a channel for the communication of the military's views to the government."[11] Moreover, "the Chief of the General Staff enjoyed a position of cardinal importance in the government, taking precedence over the cabinet ministers and ranking just below the prime minister."[12]

Before 1878 there was no clear distinction between bureaucrats with civil and military backgrounds in Japan, as the samurai had performed both functions under the old regime. But in 1885-1945, about half of all the prime ministers were former military officers (most of the rest were civil bureaucrats), and about one-third of all civilian ministries were led by men with a military background.[13] The heart of the civil bureaucracy, the Home Ministry, was shaped by General Yamagata, who retained his military position. As in Turkey, the army, navy, and air force remained outside cabinet control and the chiefs of staff had important political influence.[14]

Political Compromise with Class Interests Rule by autonomous bureaucrats who actively promoted industrialization was inherently unstable. To consolidate their political power in a changing society, those bureaucrats who initiated revolution from above needed a solid social base. Because modernizing bureaucrats in Japan and Turkey promulgated a revolution from above without mobilizing mass support, they were forced to gain at least tacit cooperation from the most influential local interests in order to institutionalize the power of the new regimes. To win their support, the Meiji bureaucrats helped the richest peasants to consolidate their economic and social control in the countryside and to become landlords. They did not, however, give the landlords political control even on the local level. Rather, all local officials, were career bureaucrats appointed by, and responsible to, the Home Ministry.[15] Taxation and the provision of schools and police forces were also controlled by the central government. Ataturk also acted to consolidate the economic and social control of local landowners who were descended from religious officials (ulema) or from tribal and warlord leaders.[16] While the Turkish government appointed local officials from career bureaucrats who were responsible only to the central government,[17] Ataturk did use the landed notables to staff the local party machine.[18] During Ataturk's lifetime (to 1938) these landlords had little political influence in the party and were not elected to national office, but their potential for increased political influence was institutionalized in the party structure.

As landlords in Japan consolidated their social and economic power at the local level, they also sought greater political influence. Japanese landlords became politicized against the heavy agricultural tax. Landed interests were the backbone (if not necessarily the leaders) of the first political party in Japan. This party led a popular movement for a constitution and a parliament.[19] When the peasants and some dissident samurai in the movement became too radical, the landowners dissolved the party (in 1884) and formed a more conservative party to contest the first national election in 1890.[20] Of 300 members elected to the first Diet, 129 represented landed interests.[21] Landlords increased their dominance of the legislature up to 1912, primarily because suffrage laws established the electorate on the basis of national taxes which were heavier on rural than on urban interests.[22] But landed control of the national legislature did not have much political impact. The Meiji oligarchs were careful to promulgate a constitution and establish the parliament in a way which kept decision-making power in their own hands. During the ten years they took to plan constitutional government, the bureaucratic leaders strengthened and rationalized executive authority.[23] The Diet as established under the constitution only had power to advise the emperor (in reality, the bureaucratic clique). The cabinet and prime minister were appointed by the emperor, independent of the majority party. The cabinet was not responsible to the legislators, and could not be removed by them. It was not until 1895 that a party leader was made a member of the cabinet, and not until the 1920s that a party dominated the cabinet from time to time. But even such a party-controlled cabinet could not dominate the executive and the military. Thus, the small group of samurai bureaucrats who led the Meiji Restoration retained control of the state apparatus until well into the twentieth century. The landlords of the Diet were capable of little more than obstructionist tactics which usually were ineffective.[24]

Nor did Japanese urban capitalists combine politically with the landed interests. Industrialists wanted cheap rice for the workers and a high land tax, policies inimical to the precapitalist, rentier landlords. Japanese capitalists had close ties to state bureaucrats, but they remained politically subordinate. "The social stigma attached to commercialism was not to be cast off lightly, and this, supplemented by the very great obligations of commerce and industry to government, tended to produce strong notes of apology and deference in the attitude of the business class toward public officials."[25] Thus, "the owners and executives of the big banks, factories, and trading concerns never attained a decisive position in prewar Japanese politics .... They were influential in economic affairs, but insecure and lacking the power to make the great political decisions shaping the destiny of the country."[26]

In contrast, Turkish landlords allied with small-town merchants captured state power only twenty-five years after the Ataturk Revolution. During his lifetime, party, civil, and military bureaucrats worked closely together. After Ataturk's death in 1938, more landlords were recruited into top party positions, and local party branches gained more autonomy.[27] These rural interests were opposed to state control of the economy, and more open to foreign investment.[28] One reason that the bureaucratic leaders came to permit the organization of an opposition party in 1946, was to purge the Republican party of the rising leaders supporting landlord interests. The four members of the Republican party who left to found the new Democratic party first banded together in 1945 to oppose a bill for land reform.[29] The leader of the Democratic party, Menderes, was a large landowner, and the new party ran primarily on a platform advocating free enterprise and more power for the provinces. This party, which won control of Parliament (and hence of the bureaucracy) in 1950, changed Turkey's political leadership "from being primarily a national elite group, oriented toward the tutelary development of the country, to being primarily an assemblage of local politicians, oriented toward more immediate local political advantages." [30] As another commentator put it: "The great Rumelien bureaucratic, religious, and military families are dwindling and losing their importance. The Anatolian (interior) country boys—and still more the Anatolian country lords and gentry—are inheriting their places." [31] While representing primarily the economic interests of the landed class, the Democratic party won because it also mobilized peasant support by appealing to the traditional values and way of life of peasants who had not been transformed by the revolution from above.

The political power won by traditional landlords in Turkey was directly conditioned by the failure of the Ataturk Revolution to destroy the economic base of the local notables. Because landlords in Japan came primarily from peasant backgrounds, they had no traditional status to challenge bureaucrats at the national level. Conversely, Turkish landlords with traditional noble and religious status became more powerful more quickly. The political coalition of bureaucrats with a landlord class led to the depoliticization of the peasants in both Japan and Turkey and precluded the mobilization of a mass base of support for the bureaucratic government.

Depoliticization of the Masses   To help consolidate and maintain the social and economic power of local landowners over the peasants, the revolutionary bureaucrats either incorporated traditional and paternalistic appeals into their new doctrines of nationalism (as in Japan), or they excluded peasants from integration into the nation (in Turkey). In either case, nationalism acted to maintain the peasant's way of life as it had been for centuries, and prevented any mass identification with modernizing reforms of the revolutions. Both traditionalist and elitist nationalism also blocked mass legitimacy for modern political institutions.

The primary ingredient of Japanese nationalism was traditional religious cultural values. The fundamental concept of Japanese nationalism, kokutai, appealed to the sacred and primordial Shinto myth of the emperor and to the feudal-Confucian values of loyalty to the lord and family. Kokutai pictured Japan as a sacred family-nation with the emperor as father and lord. According to this conception, Japan's unique national essence stemmed from its unbroken line of emperors descended from the sun god, and from the subsequent descent of all Japanese families from the imperial line. The whole nation was one hierarchical lineage group. This doctrine of nationalism created a personal, racial, and quasi-religious commitment of the populace to the emperor, and hence to the polity.

The advantage for the Meiji oligarchs of this concept of nationalism was that they did not have to create new political loyalties. "The nation-state, they said, was a family writ large. A man incurred 'on' [obligations] to his parents; by the same token a subject has incurred 'on' to his emperor, the 'father' of the nation."[32] In the early Meiji period, submissive respect for parochial authorities (family ancestors, the father, village leaders, local lord) precluded the need for nationalist education. Later, the state took active measures to strengthen these traditional values and loyalties, through, for example, the Imperial Rescript on Education, the Rescript to Soldiers and Sailors, and ethics courses in public schools. "The emperor-system or concept of the family state represented neither an inevitable nor a popular feudal legacy to modern Japan, but rather, the conscious, calculated and belated popularization by the early Meiji ruling group of a waning and elite tradition."[33]

Nationalist values did not ascribe legitimacy to the bureaucratic oligarchy which actually ruled in Meiji Japan. Japanese nationalism, with its emphasis on family and communal loyalty, failed to incorporate and subordinate primordial and local loyalties to a new national identity. "Family and village consciousness could not be extended smoothly to national consciousness. Primary group values tended to foster sectionalism, which in turn weakened national solidarity."[34] The reinforcement of these primordial loyalties increased the symbolic cleavage between modernizing elites and rural masses. "This dualism in Japan, the great gap between the outward-looking apex and the tradition-bound base, was inherent in the development of Japanese nationalism and constitutes one of its main weaknesses."[35] The peasants remained "a huge apolitical and submissive mass."[36]

The emphasis in Japanese nationalism on a strong integration into family, local, and corporate groups also prevented the development of a civic consciousness. In Japan, "a citizen does not have the feeling that the streets, districts, and towns belong to him. The world does not belong to him outside his village, in the country; outside his family, in a large town."[37] The Japanese, while cultivating an ethic of extreme courtesy and politeness in personal relations, did not maintain such civility in their public behavior.

Turkish nationalism with its emphasis on republicanism, secularism, etatism, and populism did try to create a common national consciousness that broke with traditional values—especially Islam as a basis of political identity and legitimacy. But the universal values of Turkish nationalism did not really appeal to the peasants. "Turkish nationalism during the first twenty-five years of the Republic appeared to be rationalist, secularist, and materialist—that is, in a form acceptable only to a rather small intellectual group."[38] The Turkish peasant continued to view the nation-state as a religious community and not as a political one. Ataturk himself was seen in the village "as a latter day Islamic saint in direct line from the early Caliphs."[39]

The Turkish Revolution did not try to change the peasants or integrate them into the new polity. "No member of the Turkish elite ever constructed an operational theory of peasant mobilization. Rather, the Republican program implied that peasants were 'backward' and would only be changed by transforming the laws of the land. Integration from the top down by imposing regulations had been the general approach also behind Ottoman social engineering."[40] In continuing this bureaucratic style, Kemalism was "profoundly unrevolutionary despite the populist themes which the Republic developed."[41] Kemalism did not even try to break down the centuries-old antipathy that villagers felt for the central state and its representatives. "The peasants had led a traditional, isolated existence, suspecting any stranger who wandered into their community of being tax collectors, or a similar evil species. This feeling of apathy towards the government had been strengthened by the efforts of the Republican People's Party, led by the great Ataturk, to bring about basic changes in the social and religious life of the Turkish people. These had had little impact on the area . . . . The villagers' admiration of Ataturk had been tempered with a dislike for many of his reforms."[42] In fact, "a major effect of the Kemalist program was to create two nations: one rural, traditionalist and underdeveloped; the other urban, modernist, and developing."[43]

By not mobilizing the peasants, Kemalism strengthened the traditional bond between local notables (usually landlords) and peasants as antagonists to the state. In Ottoman times "the gentry (ayans) and the peasantry were driven into the same camp if only because their antagonism to official policy was more enduring than their differences."[44] Because the gentry had a long-time commitment to the provinces, their oppressiveness had to be tempered with measures to gain peasant support. "This is one of the reasons for which even today well-established families who do not want to squeeze their subjects like lemons—as did official appointees—have retained the allegiance of the peasants."[45] By failing to bring new cultural values to the peasants, the Ataturk Revolution reinforced that local culture that integrated lord and peasant. "The villager visits the guest room of the village aga (lord), just as his wife uses the same methods of cooking, fetching water, bedmaking, and child care as the aga's wife. Both are interested in the same gossip and the same set of people. Both see themselves primarily as members of their village."[46]

This depoliticization of the masses effectively precluded any real democratization of the bureaucratic-authoritarian regime even when later, political parties with democratic aspirations came into existence. Either these parties made no attempt to gain peasant support—preferring to work with the local elites (as in Japan)—or they mobilized the peasant masses on the basis of traditionalistic appeals. Such appeals obscured the true socioeconomic interests of party leaders and precluded effective peasant participation in politics. The continuing traditionalism of the peasant masses also blocked the mobilization of mass support for leftist parties and movements. Communism, socialism, or even social democracy remained alien to the peasants.

Centrist political parties in Japan articulated the interests of the landlords, businessmen, and bureaucrats, but never really tried to appeal to the peasants or even urban workers. This was partly due to the strength of the bureaucracy in the Japanese state and the restricted electorate (until 1925). Because majority control of the Japanese Diet did not ensure appointment of the prime minister or other cabinet posts, the Japanese parties (in order to gain power) were induced to manipulate and bargain behind the scenes with bureaucrats and elder statesmen, rather than mobilize mass support. "In Japan it was precisely by restricting the size and quality of the base that the party politicians maximized their negotiating strength at the top."[47] But party elitism was also the result of Japanese nationalism which turned the people's attention away from politics into personal, family, and local spheres. By making people apolitical in their interests, "nationalism paradoxically had a capital effect on the country's politics, which became more and more the preserve of local bosses and professional politicians."[48] The political parties in Japan "regarded the public as passive and inchoate, to be influenced and used as a means to power."[49] The mass of the population "remained largely indifferent to the partisan struggles which raged in far-off Tokyo and cast their ballots for the parties with no more enthusiasm than they paid their taxes or answered conscription summonses."[50] Even in the 1950s the Japanese vote was always higher in local than in national elections, and "in questions of national politics, interest centered on international more than on internal politics."[51]

Even the political movements which arose in Japan after 1912 to press for universal suffrage and party control of the cabinet were primarily urban, based on the support of liberal intellectuals, student activists, and a few urban workers in the most modern industries. The Japanese leftist and proletarian parties in the 1920s also gained their primary support from intellectuals and white-collar workers. The paternalistic employee-employer relationship in most Japanese firms prevented union organization and precluded worker support for left-wing parties. Tenant farmers remained traditional and reluctant to enter organizations outside the family.[52] As a result, "the communists, like the socialists, were only dissidents on the fringes of society: they never became a mass force."[53] Nor did the level of violence from tenant unions, labor unions, or left-wing parties ever reach a level where the elites felt threatened.[54]

In the 1950s an opposition party arose in Turkey which tried to mobilize mass peasant support by an appeal to religious and primordial values, and by abolishing direct taxes on the peasants. This party opened branches and held rallies in most villages—something unheard of in the single-party era. In one village, for example, the featured speaker for the Democrats used the phrase "the golden key" to describe the villagers' position. "He said in effect: 'You have the key, for you possess the vote; we the government, are your servants, you our master' .... For weeks afterwards, no one in Erdemli discussed anything else. 'How do you like that?' they would ask. 'We are the masters, we who are only poor farmers. We can tell the government what to do.'"[55] Yet the reality of multiparty politics was quite different. A formal vote for the peasants meant that they became "occasional and manipulated voters, not critically conscious citizens."[56] In Turkish villages, as in those in Japan, personal ties, family solidarity, and obligations to authority most often determined the voters' ballot. "Even if two parties were represented in the village, they were likely to be controlled by the same families or dominated by similar interests."[57] Nor did the rural masses understand or accept the idea and ideal of opposition parties—of a clash of interests within a parliamentary and institutional framework. Observers in both Japan and Turkey noted how communal values checked democratic ones: "The clash of interests and opinions—the very lifeblood of a healthy democracy—was looked upon by believers in 'Japanism' as nothing but deplorable confusion .... Harmony between emperor and people, ruler and ruled, like the unity of religion and politics was a deeply felt nationalist ideal."[58] And "for the large masses of Turkey, these parties, and particularly the Democratic Party, were not 'opposition' parties but the incarnation of the ideal government, a government with truly popular roots which had been the secret dream of the Turkish countryside for centuries."[59]

This traditionalism meant that those peasants identified with the Democratic party were "linked to its leader rather than to the views that the party presumably stood for."[60] The peasants saw Menderes, leader of the Democratic party, as almost a god, perhaps more omnipotent than Ataturk. They did not see that the main impact of the party was to further the economic interests of landlords, traders, and commercial capitalists—interests which were antithetical to those of the peasants. A revolution from above which had not freed the peasant from tradition, paternalism, and submissive values had not educated him to recognize his own economic interests vis-à-vis landlords and emerging rural capitalists.

As in Japan, the parochialism of the peasants prevented new left-wing parties which arose in the 1960s in Turkey from mobilizing a mass base. This was especially true since the urban lower class was "composed of former Anatolian villagers crowded into the squatter areas of the large cities. These squatters shared the aspirations of the peasantry, as many of them maintained ties with their home villages and tended to maintain their former voting patterns." [61] Youth from elite families came to espouse socialist ideas in the sixties, but most youth from the villages and city slums—even if they went to college—distrusted these left-wing elites. As a contemporary commentator put it: "They are aware that twenty years ago that class of persons as administrators dealt very harshly with the masses." [62]

The establishment of a bureaucratic state apparatus which compromised with and gave some political power to a rural landlord class while de-politicizing the peasant masses created a stable political order for twenty-five years in Turkey and fifty years in Japan. This political settlement eventually began to undermine the bureaucrats' attempts to build an autonomous capitalist economy. Economic conflict and contradictions in turn created political instability. Before analyzing these dynamics we must examine the process of economic development.

Contradictions in the Process of Capitalist Development

Because they had not organized a mass base of support that could be mobilized for economic development, bureaucratic revolutionaries in both countries favored capitalist industrialization based on market mechanisms and private enterprise. The process of capitalist development was initiated and led by state bureaucrats in both Japan and Turkey. Internal (class) and external (national) relations promoted Japan's success in capitalist development—for a while. Yet even Japan soon became economically dependent on the more advanced capitalist countries.

One factor limiting the success of national capitalist development in Turkey was economic and political pressure from external sources. The consolidation of world capitalism by the 1930s, the greater technological gap between Turkey and the advanced countries, and Turkey's geographic proximity to Europe, all restricted opportunities for development. Turkey's economy—unlike Japan's—had also been opened to imperalist economic penetration for one hundred years before its revolution from above. Turkey's economy at the end of World War I was decimated not only by the war, but by years of European capitalist encroachment. Starting in 1838, when Turkey signed a commercial convention setting low import tariffs and allowing British merchants free access to the Empire,[63] the flow of cheap Western manufactured goods and then Western capital ruined native handicrafts. Turkey became a backward supplier of raw and agricultural materials (tobacco, cotton, raisins, and livestock) for Western nations.[64] By 1870, British and French banks had gained nearly complete control over Ottoman state resources and the state budget.[65] By 1914, Europeans administered the major ports, owned the most important mines and 87 percent of the rail lines, and had a majority share in Turkey's public utilities.[66]

External factors alone cannot explain the fate of state-initiated economic development. Japan was under equal or greater pressure from external capital in the mid–nineteenth century than China or Indonesia—countries which failed to industrialize. Japan's capitalist development cannot be explained by its isolation from Western economic penetration.[67] Nor was its traditional economy spontaneously generating capitalist forms sufficient for economic takeoff.

Benjamin Higgins, Jr. has assembled convincing empirical data to demonstrate that the economic development of China in the 1850s was equal to or higher than that of Japan. He shows that the grain output per capita in China was probably higher than in Japan around 1850,[68] and Chinese urban merchants more innovative.[69] Moreover, he provides evidence to demonstrate that at mid-century the Western powers had an economic impact only in the Chinese coastal cities.[70] Until 1895, the Chinese entrepreneur did not face serious foreign competition from direct investment.[71] If anything, handicraft production in Japan was damaged more by foreign imports than in China.[72] Clifford Geertz has also shown that in 1868 the per hectare rice yields were about equal in Japan and Java.[73] Indonesia was not clearly an economically dependent country before the 1870s.[74] Japan in the 1850s and 1860s was subject to about the same economic pressure from the West as other Asian countries, and its economy was no less backward. Left to itself, Japan's economy under the Tokugawa regime would not have spontaneously generated capitalist industrialization.[75] Without state intervention, it too would have succumbed to external economic penetration.

More important than external opportunities or blocks to capitalist development are internal class forces fostering or hindering economic change. Initially, class forces opposed to the measures necessary to promote capitalist industrialization were weaker in Japan than in Turkey.

Bureaucratic revolutionaries employed similar techniques to foster capitalist development in Japan after 1868 and in Turkey after 1923, but the opposition to industrialization by rentier landlords was more effective in the parliamentary party system of Turkey than in the more bureaucratic Japanese polity. Parliamentary party supremacy in Turkey permitted pre-industrial landed and commercial interests (allied with foreign capitalists) to take over the Turkish state apparatus and use it to thwart autonomous capitalist development. A liberal political system in a late-developing state is antithetical to sustained economic development. The political system created by the Meiji oligarchs was better able to maintain an autonomous bureaucracy and hence was more effective in promoting economic development, for a while. Yet the political compromise with the Japanese landed class later began to undermine the conditions for autonomous industrialization. Because the large peasant population was kept on the land producing as rentiers and tenants on small plots, they could not be drawn into the industrial economy as producers or consumers. As a result, Japanese capitalists had to seek markets overseas. This process of external expansion drew Japan into conflict with and dependency on the advanced capitalist nations to Japan's economic and political detriment.

In the following pages I will examine the initial success of state-initiated capitalist development to make both Japan and Turkey dependent economies, subordinate to the needs of Western capitalism.

State Initiative in Early Capitalist Development Once in power, autonomous bureaucrats acted to diminish foreign interference in their economies. The Japanese state was bound by treaties to a low tariff on foreign goods until 1899, but the Meiji oligarchs discouraged foreign business and did not borrow abroad.[76] They also forbade foreigners to own land or operate mines.[77] Through taxation, the state bureaucrats drained off the peasants' surplus, preventing consumption of foreign goods. Ataturk abolished the capitulations to foreign powers and nationalized all major foreign businesses—especially mines, utilities, and railways.[78] Most Greek and other minority businessmen left the country. The Turkish government employed foreign technical specialists, but restricted foreign capital—public and private. "Turkey wanted self-sufficiency and was willing to pay with austerity. Except for a British and Russian loan, the programs were financed domestically through heavy taxation, issuance of credits, etc."[79] Unlike Japan, Turkey was soon able (in 1929) to construct high tariffs against imports competing with its native industries.

Although both the Meiji and Turkish bureaucrats advocated private capitalist industrialization, they were forced to take the economic initiative because of a lack of private capital or its conservatism.[80] It was only after the state had overcome many initial problems of capital accumulation, and the technical and organizational difficulties in establishing industry, that private capital entered. Before 1880 in Japan and 1945 in Turkey almost all modern industrial enterprises were founded by the state. The Japanese government broke down feudal barriers to trade and industry, and then went on to build railways and telegraphs, open new coal mines and agricultural experiment stations; set up iron foundries, shipyards, and machine shops; import foreign equipment and experts to mechanize silk reeling and cotton spinning; and open model factories in cement, paper, and glass.[81] Throughout the nineteenth century 50 percent of investments in Japan came from the government.[82] Likewise, the Turkish state built railways and roads, electrical plants, coal and chrome mines, and mechanized sugar and cotton production.[83] The Turkish government placed many of its modern factories in provincial towns where they would stimulate economic change in formerly isolated areas. In decentralizing industry, the Ataturk planners "aimed to utilize raw materials at hand, disperse industrial activity, alleviate rural unemployment, and encourage new consumer industries."[84] Military industries were also located in the interior for reasons of national defense.[85]

Both governments also established a framework of political order and legal security conducive to economic development. Equally important, the state sponsored a universal education system which inculcated technical skills along with a nationalist doctrine calling for self-sacrifice for the national good.

All these policies of state-financed and state-directed industrialization were designed to act as a stimulus for private investment. In both countries, the government established a number of large banks which mobilized private savings for industrialization. These banks were created in advance of private demand for loans and services, and were designed by the state to foster development.[86] Once established, the state also transferred its industries to the banks (in Turkey) or sold its firms to private entrepreneurs with close ties to finance capital (in Japan). These large banks with close ties to state bureaucrats and to large private capitalists became uniquely characteristic of Turkish etatism and *zaibatsu* capitalism in Japan.

A substantial group of Turks who had been trained as managers in state enterprises left to start their own businesses with financing from development banks.[87] These capitalists retained close ties to the political elite.[88] In Japan, the Meiji government sold its businesses in 1882 because of financial strain on the government budget.[89] The state firms were sold primarily to a small number of bankers and financial brokers who had close ties to top government bureaucrats.[90] The combination of banking capital and control over industry became the core of the small number of zaibatsu (literally "money cliques"). These zaibatsu increasingly came to coordinate and control the whole economy. The state gave them further support through trading contracts, tax incentives, and monopoly powers.[91]

In both Japan and Turkey private owners of the most technologically advanced industries often started out as government bureaucrats and once in business retained close personal and ideological ties to the state. In both countries political initiative in capitalist development created a concentration of financial and industrial control that was much greater than in the earlier rise of Western capitalism.

Another similarity in state-directed industrialization in Japan and Turkey was that agriculture was not capitalized (but retained its traditional social organization), while productivity was increased through opening of new land, expanded farm credit, the use of fertilizers, etc.[92] Both countries relied on agricultural exports to finance the import of heavy machinery, but neither set of state planners sought to modernize agriculture itself.[93] The rise of capitalism in England forced small peasant farmers off the land and into the cities. Capitalist development in Japan and Turkey absorbed the population increase into the cities, but kept a large number of small peasant farmers in the countryside.[94] Rather than becoming a capitalist farmer who used machinery and hired labor, landlords in Japan and Turkey rented their estates out to tenants for high rents.[95] Both the small size of independent holdings and the rise of small tenant farms on large estates "blocked the flow of capital, enterprising ability, energy and knowledge into agriculture and thus prevented advancement."[96] This maintenance of a precapitalist structure in the countryside came to be an important block to autonomous capitalist development. Its effects were first seen in the inability of either Turkish or Japanese bureaucrats to solve the contradiction between the need for internal accumulation of capital and for internal markets for capitalist products.

The Turkish system of state-led capitalist development achieved considerable success. Turkey maintained a foreign trade surplus in 1930-46,[97] and in 1950 was moving toward economic self-sufficiency.[98] The government fostered capital accumulation by keeping consumption down through rationing and by heavy taxes on urban industrial and commercial concerns.[99] One of the key points of Ataturk's economic program was relief from heavy taxation on the peasantry. The traditional tithe on agriculture was repealed in 1925, and since then agricultural contribution to tax revenues in Turkey has been minimal.[100] As agricultural productivity increased,[101] the peasant's consumption level also rose.[102] This meant that the problem of adequate capital formation through internal accumulation was never adequateley solved in Turkey.[103]

In contrast, the Japanese land tax provided the major sources of government revenue—and the primary source of capital accumulation—for twenty-five years. Until 1882, the land tax provided over 80 percent of government revenue, while taxes on business were kept low. After 1893, taxes on consumer goods increased, but business levies and taxes on wealth were minimal.[104] It was the income from the land tax[105] which permitted Meiji bureaucrats to borrow over 46 million yen before 1881 from internal sources and to liquidate this debt before 1892.[106] This heavy levy on the agricultural population was maintained in spite of the fact that agricultural productivity in Japan never reached levels comparable to those in Europe and America. Productivity per man declined in 1878-1914, driving many peasants into debt, tenancy, and poverty.[107] The housing, food, and clothing of most of Japan's rural population in 1914 was about the same as in 1868.[108] State accumulation of capital through a regressive tax restricted the purchasing power of the mass of peasants and also kept urban wages low. This necessitated a growing foreign market, and led directly to Japanese militarism and foreign expansion.[109]

These economic contradictions directly undermined the autonomy of Japanese capitalism. In Turkey, by contrast, landlords used their political power to deter capitalist development.

Destruction of the Autonomy of Turkish Capitalism

To begin this analysis some important facts about Ataturk's compromise with the landed class must be reiterated. The party created by Ataturk, the Republican People's party, was based on a coalition of military and civil bureaucrats with local landed elites. To pacify the landlords, the party declined to press for land reform or redistribution. But the landed elites were given little representation in Parliament and no real power in the party, and bureaucrats remained hostile to rural economic interests. In 1945 when a new generation of party and state bureaucrats tried to press for land reform, the landlords left the Republicans to form an opposition party. Reports on the founding of the Democratic party clearly indicate that its original intent was to function as the political arm of commercial and large landed interests. Major decisions on the choice of local and national leaders for the new party were made by a small group of businessmen and landholders.[110]

Neither the party, civil, nor military bureaucrats in Turkey opposed this formation of an opposition party in 1945. Some military officers actively supported it.[111] There were several reasons for this acquiescence. After 1945, both civil and military bureaucrats drew closer to the Western alliance because of fear of Russian encroachment on Turkish territory. The United States, through its military and economic aid missions, made clear its preference (often amounting to threats) for a more open political system. The bureaucratic class did not expect an opposition party to win, and even if it did, they expected it to pursue established policies. The leaders of the new Democratic party were all former ranking members of the ruling party. They had worked closely with the bureaucrats in the parliament and cabinet. They shared the same experiences and the same principles. The DP did not differ from the Republican party in program and basic ideas. Because of the strength and continuing durability of their party organization, the Turkish bureaucratic elite did not conceive that the turning over of executive control to an opposition party could mean a permanent displacement from the seats of power. The Republican party, as the party of Ataturk and the revolution, had the tradition—so they thought—to quickly regain power through the electoral process, should they temporarily lose it. Another important reason for the decision of the Turkish bureaucratic elite to permit opposition parties stemmed from the rise of rural and commercial elites within the Republican party itself. Many local elites began to challenge the positions of the bureaucratic leadership. These local politicians were more interested in pragmatic and immediate economic interests. Thus the Republican leaders permitted the formation of an opposition party in 1946 in order to strengthen their own control of the revolutionary party. In this they miscalculated, for these economic elites came to replace them and undermine their hegemony.

In the election of 1950 the opposition Democratic party won an overwhelming majority of the popular vote. They attracted the peasants through appeals to traditional values. Only in the backward eastern provinces did the landowning agas retain their commitment to the Republicans and deliver the peasant vote to them.[112] The Parliament and cabinet were taken over by representatives of economic interests, while ex-bureaucrats and ex–military officers were reduced to a tiny minority. The Democratic party became the "first ruling party to emerge under leaders who had not won their spurs in the military."[113] Before winning the election, The Democrats had tried to court military support. But once in office, the Democratic leaders "soon developed a thinly veiled contempt for the officer corps, who being denied the vote did not bulk large in the party's political calculations."[114]

The Democratic party, led by landed and commercial interests, used their control over the state apparatus to overturn the economic policies of the military bureaucrats who consolidated the Ataturk Revolution. Their first act was to terminate restrictions on foreign capital.

In the early 1950s the Democrats began to accept huge loans and credits from the United States and from international agencies dominated by Western capitalists. They also encouraged private foreign investment by passing a law in 1954 which permitted investors to export as much of their profits as they desired.[115] With foreign aid also came foreign economic advisors, mainly from the United States, who "strengthened the Democratic Party's position, particularly in the almost unanimous criticism voiced by these experts of Turkish etatism.[116] As one prominent U.S. advisor said: "If Turkey wishes Americans to participate in their economic development, it must create the conditions which Americans have learned from their own experience make success possible."[117] Likewise, the International Bank would not give loans to the Turkish government, but only to an industrial bank that would finance private industry.[118]

As a result of these sentiments, a large part of U.S. aid went to large landowners and commercial groups, rather than to industries closely tied to the state. One commentator notes that U.S. motives in directing their aid this way may also have been political: "[They] hoped to stimulate the birth of a large middle class which would, in turn, provide a stable basis for Turkey's democratic regime."[119] With foreign aid also came strings. For example, U.S. loans to build a copper mine on the Black Sea included provisos that U.S. equipment must be purchased, and an American AID representative was to be on the company board.[120] As in other underdeveloped countries, foreign aid and investment soon led to a net outflow of capital from Turkey to the foreign investors, mainly in the United States.[121]

Most important than the direct impact of foreign capital on the Turkish economy was the manner in which the Democratic government and its American advisors shaped Turkey's internal economic structure.[122] The government led by landlords and commercial interests chose to admit foreign aid and American advisors and to reverse the previous policy of independent, state-directed development. As a result, the Turkish economy in the 1950s was thrown into chaos. Even with accelerated foreign investment, the rate of economic growth in Turkey in the 1950s was less than in 1935-39.[123] This was primarily because economic decisions were now made to meet the demands of special interests without regard for any long-range economic priorities. "Parochialism, log-rolling, and lack of coordination often appeared to be replacements for elitist nationalism."[124] Because the government abolished all taxes on agriculture, at the same time that it was pressing large-scale investments, inflation ran rampant and brought near-bankruptcy to the government.[125] Taxation of agriculture (77 percent of the population who produced 40 percent of the GNP) to control inflation was a political impossibility for a party whose main support was both landowners and peasants.[126] The necessity to win votes and stay in power also led the DP government to place plants in uneconomic locations. Moreover, politicians intervened with state enterprises for partisan purposes.[127]

Despite its rhetoric for free enterprise, the Turkish government in the 1950s expanded state enterprise and state intervention in the economy, demonstrating the inadequacy of private enterprise to spark development.[128] But a state controlled by precapitalist landed and commercial interests, heavily influenced by foreign capitalists, was opposed to the measures necessary for sustained economic growth. It refused to channel the agricultural surplus into industrialization. Aid to agriculture was directed primarily to large farmers, to the neglect of the mass of the peasants.[129] No attempt was made to channel individual savings into productive enterprise. As a result, well over half the savings of individuals in Turkey came to be invested in real estate.[130] A new middle class of traders, but not industrial entrepreneurs, was encouraged. The debts incurred through foreign aid also drained future foreign exchange for Turkey and prevented the importation of heavy machinery necessary for industrialization.

Turkey in the 1960s remained an underdeveloped country with 75 percent of both its employment and exports still in agriculture. It is now faced with rapid population growth and high unemployment.[131] As one Turkish observer noted: "The Turkish economy is still an underdeveloped and dependent economy despite a planning tradition of some thirty years or longer. This is the main paradox to be observed. No other country with so long an experience and effort can now be found at the bottom of the underdevelopment scale."[132] It is my contention that the roots of this continued underdevelopment are to be found in the political power of the landed class in Turkey.

Decay of the Autonomy The failure to capitalize agriculture
of Japanese Capitalism because of political compromise
with the landed class also destroyed
Japan's early attempts at autonomous economic development. In Japan the power of the landed class worked itself out through economic forces rather than through the direct political challenge of the Turkish landlords.

Despite its ability to initiate capitalist development without an influx of foreign capital and only a moderate flow of foreign goods, Japan did not remain free from the economic control of more advanced capitalist countries. Many Marxists (as well as others) characterize Japan as the first non-Western nation to achieve "full independent industrialization."[133] Or they see Japan as charting an economic course "radically different from that of all the other countries in the now underdeveloped world."[134] In contrast, I see Japan's economic development as very similar to the path of dependent capitalist development[135] of subimperialist countries in the Third World today.[136] Like Japan—Brazil, Iran, and a few other countries are developing capitalist industry. But their economic development is always subordinate to the interests and needs of the more advanced capitalist countries. As in Japan, this subordination produces an uneven and distorted economic development internally and leads them to seek imperialist control over less developed countries in the region.

The following pages will present a model of dependent capitalist development and illustrate the similarities between Japan's course of industrialization and that of Third World nations today. Japan's great leaps in industrial development occurred during two breakdowns of the international capitalist system—World War I and the Great Depression of the 1930s. Only during these times could Japan break out of its subordination to the advanced nations. It was Japan's attempt to achieve parity with U.S. and European capital that precipitated its disastrous entry into World War II. Today Japan is the second largest capitalist economy in the world. But "the indications are that Japanese capitalism is still essentially subordinate to U.S. imperialism, and that the signs and signals of 'independence' are more shadow than substance."[137] Moreover, the costs to the Japanese people of economic "success" have been enormous. The costs for dependent capitalist development in the Third World today are bound to be even higher. As in Japan, the "success" of industrialization in these countries also depends on temporary breakdowns in the world capitalist system.

Six characteristics define dependent capitalist development for non-Western countries attempting to escape from a completely peripheral position in the world economy. Japan clearly fits this model on five of the six factors:

1. INDUSTRIALIZATION FOR AN EXTERNAL MARKET Capitalist industrialization of European countries depended on the import of raw materials and the export of manufactured goods. No process of capitalist economic development was autonomous. From the beginning, capitalism was a world system. Yet capitalist development in Europe was primarily geared to a home market. As a result European industrialization created economies that were a coherent whole made up of sectors that carried on substantial exchanges between themselves.[138] In contrast, Japan as a late-developing capitalist economy geared its industrialization primarily to the external market. As in dependent capitalist countries today, consumer products of industrial technology were restricted to a "limited, upper class internal market."[139] As a completely peripheral country in the 1870s, Japan first raised the capital to import modern technology by exporting primary products—coal, copper, and raw silk. It soon included the export of cotton cloth. Even in 1937, about 35 percent of Japan's entire manufacturing product was sold abroad.[140] Textiles accounted for 59 percent of these exports. By this time Japan had also become a subimperialist power.

It exported products to the West that would not compete with those of their more developed economies. "Trading with the West, she specialized in products requiring cheap labor, plus a minimum of capital and special skills." [141] But trading with the less developed Asian countries, Japan "built up an export business in factory goods which she could produce more efficiently than her neighbors, using them to buy food and industrial materials." [142]

2. TECHNOLOGICAL DEPENDENCE ON THE MORE ADVANCED CAPITALIST COUNTRIES Like developing countries today, Japan failed to develop its own capital goods industry. [143] Rather than manufacture its own heavy machinery, Japan imported it from the West. "In the mid 19th century, England like Japan set the nucleus of its industrial capital in the spinning and weaving industry, but heavy industry already occupied an important position backing up the spinning and weaving industry." [144] Until the 1930s Japan's industrial growth remained concentrated in the light industries, especially cotton goods. [145] Japan, like semiperipheral countries today, "largely served as a purveyor of products it was no longer worth the while of the core country to manufacture." [146] The lack of basic industries in Japan meant that the consumer goods industries were "extremely dependent on the outside world, which provided the equipment and semi-finished goods they needed." [147]

3. INDUSTRIALIZATION IN A NARROW SECTOR Until World War II, Japan remained primarily an agricultural, preindustrial and even a precapitalist country. [148] Even in 1937 "the total net output of factory industry in Japan was probably less than one-fourth of that in Britain or Germany, and less than one-twelfth of that of the U.S." [149] Japan's traditional agriculture was quite productive—providing a surplus that could be taxed off to support industrialization. The failure to capitalize agriculture supported industrialization for an external market, for the peasants had no resources to participate in a consumer society. Keeping a large percentage of the population in agriculture also supported capital-intensive industrialization. As in Third World countries today, modern industry in Japan did not need many workers. In 1937, Britain and Germany had twice as many factory workers as Japan, and the United States had three to four times as many. [150] Moreover, 95 percent of factory workers in Japan labored in plants with less than thirty workers. [151] A low level of purchasing power for the peasant masses also depressed urban wages. [152] Thus, those workers that were needed for modern industry could be had cheaply. Industrialization in Japan—as in Third World capitalist societies today—created a dual society, but one in which the "traditional" sector directly supported dependent capitalist development.

4. SUPEREXPLOITATION OF WORKERS AND PEASANTS Uneven industrialization in Japan created great economic inequality. It did not improve the level of living for the mass of the people.[153] For some, their standard of living fell as Japan advanced economically. Extreme income inequality is also characteristic of dependent capitalist countries today.[154]

5. INDUSTRIALIZATION GEARED TO MILITARY NEEDS AND TO SUBIMPERIALIST CONTROL OVER THE REGION. In the 1920s and 1930s Japan did develop heavy industry, but this was almost completely for military production.[155] This industry needed raw materials which Japan lacked. The desire for a protected market for both the import of raw materials and the export of manufactured goods pushed Japan to gain colonial control over other Asian countries (Korea, Taïwan).[156] This colonial expansion necessitated the use of military force, which increased the militarization of Japanese industry. The flow of Japanese capital to military and colonial expansion left few resources for the improvement of agriculture, health, housing, or sanitation for the people.[157] It also drained resources away from production for civilian use.

6. DEPENDENCE ON FOREIGN CAPITAL It is only in this last criterion of dependent capitalist development that Japan remains somewhat unique. Japan did borrow heavily from foreign sources between 1896 and 1913 to finance military buildup and colonial expansion.[158] But such borrowing was minimized after 1915. Moreover, Japan had very little direct foreign investment in industry.[159] Perhaps because of this, Japan's handicraft industries and small firms manufacturing traditional consumer goods remained vital during the process of industrialization. This did not prevent Japan from becoming a dependent capitalist country, but it did mitigate the impact of modernization on the mass of the people.

Japan's relative independence of foreign capital was offset by extreme dependence on raw material imports. By 1936, 60 percent of all Japan's manufactured exports depended on imports of raw materials.[160] Hence Japan's industry was probably as dependent on foreign control as that of Third World countries today.

It was only during World War I and during the depression in 1931-35 that Japan began to break out of its dependent economic position.[161] The war and depression undermined Western control of world markets and opened them to Japan's products. Japanese expansion produced countermoves from the West. The advanced capitalist countries raised tariff barriers to Japanese goods,[162] and allied to bring diplomatic and military pressure against Japanese colonialism in Asia. "Because Japan set out on the road of imperialist conquests before she had rid herself of the traces of dependence, she very often was obliged to cede the fruits of her victories to stronger birds of prey."[163] Japan's refusal to remain a subimperialist power led to its desperate entry into World War II.[164] It was an irrational leap because Japan did not have the economic resources for a long war and its sources of raw materials could be easily blocked. Japan's history demonstrates that advanced capitalist countries will fight to prevent less developed countries—whether capitalist or socialist—from breaking out of a dependent position in the world capitalist system.

This pattern of dependent capitalist industrialization in Japan was accompanied by changes in the power structure of its authoritarian state. Big capitalists who controlled the export trade and technically advanced industries were integrated into the ruling class of military and civil bureaucrats and landowners. Businessmen became active in political parties, while at the same time they cultivated direct ties to bureaucrats. In 1896 the government established the first of a long series of committees of bureaucratic, business, and academic representatives to formulate common economic policy.[165] "Increasingly, the top figures in the big business combines moved in and out of the government banks and ministries handling economic affairs. They came to exercise great influence in the Diet through the political parties on which they lavished funds. They worked closely with the army and navy in the procurement of arms and equipment, and in financing imperialism overseas. They intermarried with the families of the peerage, ranking bureaucrats, politicians, admirals, and diplomats."[166] By the 1920s there was a definite Japanese political establishment consisting of the upper civil bureaucracy, conservative political party leaders, big business interests, rural landlord interests, and the military bureaucracy.[167] This establishment was never ruled or directed by the economic interests, however. On the contrary, military and civil bureaucrats retained their hegemony. As we shall see, the establishment remained in power until 1945 despite attempts from below to overthrow it.

Political Instability as a Reaction to the Contradictions of Dependent Capitalist Development

In both Japan and Turkey the uneven, unequal, and distorted economic development created by dependent capitalism resulted in political instability which threatened the authoritarian political system consolidated by revolution from above.

As high military and civil bureaucrats became tied to established economic interests and became conservative, the legacy of revolution from above—the use of the state apparatus to foster radical social and economic change—passed to younger and lower-level military officers. In both Japan and Turkey the state bureaucracy, but especially the military, recruited from all levels of society on the basis of merit. A military career—except at the very top—soon lost its elitist tradition as increasing numbers of military officers were recruited from the lower middle class. Small farmers who were not poor peasants—but not large landowners—sent their sons into military schools to become officers, as did minor urban officials and shopkeepers. These military students from the lower middle class retained a commitment to the paternal and traditional values of the masses, and through their military training internalized an intense nationalism. Many young officers also developed a keen sense of the poverty and backwardness of the countryside based on their experience at military bases in the hinterland and on the poverty and ill health of the enlisted men they led. Outrage at these conditions was reinforced by their own meager salaries and spartan lifestyle in a time of inflation. Young military officers could afford a lifestyle little better than that of the lower-middle-class families from which they came.

In the 1930s in Japan and 1960s in Turkey, young nationalist military officers attempted military coups, assassinations, and other forms of terrorism against their bureaucratic superiors, big businessmen, and party leaders. But this radicalism had a reactionary intent—to return Japan and Turkey to more traditional societies. These young officers had many of the characteristics of those military men who had earlier made revolutions from above. They were autonomous from upper-class economic interests. They were politicized around a doctrine of nationalism in reaction to civilian social movements that sought radical change. In two crucial ways, however, they were different from those who organized the Ataturk and Meiji revolutions: (1) Nationalist officers in Japan in the 1930s and in Turkey in the 1960s did not have high bureaucratic office nor training in bureaucratic skills. Rather, they resembled many of the Loyalist and Young Turk officers. But unlike them, they were not drawn into the top military bureaucracy. The military hierarchy turned against the nationalist young officers and repressed them. (2) Their nationalism was completely traditionalistic, the product of revolutions from above which successfully depoliticized the mass of the population and failed to develop new values. Let us explore these points in more detail.

Although the Turkish military had always recruited some officers from nonelite origins, the proportion rose after the Ataturk Revolution. The political and social elites in Turkey became increasingly attracted to professional, political, or technical careers for their sons. At the same time, officer training schools (which took students at age twelve) became more attractive to an education-conscious populace. Because these schools provided free board, room, and other allowances, they drew students from families which could not afford to support their children in urban secondary schools. From 1923 on, officer training schools recruited more and more students from the middle and lower-middle classes, including many boys from families of small or middle-income farmers.[168] Similarly, in Japan after World War I an increasing number of officers were recruited from the lower middle class. By 1927, about 30 percent of junior officers were sons of petty landowners and small shopkeepers.[169]

In the Japanese military after World War I and the Turkish military after World War II, officers from the lower middle class were integrated with sons of professional soldiers who did not yet have close ties to class interests. Both the former autonomy of the military elite and the open recruitment of officers helped solidify a classless ideology which reinforced nationalism. In the Japanese army, "all civilian social distinctions and family background was disregarded."[170] Likewise, a Turkish officer reported in the early 1960s: "The Turkish army takes men from all parts of the country and from all classes and makes them a single group. It doesn't matter that my father was a government clerk, and that the next man's father was a peasant . . . . We all go to the military school when we are very young and there we learn to forget about differences and become nationalists."[171] Nationalism was inculcated in Turkish military schools in compulsory courses on the Kemalist Revolution,[172] while the Japanese army used the rural family as a model for its own organization and ideologically upheld the supremacy of the rural way of life.[173] Many of the rural recruits to the Japanese army, both in the officer and enlisted corps, found an easy adjustment due to the fact that "within the army interpersonal relations followed the same pattern as in the villages."[174] The entire educational apparatus of the Japanese military was geared towards cultivating an identity of the armed forces "as being the mainstay of the nation."[175]

This classless nationalism inculcated in the military officers increasingly came into conflict with a social reality shaped by class forces. In Turkey in the 1950s "the newly rich politicians, landlords, and entrepreneurs placed emphasis on wealth, luxury, and material pursuits, all of which contrasted sharply with the ascetic idealism preached in the army."[176] In interviews and in the press, army colonels expressed resentment against rich businessmen who hung out at the Hilton Hotel in Istanbul while the colonels and their families were barely surviving.[177] Many officers left the military because of inadequate pay.[178] Others had to stay because of the lack of alternative jobs, and either worked a second job or put their wives to work.[179] Similarly, many young officers in Japan in the 1930s felt the jealousy of an "underprivileged group towards a fortunate elite."[180] Democracy and the party system were equated by many of these young officers "with political corruption, domination by vested interest, selfishness, and depression."[181]

All of these characteristics of young officers—their nationalism, continued commitment to traditional values, and their own class resentments, along with their intimate contact with enlisted men from the villages—turned them into advocates of reform in the countryside. This was true of even those officers from urban and military backgrounds. Young officers in Japan in the thirties were angered "that the army should be endangered by the poor physique of its rural conscripts and the poor morale which resulted from their constant concern with the plight of their families in the village."[182] They called attention to the "contrast between the heroic efforts of the military to safeguard the nation externally and the failure of the political leadership to provide decent living conditions and a moral example for the people."[183] Turkish officers expressed similar concern for the village population.[184]

But neither the Japanese nor Turkish young officers developed any concrete plans for rural reform. Their primary allegiance remained the nation and not a class. At their trials after 1932, army plotters in Japan spoke of the distress of the peasants "as primarily a bad thing for the nation rather than for the peasants themselves."[185] Likewise, Turkish young officers, as one of them admitted, "really looked down upon the peasantry" and wanted to control them.[186]

Even though the young officers in Japan in the 1930s and in Turkey in the 1960s had a left-wing rhetoric antagonistic to the privileged classes, anti-capitalist, and sympathetic to the peasants, they formed close ties to elitist right-wing sects and not to the peasants or urban workers.[187] This was directly tied to the earlier revolutions from above which depoliticized the masses through propagation of traditional values and social structure.

Revolutions from above which maintain the traditional agrarian social structure and values provide a much greater potential for mass mobilization by the far Right than by the Left. The agrarian values that persisted in both Japan and Turkey were used in right-wing appeals. But the depoliticization of the masses in Japan and Turkey also prevented right-wing groups from gaining mass support.

Right-wing sects had a long history in modern Japan. They arose among ex-samurai after the defeat of the Satsuma Rebellion in the 1870s. They represented a "traditionalistic reaction to the Meiji oligarchs' policy of modernization."[188] They also kept alive the tradition of the masterless samurai (ronin) who had undertaken individual acts of terrorism before the Restoration. But as I have shown, it was not these ronin who made the Meiji Restoration, and their ideals were destroyed in that revolution from above. In spite of the fact that young officers in the 1930s called for a Showa restoration modelled on Meiji, their real hero was Saigo who perished in the attempt at counterrevolution in 1878.[189]

The right-wing nationalist groups which organized against the Japanese government were also elitist. They envisioned nationalism as an elite movement consisting of small groups of heroic patriots who gave their unswerving loyalty to the leaders. Japanese nationalist sects in the 1920s and 1930s failed to inspire any mass movement; nor could they obtain any significant number of votes in elections. "Until they were finally stopped by General Tojo on the eve of the Pacific War, they continued for the most part as small, rather isolated cliques, indulging in much heady propaganda and a good deal of violence, and precariously dependent for their support on those elements in the army or elsewhere that were willing to use them temporarily as an auxiliary force for their own national missions."[190]

From the late 1950s on right-wing and fascist movements also arose in Turkey. In 1961, the Republican Peasant Nation party espoused a national socialist doctrine.[191] Colonel Turkes, the leader of this group and the prime instigator of the 1960 coup in Turkey (and also of the coup attempt in 1962), was already in the 1950s associated with small, secret, pan-Turanian sects. These sects espoused the national reunion of all Turks, especially those under Soviet rule with those in Turkey.[192] Moreover, Turkes and other nationalist military officers, while still in power and afterwards, explicitly rejected parliamentary government and proposed to establish an all-encompassing ministry of culture. This superministry, they said, would replace the Ministry of Education and the Directorates of Physical Education, Pious Foundations, Religious Affairs, Press, and Radio, and seek to create true national unity. This proposal was widely branded as fascist by the press and intellectuals.[193] Other right-wing parties combined appeals to fundamental religion with intolerant and parochial national-ism.[194] But fascist ideals in Turkey also failed to generate support from the rural masses. The Turkish peasant remained loyal to the Democratic party and its successor, the Justice party. Military officers, even when they espoused traditional values, never lost their image as the group that over-threw and executed Menderes, the first president of the DP. The peasants saw that radical ex-officers who espoused their cause really wanted to control them. As one military officer admitted: "I think that what we really need is to have a very strict government that will make the village people do the right thing. Ataturk was like that. He flattered the village people. But at the same time, Ataturk forced the villagers to build schools and pay taxes. I think that is what the NUC (military junta in 1960) should have done."[195]

The initiative taken by radical young officers in Japan in the 1930s (which resulted in military expansion in Manchuria and numerous coup and assassination attempts) and Turkey in the 1960s (which led to the 1960 coup and coup attempts in 1962 and 1963) were based on a fascist ideology that combined an appeal to social reform with traditionalistic ultranationalism and military elitism.

Reintegration of a Bureaucratic-Authoritarian State
to Repress the Fascist Challenge from Below

Representatives of the highest military elites also joined and supported the initial attempts at military intervention—the Manchurian invasion in Japan and the 1960 coup in Turkey—but they never shared the ideals which motivated the junior officers. It was these senior officers who repressed the young fascists in order to retain the conservative coalition between bureaucrats and the landlord and capitalist classes. They too tried to legitimize their repressive action by an inappropriate appeal to the traditions of the Meiji and the Ataturk revolutions from above. While the young officers were too traditionalistic to propagate a new revolution from above, the higher military officers had lost their autonomy and became too conservative. What has been said of the Turkish high command also goes for the Japanese military elite in the thirties: "The reformist and Kemalist zeal of young officers is gradually dissipated under the influence of the system. By the time they are 40, even the most reformist officers are ensnared by money and prestige. They live in dream houses and establish friendly contacts with all business circles."[196] Such officers intervened in politics to uphold the status quo through minor reform, not to push the extreme social change characteristic of the Ataturk and Meiji revolutions.

Within six months of the 1960 coup, top officers in the Turkish Junta with the support of the army high command, dismissed fourteen of the most radical junior officers in the thirty-eight-member ruling committee.[197] The fourteen had desired to prolong the military regime in order to implement basic reforms, but also to impose more unity on the country. Again, after the election of a new civil government in 1961, high military officers suppressed elements in the army who wished to dissolve the newly elected assembly and suspend political parties.[198] In 1962 and 1963 the military elites put down, with force, two coup attempts by radical junior officers who were closely connected with the fourteen radicals dismissed earlier. In 1971, senior military officers intervened in civil government to prevent a coup by junior officers.[199] After the first coup attempt, the only punishment meted out to the radicals was the retirement of some sixty-nine young officers involved in the plot. No punishment was given to cadets from the military academy who participated.[200] After the second coup attempt a public trial was convened and several coup leaders were executed. One hundred and sixty-six cadets were also convicted and the entire student body of the Military Academy, 1,459 students, was expelled for its participation.[201] Having suppressed the radical junior officers, the Turkish military elite cooperated with civil bureaucrats, party, and economic leaders to restore civil government. As a result, the 1960 coup in Turkey brought no major political, social, or economic reforms.[202] During the sixties and into the seventies the Turkish high command continued to insist that all parties adhere to the centrist line,[203] while using force against the Turkish Labor party, left-wing terrorists, and radical students.

Likewise, top military officers in Japan, who supported aggressive action by junior officers in Manchuria, suppressed internal coup attempts by young officers in 1932 and 1936. As in Turkey, sanctions against the officers who planned the 1932 coup (and in the attempt to gain power, assassinated the prime minister and other politicians) were light. As in Turkey, the second coup attempt led the military elites to execute the junior officers who planned the coup and purge many radicals from the army.[204] The suppression of army radicalism in Japan also led to a closer alliance between the military, bureaucratic, landed, and capitalist classes, and terminated any possibility of social revolution or even basic social reforms.[205] Administrative innovations under military rule in the late 1930s tightened civil and military bureaucratic controls over the countryside through new procedures. The Home Ministry organized local groups under bureaucratic guidance into a national hierarchy. "Village headmen, elementary school principals, Shinto priests, and prominent landlords, together with other local activists were the object of rural leadership training courses and hortative writing by the central bureaucracy."[206] This reinforcement of hamlet associations by the Home Ministry "involved every individual in a face-to-face pyramid of command leading through neighborhood association, hamlet association, village office and prefectural office to the Home Ministry itself."[207] Likewise, the military bureaucracy organized reserve officer associations in the countryside which reached 14,000 branches of three million members by 1936. These reserve associations stressed youth group leadership, disaster relief, aid to the local community, and the performance of patriotic ceremonies. They were "created to further the Army's goals of fusing local power structures and social hierarchies with the military and its values."[208] The reserve associations also were "seen as a way to preserve and reinforce the hierarchical order of traditional rural society."[209] When some activists in the local branches of the association became connected with right-wing sects in 1935 and began radical direct action, the reserve associations were brought "under direct army and navy control to strengthen the central headquarters discipline over local branches."[210] After 1936, the reserve association prohibited all local-level political activity.[211] Mobilization by the army and the Home Ministry sought to reinforce the apolitical controls of the bureaucracy over the masses. To back these government efforts, the zaibatsu offered financial support to some right-wing sects in order to try to infiltrate and buy off terrorist groups—a tactic that largely succeeded.[212]

Even after the threat of right-wing revolution from minor officers had been repressed, the governing coalition in Japan and Turkey sought to create a stronger state apparatus by increasing the overt power of the high military command. In neither country did this lead to a military regime or to radical departures from former patterns of rule. Rather, the coalition of business, landed, civil, and military bureaucrats continued to rule, with more power centered in the bureaucracy. In both countries, the participation of the parties in parliament (and hence the political power of landlords and small businessmen) was weakened as decision-making power became concentrated in new bureaus.

In Japan, key foreign and domestic policy decisions came to be made in superbureaus that took the place of the genro in coordinating the government. In the Cabinet Investigation Bureau, Manchurian Affairs Bureau, the Planning Board, and so on, active army and navy officers met and planned with civil bureaucrats.[213] Although the regular cabinet continued to hold legal authority, the real decisions were made in these agencies that coordinated the civil and military bureaucracy. It was these bureaus that made the decisions to go to war with China and later with the United States, and not field officers as has sometimes been charged.[214] Nor was this highly centralized government a weak or factionalized state.[215] Rather, the spread of bureaucracy at the top and also downward to the villages strengthened the state apparatus. As a result direct political participation of business and landowners decreased, but the zaibatsu retained and consolidated their private economic power over small businesses.[216] In spite of a world depression, industrial output in Japan rose from six to fifty billion dollars in 1930-41.[217]

Turkey in the 1960s and 1970s also continued its party-parliamentary government, but important decisions were made by consultation between civil, party, and military bureaucrats. The new Constitution of 1961 authorized numerous administrative councils, committees, and semiautonomous regulatory bodies to take over a number of functions previously left to the parties and the Parliament.[218] Since 1961 ex–military commanders have held the office of president,[219] and many retired officers have been given posts in the provincial bureaucracy.[220] In 1971, to prevent a coup by junior officers, senior military commanders forced the president to form a "cabinet above parties." For two years, a cabinet drawn from the three leading parties and from technocrats outside the parliament ruled in close cooperation with the military command to repress left-wing dissidents.[221] As in Japan, coalition rule by civil and military bureaucrats decreased the direct political role of business, while increasing the economic power of large private enterprise.

There are a number of reasons, then, why fascist movements failed to take political power in Japan and Turkey while they succeeded in Germany and Italy. Since fascism has only triumphed in countries with considerable industrialization, perhaps it was never an option in Turkey. But the German and Japanese bureaucratic states achieved national integration and began industrial takeoff in the nineteenth century. They have often been identified as following a similar political and economic path to modernization.[222] The triumph of a fascist movement in Germany and its defeat in Japan, however, is another factor disputing this analogy.

The political structure of Nazi Germany in the 1930s and 1940s was very different from Japan's at that time. Japan had no successful takeover of power from below and no formal change in the Meiji constitutional order.[223] There was no charismatic leader equivalent to Hitler in Japan in the thirties. "Although the Japanese army played a role more analogous to that of the Nazi Party than to that of the German Reichswar in championing middle-class socialism, it never became a totalitarian organization."[224] Communists were persecuted in Japan, but according to legal procedures, and the persecuted were usually released if they abandoned their political creed. "Although some people died under torture during Japanese investigations or as a result of maltreatment in Japanese prisons, there was no mass massacre as in Germany."[225] Japanese politics in the thirties and forties remained an elitist affair—"instead of metamorphosis to a fascist or communist movement regime, the bureaucratic, political party, and military elites who had emerged from the Meiji state composed their differences as best they could and acted as a conservative coalition to maintain the system they had inherited."[226]

The most important reason for defeat of a fascist movement from below in Japan was the strength of the bureaucratic-authoritarian state established through revolution from above in contrast to the weaker German state that evolved through bureaucratic reform without revolution.[227] The depoliticization of the masses by the Meiji state, supported by specific repressive measures, retarded both the rise of left- and right-wing mass movements in Japan. The German state was far less successful in depoliticizing the masses and failed to incorporate them into the political system in a subordinate role. The Japanese state was also more effective in integrating the bourgeoisie, by consolidating party and parliamentary institutions under bureaucratic supremacy. In Japan, the bureaucratic oligarchy formed and controlled political parties, and then let a few party leaders into the cabinet. In contrast, Bismarck and the Prussian-German bureaucrats stayed aloof from parties and Parliament and did not permit party leaders into the cabinet. Parliamentary-party government came to Germany only after the bureaucratic empire had been discredited in World War I.[228] In the Weimar Republic, the military and civil bureaucrats were set in opposition to the bourgeoisie and working-class parties.[229] The German Junkers (landed class) through their near-monopoly of the civil and military bureaucracy in the empire had much more control of the state before 1920 than the Japanese landed class, and much less political power afterward. German big business never became an important part of the stable ruling coalition as the zaibatsu did in Japan. Under the empire, German industrialists were subordinate to the Junker bureaucracy; under the republic, they had to share power with the working class,[230] and under the Nazis they lost political control.[231]

Military and civil bureaucrats drawn from all social classes retained much more political power in twentieth-century Japan than their German counterparts who were more clearly tied to a landed aristocracy. German bureaucrats were first displaced by bourgeois party government under Weimar and then by a mass party under the Nazis. The strong political role of the Japanese military command in the 1930s contrasts with the weak and subordinate role of the German military under Hitler.[232]

The Costs of a Conservative Bureaucratic-Class Coalition

Prior to the Meiji and Ataturk revolutions, high-level military bureaucrats repressed traditionalist radical movements among their lower and younger officers. These military elites then went on to lead revolutions in support of modernization. But the military bureaucrats who repressed right-wing movements led by junior officers in the 1930s in Japan and 1960s in Turkey could not imitate the bureaucratic revolutionaries. Faced with external threats to their national goals and internal turmoil, the ruling class coalition of landlords, industrialists, and civil and military bureaucrats failed to find innovative solutions. The autonomous bureaucrats who made the Meiji and Ataturk revolutions focused on consolidating national power vis-à-vis the international order, even if this meant undermining a traditional upper class. Their bureaucratic successors, in contrast, sought to protect upper-class interests even if this meant abdicating leadership in resolving international conflict.

The Japanese model of industrialization without modernizing agriculture restricted the purchasing power of the peasant and depressed urban wages. Industrial expansion depended on an expanding external market for Japanese goods. An Asian market was secured by military victory over China in 1894 and over Russia in 1905.[233] But as the Western powers expanded into Asia and restricted Japan's export market in both Western and Eastern countries, Japan's policymakers were boxed in.[234] If the bureaucrats had been more autonomous and less conservative they might have tried to resolve some of Japan's economic dilemmas through internal reforms. Like the Meiji oligarchs they might have removed some of the internal class barriers to the home market. As it was, they sought relief only through external military and imperialist expansion, even when they sensed that this was irrational. The lack of innovation in the Japanese ruling class in the 1930s is seen in their decision to go to war with the United States. Many of the highest officers in the Japanese general staff had grave doubts about the technical capacity of Japan to wage war simultaneously with China and the United States. Yet General Tojo, who became military dictator during the war, said: "At some point during a man's lifetime, he might find it necessary to jump, with his eyes closed, from the veranda of Kiomizu-dera (a Buddhist temple) into the ravine below."[235] That was Tojo's way of saying that he and others in the army and government bureaucracy believed that there are occasions when success or failure depended on the irrational risks one was prepared to take. "These leaders of Japan never once asked themselves why they were confronted by such a critical choice (war with the United States). They did not look to the record or otherwise seek in past policies, an explanation for their present difficulties. Their decision-making was cut to the pattern set by traditions; conformity, not independence; acquiescence, not protest; obedience, not questioning."[236] These bureaucrats were not like those who made the Meiji Restoration. Tragically, depoliticization of the masses through the nationalist ideology created by the Meiji oligarchs precluded any popular support for those (few) members of the elite who sought alternative (peaceful) solutions to Japan's problems.[237]

The conservative ruling coalition which came to power in the 1960s in Turkey continued to block effective industrialization, while protecting the economic interests of the Turkish bourgeoisie tied to international capital. This coalition could repress leftist terrorists and rightist junior officers, but it could not ally the economic discontent of the large mass of lower- and lower-middle-class citizens. As unemployment increased and large numbers of Turkish workers emigrated to jobs in West Germany, a group of young social democrats won control of the Republican party, ousted the aging General Inonu from leadership, and expelled the landlords from the party (one-third of the membership). This new Left-of-Center leadership invoked the mantle of Ataturk, but refused to cooperate with the military-sponsored government in 1971.[238] In 1973, the new Republican party for the first time won more popular votes than the more conservative Justice party. By promising land redistribution, the Republicans won many peasant votes; by supporting the small entrepreneur instead of the multinational corporations, they won the urban lower middle class. For the first time, a Turkish majority party has begun to mobilize mass support on more progressive values.[239] The Republicans also won support from far-Left students for their social democratic program. Although the new Republican party takes an anti-American line and calls for the nationalization of industry, they have not yet put these policies into practice. If this party becomes only the equivalent of the Labor party in Britain, it will probably remain acceptable to the military and business elite, but it will be unable to take the steps necessary to foster autonomous economic development. Either way, Turkey faces continuing political, economic, and social turmoil: to break with the conservative coalition and mobilize mass support for national economic development will probably involve revolutionary violence. But to remain an underdeveloped, dependent capitalist country will also foster mass discontent and violence.

The preceding pages have documented the weaknesses and failures of revolutions from above which sought to depoliticize the masses rather than mobilize them for political and economic action. Instead, military bureaucrats who led revolutions from above in Japan and Turkey chose to cultivate the political support of landlords. In Japan especially, this was a real choice and not something imposed by structural and historical circumstances. Landlords in Japan were not a powerful aristocratic estate, but former peasants. Their later economic and political strength was largely the result of support by the Meiji state. Turkish landlords had more power and status at the local level than those in Japan, but they were not an organized national class in the early years of the Ataturk Revolution. This compromise with the landed class undermined autonomous capitalist industrialization in both Japan and Turkey, promoted increased social and economic inequality, and necessitated an increasingly authoritarian state.

The next chapter will examine two contemporary revolutions from above that did not compromise with their landed class. Revolutions from above in Egypt and Peru destroyed the political and economic power of the landlords and sought to foster industrialization through support of a local capitalist class without mass mobilization. Analysis of these two cases will demonstrate how revolutions from above alter with changing historical circumstances. It will raise new questions about the future of this type of revolutionary change.

Notes

1. George Harris, "The Role of the Military in Turkish Politics," *Middle East Journal* 19 (1965): 62.
2. Roger Hackett, "Political Modernization and the Meiji Genro," in Ward, p. 69.
3. Ibid., p. 73.
4. Ibid., p. 95.
5. Peter Duus, *Party Rivalry and Political Change in Taisho Japan* (Cambridge, Mass.: Harvard University Press, 1968), p. 84.

6. Robinson, p. 235.
7. Osman Faruk Logoglu, "Ismet Inonu and the Political Modernization of Turkey, 1945-1965," Ph.D. dissertation, Princeton University, 1970.
8. Harris, "The Role of the Military," p. 55.
9. Robinson, p. 241.
10. Leslie L. Roos and Noralou P. Roos, *Managers of Modernization: Organization and Elites in Turkey, 1950-1969* (Cambridge, Mass.: Harvard University Press, 1971), p. 29.
11. Harris, "The Role of the Military," p. 58.
12. Ibid., p. 60.
13. Roger Hackett, "The Japanese Military," in Ward and Rustow, p. 346.
14. Roger Hackett, *Yamagata Aritoma* (Cambridge, Mass.: Harvard University Press, 1971), p. 127.
15. Kurt Steiner, *Local Government in Japan* (Stanford: Stanford University Press, 1965), p. 228.
16. Rustow, "Politics and Development Policy," in *Four Studies in the Economic Development of Turkey*, ed. Frederick Shorter (London: Frank Cass, 1967), p. 21.
17. Albert Gorvine, *An Outline of Turkish Provincial and Local Government* (Ankara: Ankara University, Faculty of Political Science, 1956), p. 4.
18. H. Haluk Ulman and Frank Tachau, "Turkish Politics: The Attempt to Reconcile Rapid Modernization with Democracy," *Middle Eastern Journal* 19 (1965): 159.
19. Norman, *Japan's Emergence as a Modern State*, p. 169.
20. Ibid., p. 173.
21. Robert Scalapino, *Democracy and the Party Movement in Pre-War Japan* (Berkeley: University of California Press, 1962), p. 259.
22. Ibid., p. 257.
23. George Akita, *Foundations of Constitutional Government in Japan, 1868-1900* (Cambridge, Mass.: Harvard University Press, 1967).
24. Lockwood, *The Economic Development of Japan*, p. 68.
25. Scalapino, *Democracy in Pre-War Japan*, p. 25.
26. Lockwood, *The Economic Development of Japan*, p. 564.
27. Frey, *The Turkish Political Elite*, p. 14.
28. Robinson, p. 134.
29. Rustow, "Politics and Development Policy," p. 21.
30. Frey, *The Turkish Political Elite*, p. 196.
31. Lewis, *The Emergence of Modern Turkey*, p. 479.
32. Ike, p. 34.
33. John W. Dower, "Introduction" to Halliday, *A Political History of Japanese Capitalism*, p. xxii.
34. Masao Maruyama, *Thought and Behavior in Modern Japanese Politics* (London: Oxford University Press, 1963), p. 147.
35. Ibid., p. 150.
36. Moore, *The Social Origins of Dictatorship and Democracy*, p. 308.
37. Shuicho Kato, "Postwar Japan: Society of Contrasts," unpublished paper, Center for Japanese and Korean Studies, University of California, Berkeley, 1968.
38. Karpat, *Turkey's Politics*, p. 254.
39. Dankwart Rustow, "Turkey: The Modernity of Tradition," in *Political Culture and Political Development*, eds. Lucian Pye and Sidney Verba (Princeton: Princeton University Press, 1965), p. 184.

40. Mardin, "Power, Civil Society, and Culture in the Ottoman Empire," p. 183.

41. Ibid.

42. Joseph Szyliowicz, *Political Change in Rural Turkey* (New York: Columbia University, 1966), p. 156.

43. Kenneth Fidel, "Social Structure and Military Intervention: The 1960 Turkish Revolution," Ph.D. dissertation, Washington University, 1969, p. 150.

44. Serif Mardin, "Historical Determinants of Stratification: Social Class and Class Consciousness in Turkey," *Siyasal Bilqilar Fakultesi Dergisi* (Ankara University) 22 (1967):132.

45. Ibid.

46. Paul Stirling, *Turkish Village* (London: Weidenfeld & Nicolson, 1965), p. 284.

47. Tetsuo Najita, *Hara Kei and the Politics of Compromise, 1905-1915* (Cambridge, Mass.: Harvard University Press, 1967), p. 213.

48. Ivan Morris, *Nationalism and the Right-Wing in Japan* (London: Oxford University Press, 1960), p. 142.

49. Najita, p. 214.

50. Duus, *Party Rivalry in Taisho Japan*, p. 24.

51. Ronald Dore, *City Life in Japan* (Berkeley: University of California Press), p. 222.

52. Scalapino, *Democracy in Pre-War Japan*, p. 311.

53. George Beckman and Okubo Genji, *The Japanese Communist Party, 1922-1945* (Stanford: Stanford University Press, 1969), p. 276.

54. Ronald Dore and Tsutomu Ouchi, "Rural Origins of Japanese Fascism," in *Dilemmas of Growth in Prewar Japan*, ed. James Morley (Princeton: Princeton University Press, 1971), p. 187.

55. Logoglu, p. 146.

56. Szyliowicz, *Political Change in Rural Turkey*, p. 160.

57. Fidel, p. 215.

58. Richard Storry, *The Double Patriots: A Study of Japanese Nationalism* (London: Chatto & Windus, 1957), p. 24.

59. Serif Mardin, "Opposition and Control in Turkey," *Government and Opposition* 1 (1966): 384.

60. Logoglu, p. 161.

61. W.B. Sherwood, "The Rise of the Justice Party in Turkey," *World Politics* 20 (1967): 57.

62. Ibid.

63. Issawi, p. 83.

64. Dogu Ergil and Robert Rhodes, "The Impact of the World Capitalist System on Ottoman Society," unpublished paper, State University of New York at Binghamton, 1973.

65. Issawi, p. 103.

66. Robinson, pp. 100-101.

67. The position that Japan's economic development was made possible primarily by its isolation from Western economic penetration is argued by several Marxist theorists including: Paul Baran, *The Political Economy of Growth* (New York: Monthly Review Press, 1957); Jon Halliday, "Japan: Asian Capitalism," *New Left Review* 44 (1967); and Norman, *Japan's Emergence as a Modern State*. The following non-Marxists have also advanced a similar argument: Lockwood, *The Economic Development of Japan*; and Fairbanks, Reischauer, and Craig.

68. Benjamin Higgins, Jr. "The Political Basis of Economic Development: The

Role of the Pre-Industrial Bureaucracies in Japanese Growth and Chinese Stagnation, 1850-1912," M.A. dissertation, McGill University (Montreal), 1971, p. 12.

69. Ibid., p. 32.

70. Ibid., p. 150.

71. Ibid., p. 59.

72. Ibid., p. 33.

73. Clifford Geertz, *Agricultural Involution: the Processes of Ecological Change in Indonesia* (Berkeley: University of California Press, 1968), p. 131.

74. Ibid.

75. According to Rosofsky (p. 104), Japan's economic structure was not undergoing rapid transformation in 1868. Its agriculture was only slightly commercialized, with about 20 percent of agricultural output reaching the market. France and England had a much lower percentage of population in agriculture when they began to industrialize: England in 1688 had 60 percent of its population in agriculture; France in 1789 had 55 percent. Japan in 1868 was much like underdeveloped countries today with 80 percent of its population in agriculture (pp. 111-12). The per capita product of Japan in the 1870s was only one-half to one-third that of most European countries before their entry into modern economic growth at dates ranging from the late eighteenth to the late nineteenth century. Simon Kuznets, "Notes on Japan's Economic Growth," in *Economic Growth: The Japanese Experience Since the Meiji Era*, ed. Lawrence Klein and K. Ohkawa (Homewood, Ill.: Richard Irwin, 1968), p. 394.

76. Lockwood, *The Economic Development of Japan*, p. 505.

77. Ibid., p. 322.

78. Eugene McGrummen, "The Role of Foreign Trade and Foreign Investment in the Economic Development of Turkey," M.A. dissertation, University of California, Berkeley, 1962, p. 10.

79. Malcolm Rivkin, *Area Development for National Growth: The Case of Turkey* (New York: Praeger, 1965), p. 68.

80. Smith, *Political Change and Industrial Development in Japan*, p. 36; Sugar, p. 164.

81. Lockwood, *Economic Development of Japan*, p. 507.

82. William McCord, "The Japanese Model of Development," in *Political Economy of Development*, ed. Charles Wilber (New York: Random House, 1973), p. 279.

83. Hakki Kestin, "Imperialismus, Unterentwicklung, Militarregierun in der Turkei," *Problems des Klassenkampfs* (1973): 77.

84. Howard Ellis, *Private Enterprise and Socialism in the Middle East* (Washington: American Enterprise Institute for Public Policy Research, 1970), p. 49.

85. Rivkin, p. 92.

86. Higgins, p. 82.

87. Sugar, p. 168.

88. Rustow, "Politics and Development Policy," p. 14.

89. Smith, *Political Change and Industrial Development*, p. 98.

90. Norman, *Japan's Emergence as a Modern State*, p. 114.

91. Hirschmeier, p. 24.

92. Robinson, p. 113; Lockwood, *Economic Development in Japan*, p. 16.

93. McGrummen, p. 11; Higgins, p. 91.

94. Robinson, p. 117; Norman, *Japan's Emergence as a Modern State*, p. 149.

95. Resat Aktan, "Problems of Land Reform in Turkey," *Middle Eastern Journal*

19 (1965): 323; Dore, *Land Reform in Japan* (London: Oxford University Press, 1959), p. 17.

96. Aktan, Ibid.

97. Richard Pfaff, "Political Factors Influencing the Economic Development of Turkey, Iraq, and Iran," Ph.D. dissertation, University of California, Berkeley, 1960, p. 102.

98. Rivkin, p. 79.

99. Ibid., p. 80.

100. Lee Seidler, *The Functions of Accounting in Economic Development: Turkey as a Case Study* (New York: Praeger, 1967), p. 33.

101. Productivity in Turkish agriculture doubled from 1927 to 1938, mainly due to an increase in land under cultivation and not because of improved techniques. Productivity could have increased much more. Ellis, p. 54.

102. Nuri Eren, *Turkey Today and Tomorrow* (London: Pall Mall, 1961), p. 130; A.J. Meyer, *Middle Eastern Capitalism* (Cambridge, Mass.: Harvard University Press, 1959), p. 77.

103. Sugar, "Economic Modernization in Turkey," in Ward and Rustow, p. 164.

104. Lockwood, *The Economic Development of Japan*, pp. 521-22.

105. The land tax took an average of 34 percent of the agricultural product. Smith, *Political Change and Industrial Development in Japan*, p. 82.

106. Ibid., pp. 75-76.

107. Higgins, p. 71.

108. Lockwood, *The Economic Development of Japan*, p. 301.

109. Dore, *Land Reform in Japan*, p. 117.

110. Fidel, pp. 98-99.

111. Ibid., p. 205; Kemal Karpat, "The Military and Politics in Turkey, 1960-1964: A Socio-Cultural Analysis of a Revolution," *American Historical Review* 80 (October 1970): 1661.

112. Michael Hyland, "Crisis at the Polls: Turkey's 1969 Elections," *Middle Eastern Journal* 24 (1970): 2.

113. George Harris, "The Causes of the 1960 Revolution in Turkey," *Middle Eastern Journal* (Fall 1970): 441.

114. Ibid.

115. McGrummen, p. 34.

116. Pfaff, p. 271.

117. Max Thornberg, Graham Spry, 'and George Soule, *Turkey: An Economic Appraisal* (New York: Twentieth Century Fund, 1949), p. 184.

118. Pfaff, p. 275.

119. Karpat, *Turkey's Politics*, p. 60.

120. Ference Vali, *Bridge across the Bosporus: The Foreign Policy of Turkey* (Baltimore: Johns Hopkins Press, 1971), p. 328.

121. George Harris, *Troubled Alliance: Turkish-American Problems in Historical Perspective* (Palo Alto: Hoover Institute, 1972).

122. An American political scientist notes that American advisors and consultants must be held partly responsible for Turkey's economic chaos in the 1950s, for they "had a very substantial hand in helping to chart Turkey's course of development in these years." Dwight Simpson, "Development as a Process: The Menderes Phase in Turkey," *Middle Eastern Journal* 19 (1965): 143.

123. Ibid., p. 145.

124. Frey, *The Turkish Political Elite*, p. 15.

125. Harris, *Troubled Alliance*, p. 72.

126. Robinson, p. 221.

127. Edwin Cohn, *Turkish Economic, Social, and Political Change* (New York: Praeger, 1970), p. 124.

128. Robinson, p. 151.

129. Karpat, *Turkey's Politics*, p. 306.

130. Seidler, p. 154.

131. Z.V. Hershlag, *Turkey: The Challenge of Growth* (Leiden: E.J. Brill, 1968), p. 243.

132. E. Gunce, "Early Planning Experiences in Turkey," in *Planning in Turkey*, ed. S. Ilkin (Ankara: Faculty of Administrative Science, Publication no. 9, 1967), p. 25.

133. Bob Sutcliffe, "Imperialism and Industrialization in the Third World," in *Studies in the Theory of Imperialism*, ed. Roger Owen and Bob Sutcliffe (London: Longman, 1972), p. 185.

134. Baran, p. 159.

135. Fernando H. Cardoso, "Imperialism and Dependency in Latin America, in *Structures of Dependency*, ed. Frank Bonilla and Robert Girling (Stanford University: Latin American Studies Institute, 1973).

136. Ruy Maurio Marini, "Brazilian Subimperialism," *Monthly Review* 23 (February 1972).

137. Jon Halliday and Gavan McCormick, *Japanese Imperialism Today* (New York: Monthly Review Press, 1973).

138. Samir Amin, *Accumulation on a World Scale*, vol. 1 (New York: Monthly Review Press, 1974), p. 16.

139. Cardoso, p. 12.

140. Lockwood, *The Economic Development of Japan*, p. 365.

141. Ibid., p. 403.

142. Ibid., p. 403.

143. Halliday, *A Political History of Japanese Capitalism*, p. 53.

144. Terucka Shuzo, "Japanese Capitalism and Its Agricultural Problems," *Developing Economies* 4 (1966): 473.

145. Lockwood, *The Economic Development of Japan*, p. 53.

146. Immanuel Wallerstein, "Dependence in an Interdependent World: The Limited Possibilities of Transformation within the Capitalist World Economy," *African Studies Review* 17 (April 1974): 13.

147. Amin, vol. 1, p. 16.

148. Halliday, *A Political History of Japanese Capitalism*, p. 53.

149. Lockwood, *The Economic Development of Japan*, p. 177.

150. Ibid., p. 177.

151. Halliday, *A Political History of Japanese Capitalism*, p. 57.

152. Dore, *Land Reform in Japan*, p. 117.

153. Lockwood, *The Economic Development of Japan*, p. 140.

154. See Irma Adelman and Cynthia Taft Morris, *Economic Growth and Social Equity in Developing Countries* (Stanford: Stanford University Press, 1973), p. 189.

155. Halliday, *A Political History of Japanese Capitalism*, p. 57.

156. Ibid., p. 101.

157. Lockwood, *The Economic Development of Japan*, p. 292.

158. Ibid., p. 252.

159. Ibid., p. 49.

160. Ibid., p. 68.

161. Ibid., p. 117.

162. Ibid., p. 74.
163. O. Tanin and E. Yohan, *Militarism and Fascism in Japan* (London: Martin Lawrence, 1934), p. 54.
164. Halliday, *A Political History of Japanese Capitalism*, p. 129.
165. Arthur Tiedmann, "Big Business and Politics in Prewar Japan," in Morley, p. 271.
166. Lockwood, *The Economic Development of Japan*, p. 563.
167. Hall, *Japan*, p. 310.
168. Nur Yalman, "Intervention and Extrication: The Officer Corps in the Turkish Crisis," in *The Military Intervenes*, ed. Henry Bienen (New York: Russel Sage Foundation, 1968), p. 129; Ergum Ozbudun, "The Role of the Military in Recent Turkish Politics," Occasional Paper no. 14, Center for International Affairs, Harvard University, 1966, p. 29.
169. Storry, p. 43.
170. George Totten, *The Social Democratic Movement in Prewar Japan* (New Haven: Yale University Press, 1966), p. 83.
171. Fidel, p. 609.
172. Harris, "The Role of the Military in Turkish Politics," p. 62.
173. Ward, *Political Development in Japan*, p. 200.
174. Ibid., p. 201.
175. Maruyama, p. 14.
176. Karpat, "The Military and Politics in Turkey," p. 1663.
177. Fidel, p. 594.
178. Harris, "The Role of the Military in Turkish Politics," p. 170.
179. Fidel, p. 581.
180. Storry, p. 140.
181. Scalapino, *Democracy in Prewar Japan*, p. 29; Fidel, p. 512.
182. Dore and Ouchi, p. 192.
183. Ben-Ami Shillony, *Revolt in Japan: The Young Officers and the February 26, 1936 Incident* (Princeton: Princeton University Press, 1973), p. 9.
184. Fidel, p. 581.
185. Dore, *Land Reform in Japan*, p. 94.
186. Fidel, p. 627.
187. Civilian right-wing sects in Japan found support mainly among the lower middle class, from "small factory owners, building contractors, retail shop owners, master carpenters, small landowners, independent farmers, primary school teachers, village officials, and low grade bureaucratic officials." Maruyama, p. 64.
188. Michael Leiserson, "Political Opposition and Political Change in Modern Japan," unpublished paper, Center for Japanese and Korean Studies, University of California, Berkeley, 1968, p. 24.
189. Shillony, p. 67.
190. Maruyama, p. 73.
191. Ozbudun, p. 40.
192. Yalman, "Westernized Reformers and Reactionary Conservatives," p. 47.
193. Weiker, *The Turkish Revolution*, p. 136.
194. Frank Tachau and Mary-Jo Good, "The Anatomy of Political and Social Change: Turkish Parties, Parliaments, and Elections," *Comparative Politics* 5 (July 1973): 571.
195. Fidel, p. 582.
196. Report on an article in *Le Figaro* on the Turkish army as published in the Turkish paper *Yanki* on October 22, 1973. Translated into English by the Joint Publications Research Service, Jan. 17, 1974, bulletin.

197. Weiker, *The Turkish Revolution*, p. 116.

198. Ozbudin, p. 33.

199. Robert Olson, "Al-Fateh in Turkey: Its Influence on the March 12 Coup," *Middle Eastern Studies* 9 (1973): 200; Feroz Ahmad, "The Turkish Guerrillas," *New Middle East* (April 1973): 16.

200. Walter Weiker, "The Aydemir Case and Turkey's Political Dilemma," *Middle Eastern Affairs* 14 (1963): 259.

201. Ibid.

202. Weiker, *The Turkish Revolution*, p. 146.

203. Simpson, p. 41.

204. Maruyama, p. 71.

205. Ibid., p. 71.

206. Kenneth Pyle, "The Technology of Japanese Nationalism," *Journal of Asian Studies* 33 (1973): 65.

207. Dore, *Land Reform in Japan*, p. 104.

208. Richard Smethurst, "The Creation of the Imperial Military Reserve Association in Japan," *Journal of Asian Studies* 30 (1971): 819.

209. Ibid., p. 818.

210. Richard Smethurst, "Military Reserve Associations and the Minobe Crisis of 1935," in *Crisis Politics in Prewar Japan*, ed. George Wilson (Tokyo: Voyagers' Press, 1970), p. 23

211. Ibid., p. 23.

212. Shillony, p. 81.

213. Before this time in the late thirties, military officers had to resign their commissions if appointed to a civil bureau. Robert Spaulding, "Japan's New Bureaucrats, 1932-1945," in Wilson, pp. 56-57.

214. James Crowley, *Japan's Quest for Autonomy: National Security and Foreign Policy, 1930-1938* (Princeton: Princeton University Press, 1966), p. 380.

215. Those who have emphasized the weakness of the Japanese state in the thirties include Maruyama; Robert Butow, *Tojo and the Coming of War* (Princeton: Princeton University Press, 1961); and Yale Maxon, *Control of Japanese Foreign Policy*, 1930-1945 (Berkeley: University of California Press, 1957).

216. T.A. Bisson, "The Zaibatsu's Wartime Role," in *Imperial Japan, 1800-1945*, ed. Jon Livingston, Joe Moore, and Felicia Oldfather (New York: Pantheon, 1973), p. 459.

217. Moore, *Social Origins of Dictatorship and Democracy*, p. 301.

218. Weiker, *The Turkish Revolution*, p. 67.

219. Michael Hyland, "Crisis at the Polls: Turkey's 1969 Elections," *Middle Eastern Journal* 24 (1970): 14.

220. Fidel, p. 607.

221. Tachau and Good, p. 553; Dwight Simpson, "Turkey: A Time of Troubles," *Current History* 62 (January 1972): 51.

222. Moore in *Social Origins of Dictatorship and Democracy* sees German and Japanese history as analogous.

223. George Wilson, "A New Look at the Problem of Japanese Fascism," *Comparative Studies in Society and History* 10 (1965): 405.

224. Kentaro Hayashi, "Japan and Germany in the Interwar Period," in Morley, p. 483.

225. Ibid., p. 486.

226. Wilson, "The Problem of Japanese Fascism," p. 411.

227. German history is remarkable for its lack of revolutionary discontinuity in

the nineteenth century, compared with its great discontinuities in the twentieth century. The Japanese experienced their revolution in the nineteenth century and had a conflictful but continuous political history in the twentieth century until the defeat of 1945.

228. Hayashi, p. 465.

229. Under the German monarchy, aristocrats (mainly landlords) held 65 percent of cabinet posts; under the Weimar Republic they held 12 percent. Maxwell Knight, *The German Executive, 1890-1933* (Stanford: Stanford University Press, 1952).

230. In the 1920s, 29 percent of elected Reichstag deputies in Germany identified themselves as workers. David Shoenbaum, *Hitler's Social Revolution* (New York: Doubleday, 1966), p. 242.

231. Under Hitler "the industrialists made concessions not even demanded of them by a revolutionary socialist party . . . and the Reich was represented by a set of 'new men' compared to whom the revolutionaries of 1792 appear in retrospect like representative of the ancient regime." Ibid., p. 278.

232. In the 1930s "the army capitulated to a civilian administration like no other army in German history." Ibid.

233. Tanin and Yohan, p. 34.

234. Akira Iriye, "The Failure of Military Expansionism," in Crowley, p. 138.

235. Botow, p. 267.

236. Ibid., p. 315.

237. Edwin Reischauer, "What Went Wrong?" in Morley, p. 506.

238. Simpson, "Turkey in a Time of Troubles," p. 43.

239. Ahmed, "The Turkish Guerrillas," p. 14.

Chapter 5
Current Attempts at Revolution from Above: Nasser and the Peruvian Generals

The utility of a model of revolution from above is further validated by examining Nasser's regime in Egypt during 1952-67 and the Peruvian military junta in power from 1968 to the present writing (1975). All analysts of these two military takeovers recognize that they were not ordinary coups. Both Abdul Gamal Nasser and Juan Velasco led military coups which established a stable authoritarian regime, sought national economic autonomy, and initiated basic social and economic change. Both regimes won popular approval through expropriation of a major foreign enterprise which epitomized the nation's economic dependence on Western capitalism—the Suez Canal in Egypt and the International Petroleum Company in Peru. More importantly, these two regimes implemented significant land reform which destroyed the economic and political power of the landed upper class. In so doing, they turned a political and nationalist coup into a social and economic revolution.

It is my contention that the radicalism of—and the limits to—the change initiated by these two military regimes can best be understood through application of a model of revolution from above. Succeeding pages document the close fit between preconditions, processes, and results of revolutions from above in Japan and Turkey and those in Egypt and Peru. I will demonstrate that the autonomy of military bureaucrats from class forces in Egypt and Peru parallelled that in Japan and Turkey; it was the crucial variable in permitting revolution from above. It will show that my specification of the preconditions for revolution from above presents a better theoretical explanation than recent literature on why the military in Third World countries acts to prop up a declining social and economic order or to initiate comprehensive economic and social change.

Consideration of these two new cases also permits me to refine the model and specify how the results of revolution from above are altered by changing historical conditions. Even though military bureaucrats in Egypt and Peru destroyed the landed class and placed significant controls over the rising bourgeoisie, they chose to promote capitalist industrialization without mass mobilization for economic and political change. This produced many of the same failures as revolution from above in Japan and Turkey. Military bureaucrats in Egypt and Peru were more revolutionary in destroying internal blocks to capitalist development, but the increasing external interdependence of the world capitalist system mitigated the impact of their action. Analysis of the weaknesses of revolution from above in Egypt and Peru permits us to specify what alterations in methods would be necessary for future attempts at such revolution. In the concluding chapter, I will try to evaluate whether future revolutions from above are bound to repeat these failures or whether such modification in their methods is possible. I will evaluate both the probability and costs of revolution from above versus revolution from below in the Third World in the last quarter of the twentieth century.

The Process of Revolution from Above in Egypt and Peru

Despite the absence of civil war in Egypt and Peru, the manner in which military bureaucrats displaced the old regime, consolidated their own power, and initiated fundamental social and economic change was very similar to such processes in Japan and Turkey.

Nasser had a charismatic personality, but he was as much a bureaucrat as the Peruvian generals. Although charismatic leaders (like Ataturk and Nasser) may lead a revolution from above, success in consolidating an alternative regime and initiating radical change is based not on personal qualities but on the organizations they lead. One commentator aptly characterized the Nasser coup: "Nasser realized that the success of his coup depended on the extent to which 'good organization men' could be brought into it. Nasser himself and some of his conferees may have been 'rebels' in the Brian Crozier sense, but on down the line there were few or none . . . Nasser had singled out officers who were both serious and in key positions of command; his secret society consisted of these officers. His coup was not a matter of upsetting discipline, but a matter of establishing it. His pre-coup conspiracy was not concerned with building a rebellious force with which to seize power, but with easing officers of his political persuasion into key positions so that they could seize power by issuing orders through ordinary administrative channels."[1]

Even though there were highly sophisticated mass political organizations in Egypt in the 1950s and Peru in the 1960s, these two revolutions from above involved even less mass involvement than those in Japan and Turkey. As in Japan and Turkey, the new military government sought mass legitimacy through nationalist appeal. The Free Officers presented themselves as the first Egyptians in nearly twenty-five hundred years to rule Egypt.[2] After their consolidation of power in the state bureaucracy, the Free Officers outlawed former mass parties and movements of the Right (Moslem Brotherhood), Center (Wafd), and Left (the Communist party). There were some, but not massive, arrests, and little resistance. The Peruvian Junta permitted the continued existence of established parties, unions, and movements, but excluded their leaders from positions of power in new organizations. The military rulers in Egypt and Peru went beyond their Japanese and Turkish counterparts in seeking to organize their own mass organizations. But even when these new organs proved less than successful in mobilizing mass support, there was little mass resistance to the military government. The question remains whether revolutions from above in other settings would face more resistance. Were mass organizations especially weak in Peru and Egypt? Can revolutions from above succeed only when there is little prospect of mass resistance? Or can military bureaucrats in any situation win at least temporary mass assent by their nationalist words and deeds, while they consolidate bureaucratic power which can then be used to control the masses? These questions are important in considering the prospects for revolutions from above in the future. All require research and inquiry.

In all four revolutions from above, military bureaucrats consolidated their political power before initiating social and economic change and before developing an ideology. This pragmatic approach precluded the consolidation of an opposition. Neither foreign powers, the upper classes, nor the masses saw any of these regimes as "radical" in their initial stages. The destruction of traditional political organizations (parliament in both Egypt and Peru, and the monarchy in Egypt) was accomplished slowly, one step at a time. Even after the abolition of some of these political organs, it was unclear how long the military would rule directly and what kind of political order they favored. Some of this ambiguity was the result of a search for new political forms by military leaders; some of it was deliberate obfuscation to prevent the mobilization of an opposition. It was only after they consolidated political power in an authoritarian bureaucracy that Nasser and Velasco moved against the economic interests of the landed upper class.

Destruction of the economic and political power of the landed upper class made the Egyptian and Peruvian regimes revolutionary. Their complete expropriation of landed estates is all the more striking since many landlords in both Egypt and Peru were efficient capitalists growing cash crops for export.[3] Peru's land reform was more radical and more rapid than any in Latin America except Cuba.[4] As in Japan and Turkey these moves against class power were not the result of prior ideological commitment by the coup leaders. Nor were they aimed primarily at redistribution of resources to the peasants and working class. Rather, upper classes were abolished only after the military leaders became convinced that they were an irreconcilable impediment to industrialization.

Yet how could the military regimes initiate these drastic actions against the landed class without provoking violent resistance? The pragmatic style of military bureaucrats in Egypt and Peru, like that of the Meiji oligarchs and Ataturk, confused the conservatives. Landlords were mollified by compensation for their property. In both Egypt and Peru such compensation was in government bonds which would increase in value if invested in industry.[5] As in Japan, such incentives for landlords to become industrialists were not very effective,[6] but they temporarily defused landlord opposition. Yet even if such tactics had not disarmed the landed class, it is unlikely that they could have offered effective resistance.

The traditional classes excluded from power in Japan and Turkey did not have independent control of economic resources they could mobilize for resistance. They did uphold traditional values with which they mobilized some mass support. The brief rise of counterrevolutionary movements in Japan and Turkey was easily crushed by the supreme power of the state. The landed class in Egypt and Peru had control of material resources, but no legitimacy at all with the mass of the population. They had long since lost their legitimacy with peasants, workers, and even the lower middle class through their collaboration with foreign interests and their foreign lifestyle.

A final characteristic of the process of revolution from above in its relatively nonviolent character. All four military regimes used selective repression against right- and left-wing dissidents. In Egypt, landlords were jailed but soon released.[7] A few leaders of the Moslem Brotherhood were hanged and a few communists died of torture in prison, but these were exceptions. All through the fifties and sixties Egyptian leftists were alternatively jailed, released, and sometimes integrated into high positions in the regime.[8] A similar process has been used in Peru: left-wing critics of the regime are jailed or sent into exile, but periodically they are permitted to return.[9] They too are sometimes given positions in the regime. In both Egypt and Peru civil liberties are regularly revoked, but soon reinstated. Thus revolutions from above are not completely repressive nor do they institute a reign of terror.

Preconditions for the Genesis of Revolution from Above in Egypt and Peru

Revolutions from above are possible only in a state where both the military and civilian administration have become highly bureaucratized. Although both Egypt and Peru—like Japan and Turkey— possessed traditional polities based on patrimonial bureaucracy, military leaders in these two countries did not have the aristocratic status of the Meiji oligarchs or even Ataturk. Nasser and Velasco did not see themselves as the saviors of a polity with a continuing tradition of greatness. Rather they were out to restore some measure of dignity and autonomy to small countries whose traditions had been altered by long periods of direct and indirect imperialist control. It is not the aristocratic or elitist nature of state functionaries that is a precondition for revolution from above, but their degree of bureaucratization. Countries without a strong state based on patrimonial bureaucracy will still have the potential for revolution from above after the institutionalization of a modern bureaucratic polity. A tradition of patrimonial bureaucracy may indirectly facilitate this potential, however, through its impact on the class structure. To the extent that patrimonial states weakened the corporate organization of landlords, they facilitate the creation of an autonomous military bureaucracy necessary for revolution from above. Patrimonialism may also weaken the cohesion of groups that could make a revolution from below.[10]

Given a bureaucratic state, study of Japanese and Turkish history led to the hypothesis that five conditions are necessary and sufficient to generate revolutionaries from within the top ranks of the military (and often civil) administration. Four of these conditions are satisfied in Egypt and Peru prior to the military coups which turned revolutionary. Let us examine each of the four factors.

Bureaucratic Autonomy from Class Domination Military bureaucrats have the potential for leading a revolution from above (as distinct from a coup d'etat which merely changes the political structure) when the officer class—or a significant segment of it—is independent of those classes which control the means of production. Military bureaucrats are autonomous in this sense when they are not recruited from the dominant landed, commercial, or industrial classes; and when they do not form close personal and economic ties with these classes after their elevation to high office. Even in parliamentary systems controlled by such class interests (as in Peru and Egypt), military officers have the potential for breaking this institutional subordination by force.[11]

In both Peru and Egypt the civil bureaucracy, especially at its highest levels, was recruited from and maintained close personal and economic ties to the landed oligarchy and the rising bourgeoisie which fused with the landed class.[12] As a result, civil bureaucrats never initiated or supported radical action in Peru and Egypt. We have seen that the active collaboration and support of nonmilitary bureaucrats was an integral part of revolution from above in Japan and Turkey. Yet military bureaucrats in Egypt and Peru were able to implement revolutions without such support. This was true for several reasons. The higher level of modernization by the mid–twentieth century in Peru and Egypt permitted military bureaucrats to recruit autonomous technocrats from outside the civil bureaucracy. They also found support among lower-level officials who had been recruited on merit into the vast civil service of the two countries. Despite class domination of the civil bureaucracy in Peru and Egypt, the possibility of revolution from above was preserved by the weakness of the landed class in both countries and the autonomy of the military bureaucracy from class ties.

For at least the past hundred years, neither the landed class in Egypt nor Peru has been a true ruling class. In neither country was there the equivalent of a "Junker"-controlled state. A class of large private landowners has only existed since the 1840s in Egypt, and by that time Egypt was subject to imperialist control of its polity.[13] The Peruvian landed oligarchy was of longer traditional standing, and Peru has been technically independent for the past century. Yet the weak class organization of the Peruvian landed oligarchy is evidenced by the fact that it never organized a major conservative party.[14] Nor did it try to gain direct control over the military. Even after its incorporation of urban capitalists, the Peruvian oligarchy was content to work behind the scenes to manipulate the parties in parliament and various military rulers.[15] It also condoned similar manipulation by imperialist powers and foreign businessmen.[16]

The Egyptian officer corps did not begin to develop autonomy until after 1936. Before that time it was either under the direction of the British or commanded by officers from a landed upper-class background. Nasser and many of the Free Officers were members of one of the first officer classes recruited from a wider social base. By the late 1940s most of the middle- and lower-rank officers were without traditional links to the ruling class.[17] In 1948 two-thirds of the Egyptian officers were sons of salaried officials—army officers, middle-grade civil servants, and free professionals. They were drawn from the same social background as Egypt's intellectuals and thought of themselves as "intellectuals in uniform." The remaining third of the officer class were mainly sons of small farmers who lived and worked their land (in contrast to the large landowner).[18] Of the one hundred families which owned the largest estates in Egypt,[19] thirty were represented in Parliament in 1942-52, eighteen provided cabinet ministers in 1924-50, but none provided an army officer.[20]

The Peruvian military has a somewhat longer history of autonomy. The oligarchy has traditionally looked down on the military and refused to mix socially.[21] The Peruvian military has long recruited most of its officers from lower-middle-class provincial families, while the social and economic upper class lives on the coast.[22] More importantly, there were few social and economic ties between the military elite and the social and economic upper class. Military officers did not belong to the most exclusive social clubs in Peru, nor did they sit on the boards of directors of the largest corporations. "Of the 630 men who in 1963 belonged to the boards of directors and top management of the 86 largest business enterprises in Peru, only four were military men and only these four had ever served in the military."[23] The divorce between the military and financial-industrial circles also holds true in large agriculture. "None of the 51 members of the board of the National Agrarian Society in 1963 was a military man. Similarily, fewer than 1% of the member of the exclusive Club Nacional were military officers."[24]

Such class autonomy of military bureaucrats provides the potential for their radicalization. On the one hand, their status and fortune depends on a strong state, which necessitates industrialization. On the other hand, they will not personally suffer from the abolition of the existing economic structure. Yet such autonomy alone will not guarantee the precipitation of revolution from above. For years, the autonomous Peruvian military upheld the economic interests of the landed oligarchy and their urban bourgeois supporters despite the social and economic chasm between them. Other conditions are necessary to generate a revolution from above.

Politicization of the Military Bureaucracy

As bureaucrats, military officers are trained to be specialized professionals working in a hierarchy and isolated from general political concerns. As in Japan and Turkey, however, important segments of the Egyptian and Peruvian military became politicized and developed specific ideas on how to deal with the crises of their countries. In all four countries, this politicization was linked to the decay of traditional military functions and in some cases (Turkey and Egypt) to military defeat. Like the samurai, the Peruvian and Egyptian armies had not fought a foreign enemy for many years. From 1899 to 1948, the Egyptian army did not fire a single shot, and then it was ignobly defeated in the Palestinian War (analogous to the Turkish defeats in World War I).[25] In Peru, the heavy reliance on U.S. military aid and training increased officer frustration. They knew Peru would never remotely approach U.S. military strength, while any armed outbreak in Latin America would be controlled by the United States. Thus the morale and status of these armies depended upon finding a new function. National liberation through nation building became the alternative. For example, the Peruvian army by 1960 contained more engineers than cavalrymen. "Modern military skills were not very relevant to Peru, but the army was a reservoir of technical and organization skills for national development."[26] In order to put their skills to use in a constructive way, they first had to engineer political change. Hence their politicization. The Free Officers existed as a political group planning the future Egyptian state for at least three years before their coup, and many of them individually had become politicized much earlier. All through the 1960s, the advanced training school for Peruvian officers (CAEM) examined the problem of economic development and developed antiimperialist views.[27]

The Rise of Nationalist Movements from Below

Revolutions from above are national revolutions precipitated in response to international threats to national autonomy. In all four countries, the international threat was reflected in the rise of mass movements *within* the country demanding an end to national degradation.

The Muslim Brotherhood movement in Egypt and the Aprista movement in Peru were very similar to the Loyalist Movement which preceded the Meiji Restoration and the Young Ottoman and Young Turk movements in Turkey. Like the Loyalists and Young Turks, the Muslim Brotherhood and the APRA (American Popular Revolutionary Alliance) party were led by discontented elements of the middle class—downwardly mobile members of religious or aristocratic families whose social position was deteriorating in the face of modernization, and upwardly mobile students and bureaucrats with frustrated ambitions.[28] These two movements attracted the rural middle class, but unlike the Loyalists and Young Turks, they also won some urban working-class support. All these movements gave primary emphasis to cultural reform—the revitalization and renovation of traditional culture (Islamic and Inca) combined with a xenophobic rejection of Western values.[29] The Muslim Brotherhood and APRA, like the Loyalists and Young Ottomans, sought a conservative transition to modernization through the acceptance of only Western technology and science.[30] All these movements encouraged acts of individual terrorism against foreigners and Westernized government officials, while also negotiating behind the scenes with those in power. Neither the Muslim Brotherhood nor APRA ever envisioned a revolutionary takeover of power.[31]

In Japan, Turkey, and Egypt there was a direct connection between these nationalist movements based on traditional values and subsequent revolutions from above. Many of the Meiji oligarchs, Ataturk elite, and Free Officers participated in these movements earlier in their lives.[32] In Peru, an armed clash between the army and APRA in 1932 in which 200 soldiers were killed established a permanent emnity between the two. This hostility undoubtedly delayed a revolution from above in Peru until the military's contact with rural guerrilla movements in the mid 1960s.[33]

It is unlikely that autonomous military bureaucrats would become as politicized or as ready to take revolutionary action without the push of violence and disruption from below. As pointed out in chapter 3, military bureaucrats with ties to vested interests have reacted to nationalist movements with conservative repression. It is only bureaucrats without such vested interests who react positively to such nationalism by replacing movements from below by their own more rational revolutions from above.

The Opportunity for International Maneuver The international situations to which the Egyptian and Peruvian military reacted in promulgating a revolution from above were quite different from those faced by their Japanese and Turkish counterparts. Japan and Turkey were independent nations threatened by direct military takeover by an imperialist power. Egypt and Peru were technically independent, but had been subject to years of direct economic penetration and more indirect political and military dominance by Western powers. Military radicals in Egypt and Peru sought to regain national autonomy in an international arena that was more highly structured to their disadvantage than that faced by Japan or even Turkey. Yet even here there was room for maneuver. The decline of British imperial power and the cold war between the United States and the Soviet Union permitted Nasser to nationalize the Suez Canal, expropriate all large foreign business, and take a leading role in forming a third block of nonaligned nations. America's defeat in Vietnam, its preoccupation with the Middle East, and continuing rivalry between the West and the Soviet Union permitted the Peruvian generals to nationalize the International Petroleum Company and other American businesses with only minor economic and political retaliation from the United States. In both countries, it was these acts symbolizing the rebirth of national autonomy that won popular acclaim for the military governments.

The Declining Need for a Provincial Power Base Successful revolutions from above in Japan and Turkey necessitated the creation of a countergovernment in the provinces and a short civil war before the defeat of the old regime. In contrast, military radicals in Egypt and Peru staged a coup at the center which did not involve civil war. It can be hypothesized that the greater decentralization of semifeudal Japan and the heterogeneous Ottoman Empire made a provincial power base necessary for revolution from above. The prior consolidation of a centralized and relatively homogeneous nation-state in Egypt and Peru abrogated this prerequisite. Hence this fifth factor is no longer a necessary precondition for revolution from above.

Comparison with Other Theories on the Preconditions for Radicalization of the Military The preceding analysis posits four conditions that are necessary and sufficient to generate revolutionary action by military bureaucrats in a late-developing nation-state which has established effective central control. Military elites may stage coups and intervene in politics when one or more of these conditions are absent, but such political action will either maintain the given social and economic structure or attempt to restore a declining order. A military coup will promote revolutionary change only when a significant segment of the military bureaucracy is: (a) autonomous (in recruitment and structure) from those classes which control the means of production; (b) politicized around an ideology of nation building; (c) threatened by nationalist movements from below; and (d) faced with contradictions in the international power constellation which can be exploited to increase national autonomy.

Many students of the military in developing nations have tried to specify the social and political factors which promote military intervention in politics; fewer studies have attacked the question of why the military intervene to uphold the status quo or transform it. Most of the latter works hypothesize one factor that determines whether military coups are progressive or reactionary. Let us briefly review a few of these studies in order to demonstrate the superior analytic thrust of the four-factor hypothesis advanced above.

One set of theorists sees current military coups in Third World countries as either entirely progressive or conservative. José Nun predicts that all coups in Latin America defend the status quo.[34] Nun postulates that the military in all Latin American countries have close ties to the middle class and act to preserve the conservative interests of this bourgeoisie. According to Nun, the Latin American middle class is opposed to industrialization and basic social change because of its economic and social ties to the landed oligarchy which exports primary products.[35] Nun generalizes only for Latin America; he recognizes Nasserism as progressive. Writing before 1968, he concluded that a Nasserist coup was impossible in Latin America.[36] Nun was unable to predict the Peruvian revolution from above because of inadequacies in his theory. He looked only at the social origins of the military and not at the diverse manner in which the military as a bureaucratic organization could relate to class structure in different Latin American countries.

In contrast to Nun, Morris Janowitz predicts that all military coups in the Third World will be progressive; Manfred Halpern posits the same thesis for all Middle Eastern military intervention. Like Nun, they see the military as representative of the new middle class.[37] Unlike him, they view this class as antagonistic to the landed oligarchy and supportive of industrialization.[38] My contention is that the nature of the middle class is irrelevant. Recruiting army officers from this class does not automatically make the military represent middle-class interests.[39] The class interests (if any) of a military bureaucracy can only be determined by examining the economic and social ties that socially mobile officers develop once they have achieved elite positions. Neither Janowitz nor Halpern present such an analysis.

Like Nun, Janowitz, and Halpern, Irving Louis Horowitz makes generalizations about the role of the military in the Third World. In contrast to them, he denotes both progressive and conservative (positive and negative) attributes of military rule, and notes that the military can perform a distinct role in different countries.[40] But Horowitz presents no analytic concepts which permit us to predict when a military regime will be conservative or when it will promote economic, political, and social change.

Samuel Huntington develops a seemingly more sophisticated theory recognizing the possibility of both conservative and radical coups in the Third World. Whether the army plays a progressive or reactionary role depends primarily on the level of political modernization as defined by the degree of civilian participation in politics. In the "oligarchic" phase of limited citizen participation, personal military strongmen do not attempt to change the structure of political power and economic rewards, but only seek to assure their own personal benefit. Radical coups occur during a time of expanding middle-class participation. After mass political participation is achieved, a military coup will be repressive.[41] Huntington's analysis is a variation of the Janowitz and Halpern theses. He too sees the military as tied to middle-class interests which are basically progressive. The evidence in this book refutes Huntington's simplistic thesis. It is possible for a military apparatus to develop class autonomy. Military radicalism developed in both "oligarchic" Japan and in "middle-class" Egypt. The Peruvian Junta deposed a very middle-class regime.

Two other students of the military in developing nations, Alan Stepan and Abraham Lowenthal, recognize that bureaucratization of the military permits the creation of an interest cohesion which promotes military autonomy. In focusing on the internal processes of the military, however, they completely abandon a class analysis. Lowenthal predicts that the military will promote progressive social and economic action as long as this does not threaten their own corporate autonomy. In a period of mass participation, therefore, military rule will be "restrictive and regressive."[42] Alan Stepan stresses the similarities between the Brazilian and Peruvian armies in their internal bureaucratic development. Both armies are simultaneously highly professional and highly political. Both recruit primarily from the lower middle class. But Stepan never considers comparing the economic and social relationship of the military elite to the powerful classes in Brazil and Peru preceding the initiation of military government. He reverts to an ad hoc explanation for the conservatism of the Brazilian military compared to their Peruvian counterpart. He asserts that the private business sector in Brazil was so large, dynamic, and advanced, that the Brazilian military could not consider running the economy alone. In contrast, the Peruvian officers could cope with the smaller and less dynamic Peruvian economy.[43] Of course the opposite argument makes as much sense: How could the Peruvian army alone hope to overcome the greater economic stagnation and backwardness of Peru?

In contrast to other theorists, Alain Rouguie develops a multifactor analysis of how both national and international conditions structure the outcome of military coups. He tries to explain the rise of progressive or radical military regimes in Peru, Bolivia, and Panama in the late sixties and early seventies in contrast to the earlier conservatism of Latin American coups. He hypothesizes that recent changes in the international system provide room for more progressive action by all Latin American military rulers. Although he believes that these "external contingencies are the decisive variable,"[44] he also stresses the importance of intranational conditions. He predicts the revival of reformist militarism under the following conditions: (a) in socially unstable countries; (b) in societies where the weakness of the middle classes leaves the military great flexibility; (c) in economies of substantial external dependence; (d) in countries where the armed forces were most financially dependent on the United States; and (e) in countries where the state was politically weak and financially poor.[45] These reasons are theoretically vague and empirically unsupportable. Certainly both Brazil and Peru meet conditions (a), (b), and (c). Almost all Third World countries meet a number of these conditions. While I agree with Rouguie's contention that contradictions in the international system enhanced the possibility of radical military action in the Third World, I believe that it is only military bureaucrats who maintain class autonomy and develop ideological integration who will be able to lead revolutions from above.[46] Further comparative research must determine whether the hypothesis advanced in the present study stands up any better than these attempts at explanation.

Results of Revolution from Above in Egypt and Peru

Military bureaucrats in Egypt and Peru initiated radical action against class forces that exceeded the measures taken by their Japanese and Turkish counterparts. They avoided the Turkish trap of institutionalizing a liberal parliamentary and party structure that could be used later by conservative landlords and a bourgeoisie tied to external capital to thwart industrialization. Yet the long-term results of these two revolutions from above appear to be even more disappointing than those in Japan and Turkey.

In contrast to most other military rulers in the Third World today, Nasser and Velasco established relatively stable authoritarian regimes. Authoritarian structures in Japan and Turkey depoliticized the masses through ideological manipulation. But the greater urbanization and breakdown of traditional social structures in Egypt and Peru required the creation of new political organs which could channel and control political participation. Revolutions from above in Egypt and Peru, unlike those in Japan and Turkey, attempted to create *corporate* political structures. This corporatism promoted more social welfare measures than the Meiji and Ataturk states, but it was equally inimical to the values of democratic participation and social equality. Corporatism depoliticized the mass of the population.

Military bureaucrats in Egypt and Peru sought to move their countries from dependent suppliers of raw materials and primary products to an industrializing nation. As in Japan, Nasser and Velasco sought to use the state apparatus to foster a capitalist bourgeoisie without mobilizing the mass of the population. This commitment to capitalist industrialization undermined their attempts at autonomous development. As in Japan, industrialization in Egypt and Peru remained dependent upon the more advanced capitalist countries. The policy of capitalist industrialization also undermined the autonomy of the state bureaucracy and created a more conservative political coalition of bureaucrats with an urban and rural capitalist bourgeoisie. The inequities of dependent capitalist development and the conservatism of a bureaucratic class coalition seems to be undermining both the political stability and the industrialization goals of Egypt and Peru. Let us examine some of these problems in Egypt and Peru in more detail.

Consolidation of Military Supremacy in an Authoritarian-Bureaucratic State

Military bureaucrats in Egypt and Peru like those in Japan and Turkey consolidated their political power in the civil bureaucracy.[47] In both countries, large numbers of military bureaucrats resigned their military posts to accept cabinet posts, along with high, and even middle, positions in a number of civilian ministries.[48] But the top levels of the civil bureaucracy in Egypt and Peru were tied to class interests and hence were more conservative than civil servants in Japan and Turkey. As a result, military bureaucrats recruited a number of technical experts from outside government to provide innovative ideas and to help consolidate their rule over the bureaucracy.[49] In this way, they created an autonomous technocratic elite to rule the country.[50]

As in Japan and Turkey the poorest and most backward sectors of the population were completely excluded from the revolution in Egypt and Peru. Neither the rural Indians in Peru nor the peasant masses in Egypt were ideologically or organizationally incorporated into the modern polity, even in a subordinate role.[51] Like the Japanese and Turkish revolutions from above, the Nasser and Velasco regimes reinforced traditional agrarian ideological and social structures.

Ideological manipulation alone, however, could not control urban industrial workers, rural wage workers on large plantations, and the salaried middle class. Their depoliticization required the creation of bureaucratic organs to replace outlawed political parties and unions. To this end, .the military regimes sought to create corporate structures. Corporatism seeks to integrate economic interest groups into the hierarchical organization of the state so as to break up and prevent the consolidation of conscious and well-organized classes. All the workers, managers, and owners at each work place are organized into a communal organization ("a corporation") in which they supposedly share decision making. The corporation also tries to channel their requests and complaints to the appropriate government agency. The state bureaucracy manipulates these corporations through: "co-optation of leaders; vertical or sectoral policy compartmentalization; permanent institutionalization of access; legalization of group conflicts through labor and administrative courts; state technocratic planning and resource allocation; extensive development of functionally specialized para-state agencies; political culture stressing formalism, consensus and continuous bargaining; symbiotic relation with clientist and patrimonialist practices; deliberate narrowing and encapsulating of 'relevant publica'; and periodic but systematic use of physical repression and anticipatory intimidation."[52] In other countries, bureaucratic party organs have been used to politicize and mobilize the mass of the population. Corporate bureaucracies seek to depoliticize and deactivate the masses. As Schmitter remarks: "Corporatism involves the process whereby state executive power becomes progressively more independent from accountability to organized social groups, that Marx so long ago suggested was the crucial element in modern authoritarian rule."[53] Let us examine the development of corporatism in Peru and its less successful counterpart in Egypt.

Two and one-half years after their coup, the Peruvian junta created a new bureaucratic organization to stimulate the development of local corporate units. This agency, the National System for the Support of Social Mobilization (SINAMOS) absorbed eight previous state agencies. Its declared purpose was to carry out "responsible" and "constructive" mobilization.[54] It is significant that it was created only after the regime withdrew its support from spontaneous mass organizations formed to support the revolution. The junta feared that the Committees for the Defense of the Revolution could not be controlled.[55] Of equal significance is the fact that SINAMOS concentrated its efforts on creating cooperative and industrial committees in the more urban and prosperous areas of the country among those workers who were the most organized and most politicized.[56]

The "nonmobilizing" purposes of this national system for mobilization can also be seen in its operational style. While the junta drew some middle-class ex–guerrilla leaders and former left-wing political organizers into the SINAMOS national bureaucracy,[57] all union and party leaders were excluded from leadership in the local industrial communities. This meant that the most qualified working-class leaders were eliminated from participation.[58] Rather, the industrial communities were presented as places where workers and management could work together like a family for the benefit of the company.[59] The private owners of all industries included in the plan are required to reinvest 15 percent of their net profits every year until workers own 50 percent of the enterprise. At this time, workers will be given 50 percent of the seats on the board of directors.[60] As critics have pointed out, the rate of worker coownership depends on the ability of firms to generate profits.[61] But capitalist profits are based on the extraction of surplus value from workers' labor. Thus these industrial communities seek to win worker acquiescence in their own exploitation.

SINAMOS also seeks to restrict mass participatory activity narrowly to the work place,[62] while channeling all mass dissatisfaction into bargaining within the local and national bureaucracy.[63] It tries to limit citizen participation to "the way in which a decision is implemented, but does not provide the opportunity to intervene in the decision-making process itself."[64] SINAMOS doctrine expounds the idea that participation in the local work place and neighborhood is training for political participation at the national level. Yet it provides no mechanisms for making this transition.[65] It is true, however, that the corporate government "through the presence of diverse social and political forces within its administrative orbit, is far more representative of the plurality of social groups in Peruvian society than any other previous regime."[66] When Peruvian workers have staged spontaneous protests against controls in the system, the corporate system has been flexible enough to back down and allow a bit more local participation.[67] Such flexibility has not damaged its overall control.

The contradiction in this system of political control in Peru is that it is also meant to act as a stimulus for the development process.[68] The Peruvian regime desires to control the masses, but also mobilize their effort for industrialization.[69] These are incompatible aims. Most of the evidence indicates that SINAMOS has been quite successful at inducing worker apathy (depoliticization) and unsuccessful at mobilizing heroic mass effort for the government's development plans. Effective mobilization requires either much more citizen participation or much more coercion than corporatism permits. Noncoercive mobilization also requires concrete evidence that the worker or his children will benefit from the heroic effort.

It took the Egyptian regime longer to develop a corporate form. The mass corporate party (the Arab Socialist Union) they finally settled on does not seem as effective as Peruvian corporatism. Nasser, like Velasco, did not consider creating organs to channel mass political participation until some years after taking power.[70] He then initiated three different party structures (and dissolved the first two) in less than ten years. All three of these parties—the Liberation Rally, the National Union, and the Arab Socialist Union—had mobilization ideologies, but all served in practice to eliminate opposition, to prevent prior political groups from regaining strength, and to depoliticize the masses.[71] The first party failed because it had no skilled cadres committed to the revolution and trained in organizational techniques. Nor "did it possess the aura of nationalist legitimacy that surrounds a party of a movement proven and tested in struggle."[72] The second party remained "merely a bureaucracy with few links to the people."[73] Finally, the Arab Socialist Union (ASU) developed the corporatist principle of "vertical segmentation of the people by professional activity to prevent their unification from below on the basis of class interest."[74] In urban areas, the local units of ASU are formed in the work place. Unlike SINAMOS in Peru, ASU also builds rural units among the peasants. But here the party relies on natural corporation by reinforcing the traditional leader's power and authority in the village.[75] The corporatist function of ASU is also seen in its lack of decision-making power at the national level. Such power remained in the administrative bureaucracy centered in the Nasser cabinet. One commentator put it well: "The ASU is not a vanguard for recruiting top political leadership, but a rearguard for retiring it."[76] Nasser used appointment to a top position in ASU as a way to ease bureaucrats out of power. As in Peru, a few former leftist leaders were coopted into the ASU bureaucracy, but only after the dissolution of the Egyptian CP in 1965.[77] Their recruitment also occurred at a time when a few ASU leaders sought to create a truly mobilizing party. In 1965-67 there was an attempt to improve the ASU hierarchy and train professional political cadres. But this emphasis lasted only two years. After Egypt's disastrous defeat in the war of 1967, Nasser reverted to a strict emphasis on political control through ASU.[78] Even during the liberal years "at no time was there any thought of allowing the urban and rural workers to make their political desires known directly or to organize themselves into parties to work for the achievement of a program of their own within the framework of 'national action.'"[79] As in Peru, the corporate structures of ASU successfully depoliticized the masses.[80] Mass apathy in the 1960s was much greater than before 1952.[81] But neither ASU nor the Peruvian SINAMOS mobilized mass enthusiasm and commitment for the rigorous tribulations of autonomous industrialization. I shall now investigate the implications of this for economic growth.

Contradictions in the Process of Capitalist Development Nasser and the Egyptian military and technical bureaucracy consciously chose to emulate the Japanese model of development.[82] There are similarities between the economic initiatives of the Meiji oligarchs and those taken by military bureaucrats in Egpyt and Peru. Both the Nasser and Velasco regimes espoused the desire for autonomous industrialization of their nations and tried to break out of imperialist economic control. Both succeeded only in renegotiating the terms of their dependence on the advanced capitalist countries.

STATE INITIATIVE IN FOSTERING AUTONOMOUS CAPITALIST DEVELOPMENT As in Japan, the Egyptian and Peruvian state bureaucracy took the initiative in raising capital for industrial development. But the constraints on industrialization in the mid–twentieth century were far greater than those on Japan one hundred years earlier. To a greater extent than even in Turkey, the economy of these two countries was integrated into the international capitalist market. Capitalist relations of production were much more advanced in Egypt and Peru than they were in Japan and Turkey prior to their revolutions from above. Not only had foreign capital entered Egypt and Peru in large amounts, but in both countries large landowners had become capitalist farmers producing cash crops for export. They were allied with a small group of commercial and industrial capitalists who worked closely with foreign capitalists.[83] Because the combined forces of agricultural, commercial, industrial, and foreign capitalists had failed to spur sustained economic development in Egypt and Peru, modernizing bureaucrats had much less faith in private capitalists than did their Japanese and Turkish counterparts.

Yet in the beginning of their revolutions, Nasser and the Peruvian military government also tried to create a class of private entrepreneurial capitalists.[84] It was only after their moral and material incentives to private capitalists to spur industrial investments proved ineffective that state bureaucrats in Egypt and Peru moved to expropriate increasing numbers of foreign and native-owned businesses. In 1962 Nasser nationalized all banks, insurance companies, and heavy industry. Soon he expropriated 228 more companies. By 1963, 80 percent of all industry was in the public sector.[85] During their first four years in power, the Peruvian junta "purchased or expropriated most telephone assets, majority control of T.V. stations, much of the importing, exporting, and distribution of food and other basic commodities, a large part of banking and railroad industries, much metals mining, refining and marketing, the reinsurance function, and the sugar industry."[86] In 1973 and 1974 other important industries were nationalized, while the economic plan for 1975-78 calls for further diminution of the private sector.[87]

Unlike the Meiji oligarchs, Nasser and Velasco had no intention of turning state industries back to private capitalists once they became productive. They did not try to build the equivalent of the Japanese zaibatsu—large private cartels which combined banking and industry. Rather, the Egyptian and Peruvian military regimes sought to break up the beginnings of such complexes, all of which were closely tied to foreign capital.

The state therefore came to play an even more important role in Egypt's and Peru's attempts at industrialization than in Japan and Turkey. Revolutions from above in Egypt and Peru tried to change a dependent capitalist economy into an autonomous state capitalism. Fifteen years after Nasser's coup, 85 percent of gross capital formation and 70 percent of savings to finance it came from the state.[88] Five years after the Velasco coup, the state was responsible for about 50 percent of net investments in Peru.[89] Eventually, Nasser proclaimed Egypt a socialist economy and Velasco called Peru a communitarian society, neither capitalist nor communist. Both regimes fostered state capitalist economies which retained elements of primitive and private capitalism. State capitalism modified the market and productive systems, but did not eliminate private profit, the market, or conditions of wage labor. The government regulated imports, exports, and investments; it set some wage and salary rates and regulated prices of some raw materials and food stuffs. But the state still used market and price mechanisms to distribute consumer goods. Profit remained the indicator of success in both public and private enterprise.[90]

CREATION OF A DEPENDENT CAPITALIST ECONOMY Despite the ability to generate its own capital and prevent foreign investment, Japan's economic development was distorted by dependence on advanced capitalist economies for heavy machinery and raw materials. Egypt and Peru never broke their dependence on foreign capital. Neither the Nasser nor Velasco regime tried to mobilize the capital for industrial investment solely from internal sources. Neither regime taxed the peasants in the Meiji manner. Even if they had tried it is improbable that they could have duplicated the success of the Meiji regime in channeling resources from agriculture into industry. Egyptian and Peruvian agriculture did not produce a surplus equivalent to that of Japanese agriculture in the nineteenth century. To raise most of their capital internally, revolutions from above today would have to mobilize mass support for a vast productive effort combined with the sacrifice of immediate consumer fulfillment. Neither the Nasser nor Velasco regime chose to implement such mass mobilization. As a result, they had to rely on continuing foreign investment.

Both countries tried to diversify their foreign investment—borrowing and accepting private investment from Europe, Japan, the United States, the Soviet Union, and Eastern Europe.[91] They complemented this by trading with a number of countries instead of primarily with one, and by controls over private capital. For example, the military government in Peru requires foreign investors to submit to the requirements of state plans for industrial development. They are given a fixed term of investment (fifteen to twenty years), after which their industries will be taken over by the state. They are also subject to fixed profit rates.[92]

Despite these attempts at diversification, neither Egypt nor Peru broke out of their integration into a dependent position in the world capitalist economy. Egypt severed its dependence on Western investment by becoming a client of the Soviet Union. Egypt's attempt to break this Soviet dependence in the early 1970s led to a new influx of private capital from the West.[93] In the past few years, the Peruvian regime also increased the inflow of private capital. "How can the Peruvian government continue to promise 'independence' as the revolutionary reward while struggling to woo foreign capital in amounts unprecedented in the country's history?"[94]

Dependence on foreign capital was accompanied by other elements of economic dependency. Both the Egyptian and Peruvian economies remained geared to export rather than to the development of internal markets. Both countries remain dependent suppliers of raw materials to the international market. Both countries are dependent on the advanced countries for the import of heavy machinery. Industrialization in Egypt and Peru is confined to light consumer industries. Egypt, for example, imported sophisticated weaponry from the Soviet Union in exchange for Egyptian cotton and sugar.[95] Neither regime has tried to modernize agriculture. Nasser and Velasco expropriated (and then managed) large agricultural plantations which had already been capitalized to produce cash crops for the market. But neither regime has paid much attention to transforming the position of small farmers and peasants. As in Japan and Turkey, dependent industrialization in Egypt and Peru has not improved the living standard of the mass of the population. This retards the development of a home market. Neither Egypt nor Peru has industrialized enough to become a subimperialist power. But both regimes have sought external markets through some economic control over the regions outside their boundaries. Nasser's union of Egypt and Syria opened up a large new market for Egyptian industry.[96] And Peru under Velasco took the initiative in forming the Andean common market.

It is not clear whether either Egypt or Peru will be successful enough at industrialization to become a subimperialist power. Only a breakdown in the world capitalist economy will permit them to duplicate the Japanese process of industrialization. Even if this happened, the costs of dependent capitalist development will be very high in human terms.

Contradictions Between Autonomous Bureaucrats and Class Forces
The need for a class base to stabilize an authoritarian regime in Japan and Turkey led bureaucratic revolutionaries to share political power with a class of rural and eventually urban capitalists. But as the bureaucrats in Japan and Turkey formed closer ties to class interests, they also became conservative and lost the reforming zeal they had as autonomous revolutionaries. They maintained political hegemony and defeated challenges from the lower middle class to state power, but they could not find truly innovative and effective solutions to the internal and external social and economic problems that inevitably plague late-developing states.

Military bureaucrats in Egypt and Peru buttressed their autonomy by taking more control over the economy and by creating corporate controls over the masses. By sponsoring capitalist development, they created the economic base for a rising bourgeois class. While they destroyed the economic base of large landowners, both Nasser and Velasco used land reform to increase the economic and social power of small independent farmers (rich peasants) who produced for the market.[97] This class did not in any way challenge the political autonomy of the military bureaucrats,[98] but their economic and social power blocked further radicalization of the regimes. The rural bourgeoisie opposed socialist development. As a class of small individual capitalists producing for the internal market, these peasant farmers provide a potential ally for the reemergence of an independent class of industrial capitalists. The large number of small independent farmers committed to traditional values provides a potential mass that could be mobilized against the modernizing goals of the revolution.[99] Expropriation of export industries weakened the prerevolutionary commercial capitalists in Egypt and Peru, but state capitalism has created the organizational base for a "new class."

There is some indication that state managers in Egypt are expropriating profits for their personal use. If this corruption becomes widespread, the new class is likely to become a private bourgeoisie, using the profits gained through corruption to invest in private property. They will try to undermine the extension of state capitalism in favor of a return to private enterprise linked to foreign capital.[100] Opposition to this tendency in Egypt arose among top bureaucrats in ASU and in a leftist-Nasserist military faction, who wanted to move in a more radical socialist direction. After Nasser's death, Sadat's support of the new bourgeoisie has undermined this autonomous opposition. But Sadat's attempt to consolidate an independent bourgeoisie still faces resistance from the masses: "The Egyptian people are well acquainted with their political past: land reform and anti-imperialist campaigns have had their full support. It will be difficult for Sadat to convince them that restoring land to large landholders, reviving the private sector, or encouraging foreign investment are positive steps, especially when they see that the new policies fail to raise the standard of living of the Egyptian masses."[101] As in Japan and Turkey, the increasing economic power of a capitalist class tied to a dependent position in the world capitalist system is likely to inspire political conflict and instability in Egypt—conflict which will increase state support of the bourgeoisie by more authoritarian controls over the people.

Observers have also predicted the rise of a new class in Peru, with the power "to control and appropriate the vast resources at the disposal of state capitalism in association with the large international monopolies."[102]

These four revolutions from above have not resolved the technical problem of how to industrialize in a world economy controlled by those nations which industrialized in an earlier era. Nor have they tried to humanize the development process. I have argued that the reluctance of military bureaucrats to actively mobilize the population is the primary limitation in their attempts to foster autonomous industrialization. Without such mobilization there is no chance that these countries will break out of their economic dependency. Is there any possibility that future revolutions from above in the Third World will be more successful? The "Conclusion" will try to answer this question.

Notes

1. Miles Copeland, *The Game of Nations* (London: Weidenfeld & Nicholson, 1969), pp. 68, 66.

2. Eliezer Beeri, *Army Officers in Arab Politics and Society* (New York: Praeger, 1970), p. 423.

3. The fact that both the Nasser and Velasco regimes acted against the private economic interests of capitalist landlords and industrialists differentiates these

revolutions from above from Prussian history. Nasser and Velasco expropriated their "Junkers": they did not form an alliance with the large landed class. It is my contention that social scientists who draw a parallel between either Nasser or Velasco and Bismarck are incorrect. For two attempts to draw such analogies see: Amos Perlmutter, Egypt: *The Praetorian State* (New Brunswick: Transaction Books, 1974), p. 59; and James Petras and Robert LaPorte, *Cultivating Revolutions* (New York: Vintage, 1971), p. 285.

4. Abraham Lowenthal, "Peru's Ambiguous Revolution," *Foreign Affairs* 52 (July 1974): 806.

5. Patrick O'Brien, *The Revolution in Egypt's Economic System* (New York: Oxford University Press, 1966), p. 210; David Scott Palmer, *Revolution from Above: Military Government and Popular Participation in Peru, 1968–1972* (Ithaca: Cornell University Press, 1974), p. 59.

6. After 1964 in Egypt all land was made state property and all remaining compensation due to the ex-landowners was cancelled. O'Brien, p. 210.

7. Anouar Abdel-Malek, *Egypt: Military Society* (New York: Vintage, 1968), p. 161.

8. Ibid., p. 116.

9. For the sixth anniversary of the revolution, the Peruvian government released a number of detained union leaders and political activists. *Latin America*, October 4, 1974.

10. There is much controversy over the degree and causes of weaknesses in mass organization at the time of the Nasser and Velasco coups. For one attempt to link such weaknesses to political traditions see Clement Henry Moore, "Authoritarian Politics in Unincorporated Society: The Case of Nasser's Egypt," *Comparative Politics* 6 (January 1974).

11. In Japan and Turkey bureaucratic revolutions occurred before the institutionalization of parliamentary-party government. In Peru and Egypt, such revolutions took place after parliamentary-party government had been discredited.

12. For documentation of this point, see the following sources: Perlmutter, p. 92; Monroe Berger, *Bureaucracy and Society in Modern Egypt* (Princeton: Princeton University Press, 1957), p. 15; Magali Sarfatti Larson and Arlene Bergman, *Social Stratification in Peru* (Berkeley: University of California, Institute of International Studies, 1969), p. 117; Julio Cotler, "The Mechanisms of Internal Domination and Social Change in Peru," in *Masses in Latin America*, ed. Irving Louis Horowitz (New York: Oxford University Press, 1970), p. 426; Aníbal Quijano, "Tendencies in Peruvian Development and Class Structure," in *Latin America: Reform or Revolution?* ed. James Petras and Maurice Zeitlin (Greenwich: Fawcett, 1968), p. 319.

13. Roger Owen, "Egypt and Europe: From French Expedition to British Occupation," in Owen and Sutcliffe, pp. 203-5.

14. Larson and Bergman, p. 271.

15. Ralph Zink, *The Political Risks for Multinational Enterprise in Developing Countries: With a Case Study of Peru* (New York: Praeger, 1973), p. 102.

16. Aníbal Quijano, "Imperialism and International Relations in Latin America," in *Latin America and the United States*, ed. Julio Cotler and Richard Fagen (Stanford: Stanford University Press, 1974), p. 70.

17. Mahmoud Hussein, *Class Conflict in Egypt, 1945-1970* (New York: Monthly Review Press, 1973), p. 77.

18. Beeri, pp. 316-21.

19. These families also had industrial and financial holdings and were closely allied with the bourgeois class.

20. Beeri, p. 317.

21. Luigi Einaudi and Alfred Stepan, *Latin American Institutional Development: Changing Military Perspectives in Peru and Brazil* (Santa Monica: Rand Corporation, 1971), p. 41.

22. In 1965, 94 percent of the directors of Peru's largest corporations were born on the coast, while 56 percent of the generals were born in the highland or jungle areas. Ibid., p. 54.

23. Ibid., p. 42.

24. Ibid., p. 43.

25. Beeri, p. 313.

26. Luigi Einaudi, *Peruvian Military Relations with The United States* (Santa Monica: Rand Corporation, 1970), pp. 5-6.

27. Ibid.

28. Richard Mitchell, *The Society of the Muslim Brother* (London: Oxford University Press, 1969), p. 331; Peter Klaren, *Modernization, Dislocation, and Aprismo* (Austin: University of Texas Press, 1973), p. 152.

29. François Bourricaud, *Power and Society in Contemporary Peru* (New York: Praeger, 1967), p. 148.

30. Mitchell, p. 331.

31. Jane Jaquette, "The Politics of Development in Peru," Ph.D. dissertation, Cornell University, 1971, p. 76.

31. Mitchell, p. 98.

33. James Petras, "Revolution and Guerrilla Movements in Latin America," in Petras and Zeitlin, pp. 343-50.

34. José Nun, *Latin America: The Hegemonic Crisis and the Military Coup* (Berkeley: University of California, Institute of International Studies, 1969).

35. Ibid., p. 26.

36. Ibid., p. 59.

37. Morris Janowitz, *The Military in the Political Development of New Nations* (Chicago: University of Chicago Press, 1964), p. 28; Manfred Halpern, *The Politics of Social Change in the Middle East and North Africa* (Princeton: Princeton University Press, 1963), p. 253.

38. Janowitz, p. 28; Halpern, p. 51.

39. As Petras and LaPorte say (p. 319): "The fact that military officers originate from and lead middle-class types of life should not obscure the fact that they have to a certain degree an independent base of power outside existing property structure which allows them political autonomy. Not linked to the existing 'mutual support societies' characteristic of the other middle-class propertied groups they are less susceptible to the log-rolling politics which undermine the formulation of a systematic development strategy."

40. Irving Louis Horowitz, *Foundations of Political Sociology* (New York: Harper and Row, 1972), p. 342.

41. Huntington, ch. 4.

42. Alan Stepan, "The New Professionalism of Internal Warfare and Military Role Expansion," in *Authoritarian Brazil*, ed. idem (New Haven: Yale University Press, 1973), p. 63.

43. Ibid.

44. Alain Rouguie, "Military Revolutions and National Independence in Latin

America: 1968-1972," in *Military Rule in Latin America*, ed. Philippe Schmitter (Beverly Hills: Sage, 1973), p. 13.

45. Ibid., p. 43.

46. Aníbal Quijano, a Marxist theorist, explains the radicalism of the Peruvian coup as due to both the decline of American hegemony and the relative autonomy of the armed forces because of: "1) the weakness of the sectors of dependent bourgeoisie engaged in the urban-industrial economy, and 2) the very limited political development attained by the popular masses." *Nationalism and Capitalism in Peru* (New York: Monthly Review Press, 1971), p. 10. In contrast, my position is that the autonomy of a military bureaucracy depends not only on the constellation of class forces in a particular society, but on the structure of the military and how it relates to weak or strong classes. Under the conditions Quijano postulates, the military bureaucracy could still be closely tied to the landed oligarchy or to the weak bourgeoisie. In neither case would it have the autonomy to initiate radical action. Quijano does not examine the specific development of the military bureaucracy in Peru, nor its structural relations to class forces.

47. The Peruvian junta permitted no representative institutions. Under Nasser, the National Assembly had little power; neither the cabinet nor the ministries were responsible to it.

48. Einaudi, p. 26; Lowenthal, p. 812; Perlmutter, p. 112; J.C. Hurewitz, "Egypt: Military Rule in a Rapidly Changing Society," in *Man, State, and Society in the Contemporary Middle East*, ed. Jacob Landau (New York: Praeger, 1972), p. 52.

49. A Study of 131 Egyptian cabinet ministers in 1952-1969 found that 34 percent of these men were military officers. The military bureaucrats were found to have power over their more numerous civilian collaborators. The ministers from civilian backgrounds were technicians; the military officers made the political decisions. However, with the emphasis on state direction of the economy after 1962, a new breed of officer technicians appeared—military officers who had received advanced technical training. R.H. Dakmejian, *Egypt under Nasser* (Albany: State University of New York Press, 1971), pp. 168-75.

59. Abdel-Malek, p. xx.; Petras and LaPorte, p. 292; Brady Tyson, "The Emerging Role of the Military as National Modernizers and Managers in Latin America: The Cases of Brazil and Peru," in *Latin American Prospects for the 1970's*, eds. David Pollack and Arch Ritter (New York: Praeger, 1973), p. 129.

51. Perlmutter, p. 127; Beeri, p. 447; Lowenthal, p. 807.

52. Phillippe Schmitter, "Still the Century of Corporatism?" in *The New Corporatism*, ed. Frederick Pike and Thomas Stritch (Notre Dame: University of Notre Dame Press, 1974), p. 101.

53. Ibid., p. 125.

54. James Malloy, "Authoritarianism, Corporation, and Mobilization in Peru," in Ibid., p. 66.

55. Palmer, p. 87.

56. Ibid., p. 125.

57. Ibid., p. 89.

58. Ibid., p. 122.

59. Ibid., p. 58.

60. Ibid., p. 116.

61. Ibid., p. 123.

62. Malloy, p. 72.

63. Petras and LaPorte, p. 288.

64 Palmer, p. 97.

65. Ibid., p. 101.

66. Petras and LaPorte, p. 288.

67. For example in June 1972, workers in the sugar cooperatives staged a strike for freer elections of workers to the governing board. Palmer, p. 242.

68. Ibid., p. 159.

69. That such mobilization is essential for industrialization in Peru and Egypt will be documented in the discussion of economic development.

70. Perlmutter, p. 151.

71. Ibid., p. 163; Dekmejian, p. 146; James Mayfield, *Rural Politics in Nasser's Egypt* (Austin: University of Texas Press, 1971), p. 106.

72. Mayfield, p. 105.

73. Perlmutter, p. 37.

74. Hussein, p. 121.

75. Mayfield, p. 118.

76. Moore, p. 197.

77. Simon Shamir, "The Marxists in Egypt: The 'Licensed Infiltration' Doctrine in Practice," in *The U.S.S.R. and the Middle East*, ed. Michael Confino and Simon Shamir (New York: Wiley, 1973), p. 307.

78. Iliy a Harik, "The Single Party as a Subordinate Movement: The Case of Egypt," *World Politics* 26 (October 1973): 94.

79. Abdel-Malik, p. 366.

80. Fouad Ajami, "On Nasser and His Legacy," *Journal of Peace Research* 11 (1974): 41.

81. Abdel-Malik, p. xxii.

82. Ibid., p. 368.

83. O'Brien, p. 228; Hussein, p. 22; Quijano, *Nationalism and Capitalism in Peru*, pp. 12-14.

84. O'Brien, p. 104; Petras and LaPorte, pp. 284-85.

85. Abdel-Malek, pp. xv-xvi.

86. Charles Goodsell, "That Confounding Revolution in Peru," *Current History* (January 1975).

87. News report in *Latin America*, October 18, 1974.

88. O'Brien, p. 188.

89. Lowenthal, p. 88.

90. O'Brien, p. 159.

91. Quijano, *Nationalism and Capitalism in Peru*, p. 40; Hussein, p. 87.

92. Quijano, Ibid., p. 66.

93. "Open Door in the Middle East," *MERIP Reports (Middle East Research and Information Project)* 31 (October 1974).

94. Robert Klitgaard, "Observations of the Peruvian National Plan for Development, 1971-1975," *Inter-American Economic Affairs* 25 (1971): 16.

95. Hussein, p. 213.

96. Abdel-Malek, p. 123.

97. Perlmutter, pp. 118-21; Hussein, p. 218; Palmer, pp. 225-27.

98. Perlmutter, pp. 124-25; Beeri, pp. 436-66; Petras and LaPorte, pp. 286-97.

99. For example there has been a recent revival of Islamic and political conservatism in Egypt. See Ajami, p. 47.

100. Hussein, p. 188.

101. *MERIP Reports*, p. 23.

102. Quijano, "Imperialism and International Relations in Latin America," p. 96.

Conclusion:
The Future of Revolution
from Above

Attempts at revolution from above will increase in Third World nations. In 1975 military regimes in Portugal and Ethiopia initiated attempts at revolution from above. Preconditions for such revolutions are becoming widespread: (1) Continued weakening of the landed classes and failure of the bourgeoisie in the Third World to promote sustained industrialization enhance the potential for revolution from above. (2) The military in many Third World countries are becoming increasingly bureaucratic, relatively autonomous, and nationalistic. Officers recognize their permanent military subordination to the great powers unless their nations achieve industrialization. The military also fear internal upheaval against dependency and underdevelopment. (3) The potential for revolution from above depends on increasing contradictions and weakness in the world capitalist system which provide room for maneuver by developing countries. In response to competition between Japanese, European and U.S. firms, Third World countries are banding together into raw product seller's cartels, organizing regional markets and undertaking competitive bidding to diversify investments and trade between Western and Communist countries. (4) Revolutions from below led by guerrilla movements have succeeded in several countries in the past ten years (Vietnam, Cambodia, Portuguese Africa). But in many other countries such movements have been repressed (in Latin America). In those countries where the prospects for revolution from below look bleak, radicals and Marxists may have no choice but to support military revolution from above and to try to force it in more progressive directions.

What is more problematic is whether future revolutions from above will be more successful in technical or human terms than the cases studied here. Analysis of revolution from above in these four countries leads to the conclusion that the use of the state bureaucracy to foster capitalist development through sponsorship of either an independent or state capitalist class will be ineffective. Capitalist development independent of foreign control was impossible even for Japan one hundred years ago. Revolutions from above may promote some capitalist industrialization, but it will be dependent, uneven, and distorted economic development. Such industrialization will be geared to export, foster inequality, and continue poverty for the mass of the population. Any capitalist, merchant, or landlord class in the Third World today has more to gain personally from cooperation with international capitalism than from trying to promote autonomous development. Nationalization of industry by a state which maintains capitalist relations of production and exchange will also recreate a capitalist bourgeoisie whose private profit will depend on relating to international capitalism in a manner which will retard and distort national development.

The only way any country today can hope to industrialize autonomously without foreign domination of its economy is through a wide mass mobilization for a vast productive effort. This will depend on state direction and planning, although to call it "socialist" is probably a distortion of the term.[1] Such mass mobilization in a relatively populous country would have at least some possibility of activating the accumulation of capital and prodigious human effort necessary to achieve autonomous industrialization. Mobilization of a mass commitment to industrialization would necessitate using some capital accumulation to provide social welfare services to the masses, in addition to building up heavy industry. Better education, medical care, housing, and food, not only increase the popular commitment to share the burdens of an industrialization effort, but also raise productive capacity. State ownership of industry, mass mobilization, and increasing social welfare benefits which decrease inequality, have at least the potential for both technically effective and more humane economic development. This is especially true if the internal market is large enough to decrease dependence on the world capitalist market.[2]

The question remains whether military bureaucrats in alliance with their technocratic supporters have the capacity (or could develop the ability) to achieve such mass mobilization for noncapitalist development. Whatever their rhetoric, no military bureaucrats in practice have mobilized genuine mass economic and political participation or abrogated capitalist relations of production. Rather, my study suggests that relatively autonomous bureaucrats who in a crisis situation become dynamically autonomous of class forces have the capacity only to constitute themselves as a new ruling class, which in a capitalist world economy, means a capitalist class. The only possibility that a revolution from above could move in a more progressive direction depends on the existence of a strong and independent mass socialist or communist movement. Such a movement might have the power to force political measures on the military. Cooperation—even antagonistic cooperation—between radical military bureaucrats and a strong left-wing movement might create a new pattern of development in the Third World.

The problem remains of how those most dedicated to noncapitalist development operate in a world economy structured by capitalist relations of production and exchange. Even China and Cuba have run into huge obstacles in their attempt to foster economic development in a more humanistic and democratic manner than in the past. Revolutions from above cannot escape these problems. But an analysis of whether or how they might solve them can only proceed after revolution from above is recognized an an alternative route between agricultural and industrial society.

Notes

1. Immanuel Wallerstein makes an important distinction: "State ownership is not socialism. Self-reliance is not socialism. These policies may represent intelligent political decisions for governments to take. They may be decisions that socialist movements should endorse. But a socialist government when it comes will not look anything like the USSR, or China, or Chile, or Tanzania of today. Production for use and not for profit, and rational decision on the cost benefits (in the widest sense of the term) of alternative uses is a different mode of production." "Dependence in an Interdependent World: The Limited Possibilities of Transformation within the Capitalist World Economy," *African Studies Review* 27 (April 1974):23.

2. Samir Amin, *Accumulation of a World Scale: A Critique of the Theory of Underdevelopment*, vol. 1 (New York: Monthly Review Press, 1974), p. 32.

Bibliography

I. Works on Japan

Akita, George. 1967. *Foundations of Constitutional Government in Japan, 1868-1900*. Cambridge, Mass.: Harvard University Press.

Beasely, William. 1963. *The Modern History of Japan*. New York: Praeger.

———. 1972. *The Meiji Restoration*. Stanford: Stanford University Press.

Beckman, George. 1957. *The Making of the Meiji Constitution*. Lawrence: University of Kansas Press.

Beckman, George, and Genji, Okubo. 1969. *The Japanese Communist Party, 1922-1945*. Stanford: Stanford University Press.

Befu, Harumi. 1968. "Village Autonomy and Articulation with the State: The Case of Tokugawa Japan." In *Studies in the Institutional History of Early Modern Japan*. Edited by John Hall and Marius Jansen. Princeton: Princeton University Press.

Bellah, Robert. 1957. *Tokugawa Religion*. Glencoe, Ill.: Free Press.

Benedict, Ruth. 1946. *The Chrysanthemum and the Sword*. Boston: Houghton Mifflin.

Borton, Hugh. 1955. *Japan's Modern Century*. New York: Ronald Press.

Brown, Sidney. 1966. "Okubo Toshimichi and the First Home Ministry Bureaucracy, 1873-1878." In *Modern Japanese Leadership*. Edited by Bernard Silberman and Harry Harootunian. Tucson: University of Arizona Press.

Butow, Robert. 1961. *Tojo and the Coming of the War*. Princeton: Princeton University Press.

Chambliss, William. 1954. *Chiaraijima Village: Land Tenure, Taxation, and Local Trade, 1818-1884*. Tucson: University of Arizona Press.

Craig, Albert. 1959. "The Restoration Movement in Choshu." In *Studies in the Institutional History of Early Modern Japan*. Edited by John Hall and Marius Jansen. Princeton: Princeton University Press.

———. 1961. *Choshu in the Meiji Restoration*. Cambridge, Mass.: Harvard University Press.

Craucour, E.S. 1970. "Changes in Japanese Commerce in the Tokugawa Period."

In *Studies in the Institutional History of Early Modern Japan*. Edited by John Hall and Marius Jansen. Princeton: Princeton University Press.

Crowley, James. 1962. "Japanese Army Factionalism in the 1930's." *Journal of Asian Studies* 21:309-26.

————. 1966a. *Japan's Quest for Autonomy*. Princeton: Princeton University Press.

————. 1966b. "From Closed Door to Empire: The Formation of the Meiji Military Establishment." In *Modern Japanese Leadership*. Edited by Bernard Silberman and Harry Harootunian. Tucson: University of Arizona Press.

————. 1970. *Modern East Asia: Essays in Interpretation*. New York: Harcourt, Brace, & World.

Dore, Ronald. 1958. *City Life in Japan*. Berkeley: University of California Press.

————. 1959. *Land Reform in Japan*. London: Oxford University Press.

————. 1964. "Latin America and Japan Compared." In *Continuity and Change in Latin America*. Edited by J.J. Johnson. Stanford: Stanford University Press.

————. 1965. *Education in Tokugawa Japan*. Berkeley: University of California Press.

————, ed. 1967. *Aspects of Social Change in Modern Japan*. Princeton: Princeton University Press.

Dore, Ronald, and Ouchi, Tsutomu. 1971. "Rural Origins of Japanese Fascism." In *Dilemmas of Growth in Prewar Japan*. Edited by James Moreley. Princeton: Princeton University Press.

Duus, Peter. 1968. *Party Rivalry and Political Change in Taisho Japan*. Cambridge, Mass.: Harvard University Press.

————. 1969. *Feudalism in Japan*. New York: Knopf.

Earl, David. 1964. *Emperor and Nation in Japan*. Seattle: University of Washington Press.

Fairbanks, John; Reischauer, Edwin; and Craig, Albert. 1965. *East Asia: Modern Transformation*. Boston: Houghton Mifflin.

Fox, Grace. 1969. *Britain and Japan, 1853-1883*. New York: Oxford University Press.

Frost, Peter. 1970. *The Bakumatsu Currency Crisis*. Cambridge, Mass.: Harvard University, East Asian Monograph Series.

Fukuzawa, Yukichi. 1966. *The Autobiography of Yukichi Fukuzawa*. New York: Columbia University Press.

Hackett, Roger. 1965. "The Meiji Leaders and Modernization: The Case of Yamagata Atiroma." In *Changing Japanese Attitudes toward Modernization*. Edited by Marius Jansen. Princeton: Princeton University Press.

————. 1968. "Political Modernization and the Meiji Genro." In *Political Development in Modern Japan*. Edited by Robert Ward. Princeton: Princeton University Press.

————. 1971. *Yamagata Aritoma: A Political Biography*. Cambridge, Mass.: Harvard University Press.

Hall, John W. 1955a. *Tanuma Okitsugu: Forerunner of Modern Japan*. Cambridge, Mass.: Harvard University Press.

————. 1955b. "The Castle Town and Japan's Modern Urbanization." *Far Eastern Quarterly* 15 (November):37-56.

————. 1960. "Foundations of the Modern Japanese Daiymo." *Journal of Asian Studies* 20:317-29.

————. 1962. "Feudalism in Japan: A Reassessment." *Comparative Studies in Society and History* 5:15-51.

————. 1964. "The Nature of Traditional Society." In *Political Modernization in Japan and Turkey*. Edited by Robert Ward and Dankwart Rustow. Princeton: Princeton University Press.

————. 1966. *Government and Local Power in Japan, 500-1700*. Princeton: Princeton University Press.

————. 1968. "Feudalism in Japan." In *Studies in the Institutional History of Early Modern Japan*. Edited by John Hall and Marius Jansen. Princeton: Princeton University Press.

————. 1970. *Japan: From Prehistory to Modern Times*. New York: Dell.

Hall, John, and Beardsley, Richard. 1965. *Twelve Doors to Japan*. New York: McGraw-Hill.

Hall, John, and Jansen, Marius. 1968. *Studies in the Institutional History of Early Modern Japan*. Princeton: Princeton University Press.

Hall, Robert K. 1949. *Kokutai no Hongi*. Cambridge, Mass.: Harvard University Press.

Halliday, Jon. 1967. "Japan: Asian Capitalism." *New Left Review* (no. 44):3-29.

————. 1975. *A Political History of Japanese Capitalism*. New York: Pantheon.

Halliday, Jon, and McCormack, Gavan. 1973. *Japanese Imperialism Today*. New York: Monthly Review Press.

Harootunian, Harry. 1958. "The Economic Rehabilitation of the Samurai in the Early Meiji Period." *Journal of Asian Studies* 2:433-44.

————. 1959. "The Progress of Japan and the Samurai Class, 1868-1882." *Pacific Historical Review* 28:255-66.

Hayashi, Kenturo. 1971. "Japan and Germany in the Interwar Period." In *Dilemnas of Growth in Prewar Japan*. Edited by James Morley. Princeton: Princeton University Press.

Higgins, Benjamin, Jr. 1971. "The Political Basis of Economic Development: The Role of the Pre-Industrial Bureaucracies in Japanese Growth and Chinese Stagnation, 1850-1912." M.A. dissertation, McGill University (Montreal).

Hirschmeier, Johannes. 1964. *The Origins of Entrepreneurship in Meiji Japan*. Cambridge, Mass.: Harvard University Press.

Holton, D.C. 1963. *Modern Japan and Shinto Nationalism*. New York: Paragon Book Reprint.

Ike, Nobutaka. 1950. *The Beginnings of Political Democracy in Japan*. Baltimore: Johns Hopkins University Press.

Iriye, Akira. 1971. "The Failure of Military Expansionism." In *Dilemmas of Growth in Prewar Japan*. Edited by James Morley. Princeton: Princeton University Press.

Iwata, Masakazu. 1964. *Okubo Toshmichi: The Bismarck of Japan*. Berkeley: University of California Press.

Jansen, Marius. 1954. *The Japanese and Sun Yat-Sen*. Cambridge, Mass.: Harvard University Press.

————. 1961. *Sakamoto Ryoma and the Meiji Restoration*. Princeton: Princeton University Press.

————. 1965. *Changing Japanese Attitudes toward Modernization*. Princeton: Princeton University Press.

————. 1970. "The Meiji State, 1868-1912." In *Modern East Asia: Essays in Interpretation*. Edited by James Crowley. New York: Harcourt, Brace, & World.

Klein, Lawrence, and Ohkawa, K. 1968. *Economic Growth: The Japanese Experience since the Meiji Era*. Homewood, Ill.: Richard Irwin.

Lebra, Joyce. 1958. "Japan's First Modern Popular Statesman: A Study of the Political Career of Okuma Shiganoby." Ph.D. dissertation, Radcliffe College.

Leiserson, Michael. 1968. "Political Opposition and Political Change in Modern Japan." Berkeley: University of California, Center for Japanese and Korean Studies, unpublished paper.

Levy, Marion. 1953. "Contrasting Factors in the Modernization of China and Japan." *Economic Development and Cultural Change* 2 (October):161-97.

Livingston, Jon; Moore, Joe; and Oldfather, Felicia. 1973. *Imperial Japan, 1800-1945*. New York: Pantheon Books.

Lockwood, William. 1954. *The Economic Development of Japan*. Princeton: Princeton University Press.

————. 1956. "Japan's Response to the West: The Contrast with China." *World Politics* 2:37-54.

————. 1965. *The State and Economic Enterprise in Japan*. Princeton: Princeton University Press.

McLaren, W.W. 1914. *Japanese Government Documents, 1868-1891*. Vol. 42, pt. 1. New York: Transactions of the Asiatic Society of Japan.

————. 1916. *A Political History of Japan During the Meiji Era*. New York: Scribner's.

Maruyama, Masao. 1963. *Thought and Behavior in Modern Japanese Politics*. London: Oxford University Press.

Maxon, Yale. 1957. *Control of Japanese Foreign Policy, 1930-1945*. Berkeley: University of California Press.

McCord, William. 1973. "The Japanese Model of Development." In *Political Economy of Development*. Edited by Charles Wilber. New York: Random House.

Miller, Frank. 1965. *Minobe Tataukuchi: Interpreter of Constitutionalism in Japan*. Berkeley: University of California Press.

Morley, James. 1957. *The Japanese Thrust into Siberia, 1918*. New York: Columbia University Press.

————. 1971. *Dilemmas of Growth in Prewar Japan*. Princeton: Princeton University Press.

Morris, Ivan. 1960. *Nationalism and the Right Wing in Japan*. London: Oxford University Press.

————. 1963. *Japan, 1931-1945*. Boston: Heath.

Najita, Tetsuo. 1967. *Hara Kei in the Politics of Compromise, 1905-1915*. Cambridge, Mass.: Harvard University Press.

Norman, E. Herbert. 1940. *Japan's Emergence as a Modern State*. New York: Institute of Pacific Relations.

———. 1943. *Soldier and Peasant in Japan: The Origins of Conscription*. New York: Institute of Pacific Relations.

Ogata, Sadako. 1964. *Defiance in Manchuria*. Berkeley: University of California Press.

Okuma, Count Shigenobu. 1909. *Fifty Years of the New Japan*. New York: Dutton.

Passin, Herbert. 1965. *Society and Education in Japan*. New York: Teachers College Press, Columbia University.

Pittau, Robert. 1967. *Political Thought in Early Meiji Japan*. Cambridge, Mass.: Harvard University Press.

Pyle, Kenneth. 1973. "The Technology of Japanese Nationalism." *Journal of Asian Studies* 33 (November):51-65.

Quigley, Harold. 1932. *Japanese Government and Politics*. New York: Century.

Reischauer, Edwin. 1965. *Japan: Past and Present*. New York: Knopf.

———. 1971. "What Went Wrong?" In *Dilemmas of Growth in Prewar Japan*. Edited by James Morley. Princeton: Princeton University Press.

Rosovsky, Henry. 1966. "Japan's Transition to Modern Economic Growth, 1868-1885." In *Industrialization in Two Systems*. Edited by Henry Rosovsky. New York: Wiley.

Sakai, Robert. 1957. "Feudal Society and Modern Leadership in Satsuma Han." *Journal of Asian Studies* 16:365-75.

Sakota, Y. and Hall, John. 1956. "The Motivation of Political Leadership in the Meiji Restoration." *Journal of Asian Studies* 16:31-50.

Sansom, George. 1950. *The Western World and Japan*. New York: Knopf.

———. 1963. *A History of Japan, 1615-1867*. Vol. 3. Stanford: Stanford University Press.

Scalapino, Robert. 1953. *Democracy and the Party Movement in Pre-war Japan*. Berkeley: University of California Press.

———. 1968. "Elections and Political Modernization in Pre-war Japan." In *Political Development in Modern Japan*. Edited by Robert Ward. Princeton: Princeton University Press.

Scalapino, Robert, and Masumi, Junnosuke. 1962. *Parties and Politics in Contemporary Japan*. Berkeley: University of California Press.

Sheldon, Charles. 1958. *The Rise of the Merchant Class in Tokugawa Japan*. Locust Valley, N.Y.: Association for Asian Studies.

Shillony, Ben-Ami. 1973. *Revolt in Japan: The Young Officers and the February 26, 1936 Incident*. Princeton: Princeton University Press.

Shuzo, Teruoka. 1966. "Japanese Capitalism and Its Agricultural Problems." *Developing Economies* 4:472-98.

Silberman, Bernard. 1964. *Ministers of Modernization: Elite Mobility in the Meiji Restoration, 1868-1873*. Tucson: University of Arizona Press.

Silberman, Bernard, and Harootunian, Harry. 1966. *Modern Japanese Leadership*. Tucson: University of Arizona Press.

Smethurst, Richard. 1970. "Military Reserve Associations and the Minobe Crisis of

1935." In *Crisis Politics in Prewar Japan*. Edited by George Wilson. Tokyo: Voyagers Press.

———. 1971. "The Creation of the Imperial Military Reserve Association in Japan." *Journal of Asian Studies* 30 (no. 4):815-28.

Smith, Thomas C. 1955. *Political Change and Industrial Development in Japan*. Stanford: Stanford University Press.

———. 1959. *The Agrarian Origins of Modern Japan*. Stanford: Stanford University Press.

———. 1961a. "Japan's Aristocratic Revolution." *Yale Review* 50:370-83.

———. 1961b. "The Discontented." *Journal of Asian Studies* 21:215-19.

———. 1968. "The Japanese Village in the Seventeenth Century." In *Studies in the Institutional History of Early Modern Japan*. Edited by John Hall and Marius Jansen. Princeton: Princeton University Press.

Spaulding, Robert. 1967. *Imperial Japan's Higher Civil Service Examinations*. Princeton: Princeton University Press.

———. 1970. "Japan's New Bureaucrats, 1932-45." In *Crisis in Prewar Japan*. Edited by George Wilson. Tokyo: Voyagers Press.

Steiner, Kurt. 1965. *Local Government in Japan*. Stanford: Stanford University Press.

———. 1968. "Popular Participation and Political Development in Japan." In *Political Development in Modern Japan*. Edited by Robert Ward. Princeton: Princeton University Press.

Stoetzle, Jean. 1955. *Without the Chrysanthemum and the Sword*. New York: Columbia University Press.

Storry, Richard. 1957. *The Double Patriots: A Study of Japanese Nationalism*. London: Chatto & Windus.

Tanin, O., and Yohan, E. 1934. *Militarism and Fascism in Japan*. New York: International Publishers.

Tidmann, Arthur. 1971. "Big Business and Politics in Prewar Japan." In *Dilemnas of Growth in Prewar Japan*. Edited by James Morley. Princeton: Princeton University Press.

Totman, Conrad. 1967. *Politics in the Tokugawa Bakufu*. Cambridge, Mass.: Harvard University Press.

Totten, George. 1965. *Democracy in Prewar Japan: Groundwork or Facade*. Boston: Heath.

———. 1966. *The Social Democratic Movement in Prewar Japan*. New Haven: Yale University Press.

Totten, George, and Kawakami, Tamio. 1965. "The Functions of Factionalism in Japanese Politics." *Pacific Affairs* 38 (no. 2):109-22.

Trimberger, Ellen Kay. 1977. "State Power and Modes of Production: Implications of the Japanese Transition to Capitalism." *The Insurgent Sociologist* 7 (Spring):85-98.

Tsukahira, Toshio. 1967. *Feudal Control in Tokugawa Japan: The Sankin Kotai System*. Cambridge, Mass.: Harvard University, East Asian Monographs.

Ward, Robert E. 1968. *Political Development in Modern Japan*. Princeton: Princeton University Press.

Ward, Robert, and Rustow, Dankwart. 1964. *Political Modernization in Japan and Turkey*. Princeton: Princeton University Press.

Webb, Herschall. 1965. "The Development of the Orthodox Attitude toward the Imperial Institution in the 19th Century." In *Changing Japanese Attitudes toward Modernization*. Edited by Marius Jansen. Princeton: Princeton University Press.

Wilson, George. 1965. "A New Look at the Problem of Japanese Fascism." *Comparative Studies in Society and History* 10:401-12.

———. 1966. "Kita Ikki's Theory of Revolution." *Journal of Asian Studies* 26 (November):89-99.

———. 1970. *Crisis Politics in Prewar Japan*. Tokyo: Voyagers Press.

Wilson, Robert. 1957. *Genesis of the Meiji Government in Japan, 1868-1871*. Berkeley: University of California Press.

Yanaga, Chitoshi. 1956. *Japanese People and Politics*. New York: Wiley.

Yutaimi, Eiji. 1972. "Peasantry and Revolution in Pre-industrial Japan." Berkeley: University of California, Center for Japanese and Korean Studies, unpublished paper.

II. Works on Turkey

Ahmad, Feroz. 1969. *The Young Turks*. London: Oxford University Press.

———. 1973. "The Turkish Guerrillas: Symptom of a Deeper Malaise." *New Middle East* (April):13-16.

Ahmad, Feroz, and Rustow, Dankwart. 1973. "The Parliaments of the Second Constitutional Period, 1908-1918." Unpublished paper.

Aktan, Resat. 1965. "Problems of Land Reform in Turkey." *Middle Eastern Journal* 19:317-34.

Allen, Henry. 1933. *The Turkish Transformation*. Chicago: University of Chicago Press.

Bailey, Frank. 1942. *British Policy and the Turkish Reform Movement, 1826-1853*. Cambridge, Mass.: Harvard University Press.

Bellah, Robert. 1958. "Religious Aspects of Modernization in Turkey and Japan." *American Journal of Sociology* 64:1-15.

Berkes, Niyazi. 1954. *Turkish Nationalism and Western Civilization: Selected Essays of Ziya Gokalp*. New York: Columbia University Press.

———. 1964. *The Development of Secularism in Turkey*. Montreal: McGill University Press.

Bisbee, Eleanor. 1951. *The New Turks*. Philadelphia: University of Pennsylvania Press.

Buxton, Charles. 1909. *Turkey in Revolution*. London: Fisher Unwin.

Caldwell, Lynton. 1959. "Turkish Administration and the Politics of Expediency." In *Toward the Comparative Study of Public Administration*. Edited by William Siffin. Bloomington: University of Indiana Press.

Cohn, Edwin. 1970. *Turkish Economic, Social, and Political Change*. New York: Praeger.

Cunningham, Allan. 1968. "Stratford Canning and the Tanzimat." In *Beginnings of*

Modernization in the Middle East. Edited by William Polk and Richard Chambers. Chicago: University of Chicago Press.

Daniel, Norman. 1966. *Islam, Europe, and Empire*. Edinburgh: Edinburgh University Press.

Davison, Roderic. 1963. *Reform in the Ottoman Empire, 1856-1867*. Princeton: Princeton University Press.

Devereaux, Robert. 1963. *The First Ottoman Constitutional Period*. Baltimore: Johns Hopkins University Press.

Edib, Halide. 1928. *The Turkish Ordeal*. New York: Century.

———. 1930. *Turkey Faces West*. New Haven: Yale University Press.

———. 1935. *Conflict of East and West in Turkey*. Lahore (India): Shaikh Mulramud Ashraf.

Eliot, Sir Charles. 1908. *Turkey in Europe*. London: Arnold.

Ellis, Howard. 1970. *Private Enterprise and Socialism in the Middle East*. Washington, D.C.: American Enterprise Institute for Public Policy Research.

Eren, Nuri. 1961. *Turkey Today and Tomorrow*. London: Pall Mall.

Ergil, Dogu, and Rhodes, Robert. 1973. "The Impact of the World Capitalist System on Ottoman Society." Binghamton, N.Y.: State University of New York, Department of Sociology, unpublished paper.

Fidel, Kenneth. 1969. "Social Structure and Military Intervention: The 1960 Turkish Revolution." Ph.D. dissertation, Washington University.

Findley, Carter. 1970. "Legacy of Tradition to Reform: Origins of the Ottoman Foreign Ministry." *International Journal of Middle East Studies* 1:334-57.

Frey, Frederick. 1963. "Surveying Peasant Attitudes in Turkey." *Public Opinion Quarterly* 28:335-55.

———. 1965. *The Turkish Political Elite*. Cambridge, Mass.: MIT Press.

Frye, Richard. 1957. *Islam and the West*. The Hague: Mouton.

Gibb, H.A.R., and Bowen, Harold. 1957. *Islamic Society and the West*, vols. 1, 2. London: Oxford University Press.

Gorvine, Albert. 1956. *An Outline of Turkish Provincial and Local Government*. Ankara: Ankara University, Faculty of Political Science.

Gunce, E. 1967. "Early Planning Experiences in Turkey." In *Planning in Turkey*. Edited by S. Ilkin. Ankara: Ankara University, Faculty of Administrative Science, Publication no. 9.

Haddad, George. 1965. *Revolution and Military Rule in the Middle East: The Northern Tier*. New York: Speller.

Harris, George. 1965. "The Role of the Military in Turkish Politics." *Middle Eastern Journal* 19:54-66, 169-76.

———. 1967. *The Origins of Communism in Turkey*. Stanford: Hoover Institution Publications.

———. 1970. "The Causes of the 1960 Revolution in Turkey." *Middle Eastern Journal* 24 (Fall):438-54.

———. 1972. *Troubled Alliance: Turkish-American Problems in Historical Perspective, 1945-71*. Stanford: Hoover Institute Publications.

Hershlag, Z.Y. 1958. *Turkey: An Economy in Transition*. The Hague: University Van Keulen, N.V.

————. 1968. *Turkey: The Challenge of Growth*. Leiden: Brill.

Heyd, Uriel. 1950. *Foundations of Turkish Nationalism*. London: Luzac.

————. 1954. *Language Reform in Modern Turkey*. Jerusalem: Israel Oriental Society.

————. 1961. "The Ottoman Ulema and Westernization in the Time of Selim III and Mahmud II." *Scripta Hierosolymitana* 9:63-96.

Hostler, Charles. 1957. *Turkism and the Soviets*. London: Allen & Unwin.

Hourani, Albert. 1968. "Ottoman Reform and the Politics of Notables." In *Beginnings of Modernization in the Middle East*. Edited by William Polk and Richard Chambers. Chicago: University of Chicago Press.

Hyland, Michael. 1970. "Crisis at the Polls: Turkey's 1969 Elections." *Middle Eastern Journal* 24:1-16.

Inalcik, Halil. 1964. "The Nature of Traditional Society." In *Political Modernization in Japan and Turkey*. Edited by Robert Ward and Dankwart Rustow. Princeton: Princeton University Press.

————. 1969. "Capital Formation in the Ottoman Empire." *Journal of Economic History* 29:97-140.

————. 1970. "The Heyday and Decline of the Ottoman Empire." In *The Cambridge History of Islam*. Vol. 1. Cambridge: Cambridge University Press.

International Bank for Reconstruction and Development. 1951. *The Economy of Turkey*. Washington, D.C.

Issawi, Charles. 1966. *The Economic History of the Middle East*. Chicago: University of Chicago Press.

Itzkowitz, Norman. 1962. "Eighteenth Century Ottoman Realities." *Studia Islamica* 16:73-94.

Karpat, Kemal. 1959. *Turkey's Politics: The Transition to a Multi-Party System*. Princeton: Princeton University Press.

————. 1963. "The People's Houses in Turkey." *Middle Eastern Journal* 17:55-67.

————. 1964. "Society, Economics, and Politics in Contemporary Turkey." *World Politics* 17:50-74.

————. 1967. "Socialism and the Labor Party in Turkey." *Middle Eastern Journal* 21 (no. 2):157-72.

————. 1968. "The Land Regime, Social Structure, and Modernization in the Ottoman Empire." In *Beginnings of Modernization in the Middle East*. Edited by William Polk and Richard Chambers. Chicago: University of Chicago Press.

————. 1970. "The Military and Politics in Turkey, 1960-64: A Socio-Cultural Analysis of a Revolution." *American Historical Review* 80 (October):1654-83.

————. 1972. "The Transformation of the Ottoman State, 1789-1908," *International Journal of Middle East Studies* 3:243-81.

Kazamias, Andrews. 1966. *Education and the Quest for Modernity in Turkey*. Chicago: University of Chicago Press.

Kemal, Mustapha. 1929. *A Speech Delivered by Ghazi Mustapha Kemal, October 1927*. Leipzig: Koehler.

Kestin, Hakki. 1973. "Imperialismus, Unterentwicklung, Militarregierung in Der Turkei." *Problema des Klassenkampfs* 6:49-120.
Kinross, Lord. 1964. *Ataturk: The Rebirth of a Nation*. London: Weidenfeld & Nicolson.
Knight, Edwin. 1910. *Turkey*. Boston: Millet.
Lerner, Daniel, and Robinson, Richard. 1960. "Swords and Ploughshares: The Turkish Army as a Modernizing Force." *World Politics* 8:19-44.
Lewis, Bernard. 1953. "History-writing and National Revival in Turkey," *Middle Eastern Affairs* 4:218-27.
———. 1959. "Democracy in the Middle East." *Middle Eastern Affairs* 6 (April):101-8.
———. 1961. *The Emergence of Modern Turkey*. London: Oxford University Press.
———. 1963. *Istanbul and the Civilization of the Ottoman Empire*. Norman: University of Oklahoma Press.
Logoglu, Osman Faruk. 1970. "Ismet Inonu and the Political Modernization of Turkey, 1945-1965." Ph.D. dissertation, Princeton University.
Lybyer, Albert. 1913. *The Government of the Ottoman Empire in the Time of Suleiman the Magnificent*. Cambridge, Mass.: Harvard University Press.
Mardin, Serif. 1962. *The Genesis of Young Ottoman Thought*. Princeton: Princeton University Press.
———. 1966. "Opposition and Control in Turkey." *Government and Opposition* 1 (May):375-81.
———. 1967. "Historical Determinants of Stratification: Social Class and Class Consciousness in Turkey." *Siyasal Bilgilar Fakultesi Dergisi* (Ankara University) 22 (December):111-42.
———. 1969. "Power, Civil Society, and Culture in the Ottoman Empire." *Comparative Studies in Society and History* (June):258-81.
———. 1971. "Ideology and Religion in the Turkish Revolution." *International Journal of Middle Eastern Studies* 2:197-211.
McGrummen, Eugene. 1962. "The Role of Foreign Trade and Foreign Investment in the Economic Development of Turkey." M.A. thesis, University of California, Berkeley.
Meyer, A.J. 1959. *Middle Eastern Capitalism*. Cambridge, Mass.: Harvard University Press.
Miller, Barnette. 1941. *The Palace School of Muhammad the Conqueror*. Cambridge, Mass.: Harvard University Press.
Olson, Robert. 1973. "Al-Fateh in Turkey: Its Influence on the March 12 Coup." *Middle Eastern Studies* 9 (May):197-205.
Ozbudun, Ergun. 1966. *The Role of the Military in Recent Turkish Politics*. Cambridge, Mass.: Harvard University, Center for International Affairs, Occasional Paper no. 14.
Pallis, Alexander. 1951. *In the Days of the Janissaries*. London: Hutchinson.
Pfaff, Richard. 1960. "Political Factors Influencing Economic Development of Turkey, Iraq, and Iran." Ph.D. dissertation, University of California, Berkeley.
Polk, William, and Chambers, Richard. 1968. *Beginnings of Modernization in the Middle East*. Chicago: University of Chicago Press.

Ramsaur, E.E. 1967. *The Young Turks.* Princeton: Princeton University Press.

Ramsey, William. 1911. *The Revolution in Constantinople and Turkey.* London: Hodder & Stoughton.

Reed, H.A. 1954. "The Revival of Islam in Secular Turkey." *Middle Eastern Journal* 8:267-82.

———. 1967. "Historical Determinants of Stratification: Social Class and Class Consciousness in Turkey." *Siyasal Bilgilar Fakultesis Dergisi* (Ankara University) 22 (December):111-42.

Rivkin, Malcolm. 1965. *Area Development for National Growth: The Case of Turkey.* New York: Praeger.

Rivlin, Benjamin, and Szyliowicz. 1965. *The Contemporary Middle East.* New York: Random House.

Robinson, Richard. 1963. *The First Turkish Republic.* Cambridge, Mass.: Harvard University Press.

Rustow, Dankwart. 1959. "The Army and the Founding of the Turkish Republic." *World Politics* 11:513-52.

———. 1964. "The Military." In *Political Modernization in Japan and Turkey.* Edited by Robert Ward and Dankwart Rustow. Princeton: Princeton University Press.

———. 1965a. "Turkey: The Modernity of Tradition." In *Political Culture and Political Development.* Edited by Lucian Pye and Sydney Verba. Princeton: Princeton University Press.

———. 1965b. "The Appeal of Communism to Islamic Peoples." In *Islam and International Relations.* Edited by J. Harris Proctor. New York: Praeger.

———. 1966a. "Turkey." In *Political Modernization in the Near East and North Africa.* Princeton: Princeton University Conference, 1966.

———. 1966b. "The Development of Parties in Turkey." In *Political Parties and Political Development.* Edited by Joseph La Palombara. Princeton: Princeton, University Press.

———. 1967. "Politics and Development Policy." In *Four Studies in the Economic Development of Turkey.* Edited by Frederick Shorter. London: Cass.

———. 1968. "Ataturk as Founder of a State." 97:793-828.

Saunders, John. 1966. *The Muslim World on the Eve of Europe's Expansion.* Englewood Cliffs, N.J.: Prentice-Hall.

Seidler, Lee. 1967. *The Function of Accounting in Economic Development: Turkey as a Case Study.* New York: Praeger.

Shaw, Stanford. 1968. "Some Aspects of the Aims and Achievements of the 19th Century Ottoman Reformers." In *The Beginnings of Modernization in the Middle East.* Edited by William Polk and Richard Chambers. Chicago: University of Chicago Press.

———. 1971. *Between Old and New: The Ottoman Empire Under Sultan Selim III, 1789-1807.* Cambridge, Mass.: Harvard University Press.

Sherwood, W.B. 1967. "The Rise of the Justice Party in Turkey." *World Politics* 20 (October):54-65.

Simpson, Dwight. 1965. "Development as a Process: The Menderes Phase in Turkey." *Middle Eastern Journal* 19:141-52.

———. 1972. "Turkey: A Time of Troubles." *Current History* 62 (January):38-43.

Stavianos, L.S. 1961. *The Balkans since 1453*. New York: Holt, Rinehart, & Winston.

Stirling, Paul. 1965. *Turkish Village*. London: Weidenfeld & Nicolson.

Szyliowicz, Joseph. 1966. *Political Change in Rural Turkey*. New York: Columbia University Publications in Near and Middle Eastern Studies.

———. 1967. "The Turkish Elections, 1965." *Middle Eastern Journal* 21:473-94.

———. 1971. "Elite Recruitment in Turkey: The Role of Mulkiye." *World Politics* 23 (April):371-98.

Tachau, Frank, and Good, Mary-Jo. 1973. "The Anatomy of Political and Social Change: Turkish Parties, Parliaments, and Elections." *Comparative Politics* (July):551-73.

Thomas, Lewis, and Frye, Richard. 1955. *The U.S. and Turkey and Iran*. Cambridge, Mass.: Harvard University Press.

Thornberg, Max. 1949. *Turkey: An Economic Appraisal*. New York: Twentieth Century Fund.

Ulman, A.E., and Tachau, Frank. 1965. Turkish Politics: The Attempt to Reconcile Rapid Modernization and Democracy." *Middle Eastern Journal* 19 (no. 2):153-68.

Vali, Ference. 1971. *Bridge Across the Bosporus: The Foreign Policy of Turkey*.

Vucinch, Wayne. 1965. *The Ottoman Empire: Its Record and Legacy*. Princeton: Van Nostrand.

Ward, Robert, and Rustow, Dankwart. 1964. *Political Modernization in Japan and Turkey*. Princeton: Princeton University Press.

Weiker, Walter. 1962. "The Free Party of 1930 in Turkey: Loyal Opposition in a Rapidly Modernizing Nation." Ph.D. dissertation, Princeton University.

———. 1963. *The Turkish Revolution, 1960-1961*. Washington, D.C.: Brookings Institute.

———. 1963. "The Aydemir Case and Turkey's Political Dilemma." *Middle Eastern Affairs* 14:258-71.

Yalman, Nur. 1961a. "Crisis in Turkey." Stanford: Center for Advanced Study in Behavioral Sciences, unpublished paper.

———. 1961b. "Westernized Reformers and Reactionary Conservatives: The Major Cleavage in the Turkish Polity." Chicago: University of Chicago, unpublished paper.

———. 1968. "Intervention and Extrication: The Officer Corps in the Turkish Crisis." In *The Military Intervenes*. Edited by Henry Bienen. New York: Russell Sage.

III. Works on Egypt

Abdel-Malek, Anouar. 1968. *Egypt: Military Society*. New York: Vintage Books.

Ajami, Fouad. 1974. "On Nasser and His Legacy." *Journal of Peace Research* 11:41-49.

Beeri, Eliezer. 1970. *Army Officers in Arab Politics and Society*. New York: Praeger.

Berger, Monroe. 1957. *Bureaucracy and Society in Modern Egypt*. Princeton: Princeton University Press.

Copeland, Miles. 1969. *The Game of Nations*. London: Weidenfeld & Nicholson.

Dakmejian, R.H. 1971. *Egypt under Nassar*. Albany: State University of New York Press.

Harik, Iliya. 1973. "The Single Party as a Subordinate Movement: The Case of Egypt." *World Politics* 26 (October):80-105.

Hurewitz, J.C. 1972. "Egypt: Military Rule in a Rapidly Changing Society." In *Man, State, and Society in the Contemporary Middle East*. Edited by Jacob Landau. New York: Praeger.

Hussein, Mahmoud. 1973. *Class Conflict in Egypt, 1945-1970*. New York: Monthly Review Press.

Mayfield, James. 1971. *Rural Politics in Nasser's Egypt*. Austin: University of Texas Press.

Middle East Research and Information Project. 1974. "Open Door in the Middle East." *MERIP Reports* (October):19-25.

Mitchell, Richard. 1969. *The Society of the Muslim Brother*. London: Oxford University Press.

Moore, Clement Henry. 1974. "Authoritarian Politics in Unincorporated Society: The Case of Nasser's Egypt." *Comparative Politics* (January):193-218.

O'Brien, Patrick. 1966. *The Revolution in Egypt's Economic System*. New York: Oxford University Press.

Owen, Roger. 1972. "Egypt and Europe: From French Expediation to British Occupation." In *Studies in the Theory of Imperialism*. Edited by Roger Owen and Bob Sutcliffe. London: Longman.

Perlmutter, Amos. 1974. *Egypt: The Praetorian State*. New Brunswick, N.J.: Transaction.

Shamir, Simon. 1973. "The Marxists in Egypt: The 'Licensed Infiltration' Doctrine in Practice." In *The U.S.S.R. and the Middle East*. Edited by Michael Confino and Simon Shamir. New York: Wiley.

IV. Works on Peru

Bourricaud, François. 1967. *Power and Society in Contemporary Peru*. New York: Praeger.

Cotler, Julio. 1970. "The Mechanisms of Internal Domination and Social Change in Peru." In *Masses in Latin America*. Edited by Irving Louis Horowitz. New York: Oxford University Press.

Einaudi, Luigi. 1970. "Peruvian Military Relations with the United States." *Rand Report*. Santa Monica: Rand.

Einaudi, Luigi, and Stepan, Alfred. 1971. *Latin American Insitutional Development: Changing Military Perspectives in Peru and Brazil*. Santa Monica: Rand.

Goodsell, Charles. 1975. "That Confounding Revolution in Peru." *Current History* (January):20-23.

Jaquette, Jane. 1971. "The Politics of Development in Peru." Ph.D. dissertation, Cornell University.

Klaren, Peter. 1973. *Modernization, Dislocation, and Aprismo*. Austin: University of Texas Press.

Klitgaard, Robert. 1971. "Observations on the Peruvian National Plan for Development, 1971-1975." *Inter-American Economic Affairs* 25 (Winter):3-22.

Larson, Magali Sarfati, and Bergman, Arlene. 1969. *Social Stratification in Peru.* Berkeley: University of California, Institute of International Studies.

Lowenthal, Abraham. 1974. "Peru's Ambiguous Revolution." *Foreign Affairs* 52 (July):799-817.

Malloy, James. 1974. "Authoritarianism, Corporation, and Mobilization in Peru." In *The New Corporatism.* Edited by Frederick Pike and Thomas Stritch. Notre Dame: University of Notre Dame Press.

Palmer, David Scott. 1974. *Revolution from Above: Military Government and Popular Participation in Peru, 1968-1972.* Ithaca, N.Y.: Cornell University Press.

Petras, James. 1968. "Revolution and Guerrilla Movements in Latin America." In *Latin America: Reform or Revolution?* Edited by James Petras and Maurice Zeitlin. Greenwich, Conn: Fawcett Publications.

Petras, James, and LaPorte, Robert. 1971. *Cultivating Revolutions.* New York: Vintage.

Quijano, Aníbal. 1968. "Tendencies in Peruvian Development and Class Structure." In *Latin America: Reform or Revolution?* Edited by James Petras and Maurice Zeitlin. Greenwich, Conn.: Fawcett Publications.

———. 1971. *Nationalism and Capitalism in Peru.* New York: Monthly Review Press.

———. 1974. "Imperialism and International Relations in Latin America." In *Latin America and the United States.* Edited by Julio Cotler and Richard Fagen. Stanford: Stanford University Press.

Tyson, Brady. 1973. "The Emerging Role of the Military as National Modernizers and Managers in Latin America: The Cases of Brazil and Peru." In *Latin American Prospects for the 1970's.* Edited by David Pollack and Arch Ritter. New York: Praeger.

Zink, Ralph. 1973. *The Political Risks for Multinational Enterprise in Developing Countries: With a Case Study of Peru.* New York: Praeger.

V. General Works

Adelman, Irma, and Morris, Cynthia Taft. 1973. *Economic Growth and Social Equity in Developing Countries.* Stanford: Stanford University Press.

Alavi, Hanza. 1972. "The State in Post-Colonial Societies: Pakistan and Bangledesh." *New Left Review* 74 (July):59-81.

Amin, Samir. 1974. *Accumulation on a World Scale: A Critique of the Theory of Underdevelopment.* Vol. 1. New York: Monthly Review Press.

Anderson, Perry. 1974. *Lineages of the Absolutist State.* London: New Left.

Arendt, Hannah. 1963. *On Revolution.* New York: Viking.

Baran, Paul. 1957. *The Political Economy of Growth.* New York: Monthly Review Press.

Bendix, Reinhard. 1960. *Max Weber: An Intellectual Portrait.* New York: Doubleday.

———. 1967. "Tradition and Modernity Reconsidered." *Comparative Studies in Society and History* 9 (April):292-346.

———. 1969. *Nation-building and Citizenship.* Garden City, N.Y.: Doubleday.

Bloch, Marc. 1961. *Feudal Society.* Vols. 1, 2. London: Kegan Paul.

Bonilla, Frank, and Girling, Robert. 1973. *Structures of Dependency*. Stanford: Stanford University, Latin American Studies Institute.
Brinton, Crane. 1938. *The Anatomy of Revolution*. New York: Vintage.
Eckstein, Harry. 1964. *Internal War*. New York: Free Press.
Edwards, Lyford. 1967. *The Natural History of Revolution*. Chicago: University of Chicago Press.
Eisenstadt, Samuel N. 1963. *The Political Systems of Empires*. New York: Free Press.
Finer, S.E. 1962. *The Man on Horseback: The Role of the Military in Politics*. London Pall Mall.
Frank, André Gunder. 1967. *Capitalism and Underdevelopment in Latin America*. New York: Montly Review Press.
Geertz, Clifford. 1968. *Agricultural Involution: The Processes of Ecological Change in Indonesia*. Berkeley: University of California Press.
Gillis, John. 1970. "Political Decay and the European Revolutions, 1789-1848." *World Politics* 22 (April):344-70.
———. 1971. *The Prussian Bureaucracy in Crisis, 1840-1860*. Stanford: Stanford University Press.
Gramsci, Antonio. 1971. *Selections from the Prison Notebooks*. New York: International Publishers.
Halpern, Manfred. 1963. *The Politics of Social Change in the Middle East and North Africa*. Princeton: Princeton University Press.
Hamerow, Theodore. 1958. *Restoration, Revolution, Reaction: Economics and Politics in Germany, 1815-1871*. Princeton: Princeton University Press.
Horowitz, Irving Louis. 1972. *Foundations of Political Sociology*. New York: Harper & Row.
Huntington, Samuel. 1968. *Political Order in Changing Societies*. New Haven: Yale University Press.
Janowitz, Morris. 1964. *The Military in the Political Development of New Nations*. Chicago: University of Chicago Press.
Knight, Maxwell. 1952. *The German Executive, 1890-1933*. Stanford: Stanford University Press.
Lenin, V. Padimir I. 1932. "State and Revolution." In idem, *Collected Works*. New York: International Publishers.
Marini, Ruy Maurio. 1972. "Brazilian Sub-imperialism." *Monthly Review* 23 (February):14-24.
Marx, Karl. 1959. "Eighteenth Brumaire of Louis Bonaparte." In *Basic Writing on Politics and Philosophy*. Edited by Lewis Feuer. Garden City, N.Y.: Doubleday.
Michael, Franz. 1955. "State and Society in Nineteenth-Century China." *World Politics* 7 (April):419-33.
Miliband, Ralph. 1969. *The State in Capitalist Society*. New York: Basic Books.
———. 1973. "Poulantzas and the Capitalist State." *New Left Review* 82 (November-December):83-92.
Mitzman, Arthur. 1969. *The Iron Cage: An Historical Interpretation of Max Weber*. New York: Grosset & Dunlap.
Moffett, John. 1971. "Bureaucratization and Social Control: A Study of the Progres-

sive Regimentation of the Western Social Order." Ph.D. dissertation, Columbia University.

Moore, Barrington. 1954. *Terror and Progress: USSR*. New York: Harper & Row.

———. 1966. *The Social Origins of Dictatorship and Democracy*. Boston: Beacon.

Mosca, Gaetano. 1939. *The Ruling Class*. New York: McGraw-Hill.

Nun, José. 1969. *Latin America: The Hegemonic Crisis and the Military Coup*. Berkeley: University of California, Institute of International Studies.

Owen, Roger, and Sutcliffe, Bob. 1972. *Studies in the Theory of Imperialism*. London: Longman.

Poulantzas, Nicos. 1973a. "The Problem of the Capitalist State." In *Ideology in Social Science*. Edited by Robin Blackburn. New York: Vintage

———. 1973b. *Political Power and Social Class*. London: New Left.

Rosenberg, Hans. 1958. *Bureaucracy, Aristocracy, and Autocracy: The Prussian Experience, 1660-1815*. Cambridge, Mass.: Harvard University Press.

Rouguie, Alain. 1973. "Military Revolutions and National Independence in Latin America, 1968-1971." In *Military Rule in Latin America*. Edited by Philippe Schmitter. Beverly Hills: Sage.

Schmitter, Philippe. 1974. "Still the Century of Corporatism?" In *The New Corporatism*. Edited by Frederick Pike and Thomas Stritch. Notre Dame: University of Notre Dame Press.

Schoenbaum, David. 1966. *Hitler's Social Revolution*. Garden City, N.Y.: Doubleday.

Skocpol, Theda. 1975. "France, Russia, China: A Structural Analysis of Social Revolutions." *Comparative Studies in Society and History* (April):175-209.

———. 1976. "Explaining Revolutions: In Quest of a Social-Structural Approach." In *The Uses of Controversy in Sociology*. Edited by Lewis Coser and Otto Larsen. New York: Free Press.

Stepan, Alan. 1973. "The New Professionalism of Internal Warfare and Military Role Expansion." In *Authoritarian Brazil*. Edited by Alan Stepan. New Haven: Yale University Press.

Tocqueville, Alexis De. 1955. *The Old Regime and the French Revolution*. Garden City, N.Y.: Doubleday.

Trimberger, Ellen Kay. 1972. "A Theory of Elite Revolutions." *Studies in Comparative International Development* 7 (Fall):191-207.

Trotsky, Leon. 1932. *History of Russian Revolution*. New York: Simon & Schuster.

Tucker, Robert. 1973. "Marx as a Political Theorist." In *Marx's Socialism*. Edited by Shlomo Avineri. New York: Lieber-Atherton.

Wallerstein, Immanuel. 1974a. *The Modern World-System*. New York: Academic Press.

———. 1974b. "Dependence in an Interdependent World: The Limited Possibilities of Transformation within the Capitalist World Economy." *African Studies Review* 17 (April):1-25.

Weber, Max. 1958. "Politics as a Vocation." In *From Max Weber*. Edited by Hans Gerth and C. Wright Mills. New York: Oxford University Press.

———. 1968. Economy and Society. Edited by Guenther Roth and Claus Wittich. New York: Bedminster.

Wertheim, W.P. 1974. *Evolution and Revolution*. Baltimore: Penguin.

Index